1
HEARTLAND
DIARIES

BY FRANK MIELE
COLUMNIST, REAL CLEAR POLITICS

2018

Volume 1: Why We Needed Trump, Part 1:
Bush's Global Failure: Half Right

Volume 2: Why We Needed Trump, Part 2:
Obama's Fundamental Transformation: Far Left

Volume 3: Why We Needed Trump, Part 3:
Trump's American Vision: Just Right

FORTHCOMING

Volume 4: The Media Matrix:
What If Everything We Know Is Fake

Volume 5: How We Got Here:
The Left's Assault on the Constitution

Volume 6: What Matters Most:
God, Country, Family and Friends

Volume 7: A Culture in Crisis:
Reviews and Reminders from the War Upstream

Collected from the author's 18 years as managing editor
of the Daily Inter Lake in Kalispell, Montana.

HEARTLAND DIARY VOLUME 1

WHY WE NEEDED TRUMP

Part 1: Bush's Global Failure: Half Right

BY FRANK MIELE

HEARTLAND PRESS
KALISPELL MONTANA 2018

Why We Needed Trump: Part 1

Foreword: Richard L. Spencer
Back cover photo: Meredith Miele

ISBN: 978-1-7329633-0-6
First Edition

Library of Congress Control Number: 2018914333

Heartland Press
Kalispell, Montana

FOR MY MOTHER
LORRAINE FRANK MIELE

To whom I owe my love of books,
my belief in God,
my respect for life,
and my willingness to work.

AND DEDICATED TO THE MEMORY OF MY FATHER
CARMEN JOSEPH MIELE

Who taught me to laugh
When there was nothing to laugh about
And to love
When all else failed.

MAY THEY REST IN PEACE

Acknowledgments

First and foremost, I have to acknowledge my debt to the publishers of the Daily Inter Lake for giving me the opportunity to write the collected columns in the "Heartland Diaries" over the course of 14 years and to Hagadone Montana Publishing Company for giving me permission to reprint them in this form. The two individual publishers who oversaw my work during my time as managing editor also deserve a word of appreciation for their diligence in overseeing my work and for giving me considerable latitude in writing about anything that struck my fancy, however uncomfortable it might have been for them personally.

Second, I need to give credit to my family, who have suffered the results of my long hours at the office, especially on Friday nights when I often worked till midnight to put the finishing touches on my columns and then assemble the Montana Perspectives opinion section for the Sunday paper. Their adaptability to my needs has been truly heroic, and my wife River must be thanked for her massive patience in allowing me the time and space I needed to accomplish the work contained herein. Each of my children — Carmen, Meredith and Huzhao — also showed great understanding of my dedication to this cause, even though they did not always agree with everything I wrote.

Likewise, I would be remiss if I did not acknowledge the readers of my "Editor's 2 Cents" columns in the Daily Inter Lake. So many of you have reached out to me over the years to thank me for my work, and now I can also say thanks to you publicly and tell you how much it meant to me to have an audience of like-minded individuals who could assure me I was not crazy!

Finally, I wish to thank Richard L. Spencer for first suggesting that my work deserved to be preserved in book form, and for providing me the inspiration to aspire to be America's diarist. Although we have never met, he has been a true mentor to me and I am grateful to him for his guidance and kindness. To say that I am humbled by the generous praise he heaps on me in the "Foreword to the Heartland Diaries" which you will read immediately following these words is a vast understatement. I only hope that I can live up to one-tenth of what he says about me.

— **FDM, November 2018**

Foreword to the Heartland Diaries

"FROM COUNTRY EDITOR TO AMERICA'S DIARIST"

BY RICHARD L. SPENCER

I began reading Frank Miele quite fortuitously some 10 years ago and have never regretted it since I was attracted to the title of one of his columns while searching the internet. I forget which article it was, but I do remember how immediately astonished I was that something as sophisticated came from a Mid-Western editor of a small town newspaper called the Daily Inter Lake published out of Kalispell, Montana. As one begins reading these weekly articles from the past decade, you will find them still true, even more so. They are forever prescient, and a stark warning to our Republic: Follow the Constitution. One can ignore reality, but one cannot ignore the consequences of ignoring reality; and, that is the style you will find in Mr. Miele's fundamental thinking and comments, and that is what makes them so valuable for all of America. They are now to be published in the first three volumes of "The Heartland Diaries," entitled "Why We needed Trump," and in subsequent volumes critiquing the media, studying the history of the Progressive movement's subversion of the Constitution, and praising America's heartland values.

I quickly became a consistent reader and also was leaving comments. After that I was sending the articles to friends who replied, "they were going to become a follower." My Sunday mornings soon became one of coffee, Frank's article of the week, and my wife reading to me followed by discussion of its content. We were always amazed at the deepness of his thoughts as they went beyond the political realm and were loaded with Common Sense that is a rare commodity in journalism, especially when it relates to problem-solving policies.

What is so alluring about Mr. Miele's "Heartland Diary" entries is that they come from the soul, they are thoroughly researched, and they always have a critical point that causes the reader to evaluate his own opinions. That is one of the major clues of a solid thinker — soul in his writing that stands the test of time. Now, as the decade has passed, I seldom read other editors because when it comes to philosophic intent or critical thinking, Frank is the master. I am always astounded by how rich his mind is and how he has had the energy and intellect to produce such readable articles week after week for the better part of two decades. No one can match him. However, his readers are the winners, as they have the wisdom needed to appreciate such work.

It is a feather in Frank's cap to be known as one who pursues the truth, week after week, no matter the public derision. Mr. Miele has been the country's most courageous editorial writer through some of our most troubled times and a fine example of the best that journalism has to offer.

The difference between Frank and the national herd of editors is clear — that when he speaks of the principles of government he knows that of which he speaks. The others speak merely of their own bias rather than the principles elucidated by our Founders.

Most journalists have lost their way to the detriment of our country; Frank never has, and that is a difficult public road for him to travel. Courage and truth are his first line of defense against the naysayers, as it should be for all. Unless we honestly admit, as a whole, to the "why" we have allowed our country and its society to be slowly devoured by this monster of Moral

Relativism, we will never come close to resolving our political divide.

This basic conflict about governance in the "Heartland Diaries" that you are about to read has been the fuel for the best of mankind and the worst; and, it is at the forefront of our democratic world that struggles to govern mainly through political parties. However, the folly of the argument between the two views of governance lies in the fact that the U.S. Constitution is largely one of a constrained view of the people to be governed, not an unconstrained view. "Heartland Diaries" is clear on that point.

There should be no argument that our Founders' goal was to construct a governance system that allowed man his individual freedom to be all that he can be. The constrained vision sees freedom as finite and argues that government power is accumulated at the expense of private freedom. It is not a living Constitution as many progressives believe it should be. One must never underestimate a country's inability to imagine its own destruction fostered by its political elite through their selfish quest for power with means that are morally unjustifiable, but best serve their desired outcomes. The Constitution, as written, is Frank's map — forming the basis for his thinking and writing as highlighted in the "Heartland Diaries."

That single attribute of a principled search for truth is so lacking by others in journalism, even though they have been given a special constitutional mandate to protect the public, that Frank comes to the party almost alone in his efforts to inform. And, that in my opinion, makes him one of the outstanding and finest examples of his profession. He, unlike others, never blinks at the truth! Frank is only conservative in his protection of the U.S. Constitution and strives for resolutions to problems that have to be pulled like weeds from the garden and replanted with workable policies.

The readings in "Heartland Diaries" are a serial history beginning with the advent of the 9/11 terrorist attack that briefly united all of America and then fell apart because of the Progressive lust for power. Mr. Miele writes from the point of view of a serious, honest, patriot of America's founding and its growth to become a world power. Now, we are faced with the current Progressive movement by the left to embrace socialism, and no clear distinction can be drawn between "socialism" and "communism." That comment is certainly to be heeded by the country at large.

The historical outcome defining socialism is how the few have managed to plunder the many through the sophistry that persuades the victims that they are being robbed for their own benefit. It belies the basic foundation of all that we believe, all that we cherish, and all that the goodness of American citizens has provided for the world.

Progressives are degrading Western Civilization from inside our democratic walls through the "Political Correctness'" that destroys Good and substitutes Evil. They have set out to recreate America and Mr. Miele takes that head-on throughout the "Heartland Diaries" within the administrations of Bush, Obama, and Trump. Reading Mr. Miele's articles will give you great insight into our country from the Middle of America which is the backbone of all that is good and sane, but continually rebuffed by the Elites of the Far West Coast and the Northeast corridor.

Frank Miele has written a true history of the political thoughts of the American people since 9/11 with the publishing of the "Heartland Diaries." It is far and beyond the scope of anything else that I have seen published or read. It is educative, truthful, and helpful to all in sorting out their thoughts about the political time-bombs that we harvest now in keeping with the divisiveness we have sown during the past decade.

Lastly, enjoy Mr. Miele's critical writing and analysis that form the first three volumes of the "Heartland Diaries" about the last three presidential administrations and the vast change of heart since 9/11 concerning the impact of that terror attack upon our soil. It has turned into a political battle among our governing bodies, and the radical left with the American people. A quote by Thucydides the Greek (471-400 B.C.), "... Peace is an armistice in a war that is continually going on...." Many reject that, but it has been world history forever, and some forget that.

"Heartland Diaries" will make excellent reading and should encourage productive discussion as it is a picture of our country in political turmoil. Mr. Miele has created a Tour de Force with his "Heartland Diaries," a multi-volume book that once one begins to read it they will not want it to end. It is really that good.

— RLS, November 2018

Richard L. Spencer, Ph.D., is a retired lieutenant colonel in the U.S. Air Force, who served as a combat navigator during the Vietnam War delivering needed military supplies, ammunition, tanks, helicopters, etc., to every hot spot in the world. Counting his reserve service, Spencer devoted 27 years to his military career. As a civilian, Spencer has focused on an academic career as an economist and administrative professional, including stints as vice president of the Community College of Philadelphia and the Community College of Delaware County. He resides in Delaware with his wife Susan, and they have four grown children. Spencer is a devoted student of history. You can read more of his analysis and critiques in book reviews he published on his old squadron's webpage at http://cargomasterraster.blogspot.com/

Introduction to the Heartland Diaries

"HOW I GOT HERE"

BY FRANK DANIEL MIELE

For the most part I am irrelevant. Boswell had his Samuel Johnson to give his life meaning and import; I have had America. When Richard L. Spencer first christened me as "America's diarist" back in 2011, I was humbled but did not really have time to stop and think about it. Duty called.

Back then, I was the managing editor of the Daily Inter Lake, a position I held from April 2000 until September 2018. I had plenty to keep me busy managing a staff of as many as 23 reporters and photographers and directing news operations for not just our daily paper, but for a half-dozen weekly newspapers also owned by the Hagadone Montana Publishing group. One of the labors of love for me was editing the Opinion pages of the Inter Lake, which I envisioned as an open forum for all viewpoints. I didn't look down my nose at anyone's opinion because I had learned the hard way (around the tables of a 12-step program) that everyone had something valuable to share and that my own story wasn't so unique after all.

When, in 2004, I proposed a new expanded Sunday opinion section for the Daily Inter Lake called Montana Perspectives, my goal was to incorporate more voices into the mix. It seemed to me that any one of those down-home Montanans with their coveralls and dirty fingernails had more wisdom and common sense about a life well lived than all of the high-paid East Coast syndicated columnists put together. I grew up in the Hudson River Valley, in the shadow of the skyscrapers of New York, but that seemed like a hundred years ago. By 2004, I had been living in Montana for most of 30 years, had sobered up, and started to shed the blinders that a college education seems designed to equip people with as they tread the scary road of destiny.

Call me crazy, but I saw my job as an editor being to ensure that my newspaper told the stories of the people in our community, not to tell the people in our community stories. It seems to me, now more than ever, that too many American newspapers and too many editors have mistakenly decided that their sacred trust is to shape their community rather than to take the time to learn its intrinsic, brilliant shape and shine a light on it. The more I got to know Kalispell and Montana, the more I was convinced that I was blessed to be a part of the fabric of life here. In a sense I was content to be a Henry David Thoreau and spend my remaining years learning about the grand acre I inhabited in the heart of America and seeing through its magnifying lens the picture of a universe full of mystery, magic and mirth. "America's diarist?" I was too busy raising two young children, running a newspaper, and staying sober through a divorce, the unexpected and tragic death of my mother, and a personal debt crisis that seemed to rival the one in Washington. Life was grand, but it was all I could handle.

But then my boss, publisher Tom Kurdy, advised me with his impish grin that if I were going to start a new Sunday opinion section, it would need to include a weekly column by the editor — namely me. That didn't terrify me, but it did leave me feeling inadequate. What could I possibly write about every week that would justify the space in the daily newspaper — or the time of the readers whom I would be asking to read it? "Other editors do it," Tom reminded me. "You'll think of something." More than 700 columns later, it turns out that Tom — as usual — was right. I did think of something, and as the column that serves as the Prologue to this book and this series will tell you, fairly quickly I was driven by one reader to think of my column as a higher calling — an opportunity I should not waste. I was lucky enough to be in a position where I could devote considerable time to observation of the news cycle, and felt that it might be useful to share some of what I had learned with my readers. Nonetheless, I did not ever forget that my opinions were just the "Editor's 2 Cents," as my column was titled. I always recognized that I was just one voice in the choir and that, as Bob Dylan poignantly said, "You're right from your side, and I'm right from mine."

My column ultimately was informed by love of country, gratitude for family and friends, humility before God, and an acute awareness of the cussedness of politicians and other wild animals. I repeatedly called on the American people to live up to the mandate set upon them by the Founding Fathers — to educate themselves and govern the governors — and I publicly repudiated presidents, both Democratic and Republican, who betrayed their own sacred trust to the Constitution. All along, as I wrote of the greatness of America, I felt our country willingly slipping away into mediocrity — and looked for solutions that would come from the people, not the politicians. If you look up the "Tea Party Movement" in Wikipedia, you will find it asserted that "The movement began following Barack Obama's first presidential inauguration (in January 2009) when his administration announced plans to give financial aid to bankrupt homeowners." Maybe so, but when you look at the column I wrote on June 6, 2006, entitled "It's time to send a message," you will find this declaration: "We need a symbol that reaches to the heart of American freedom and identity. A symbol that tells the powers that be, 'We won't take it any more.' A symbol of grass-roots resistance to imperious foolishness. We need, in short, a new Tea Party."

It is no accident that the subject of that column was the Kennedy-McCain immigration "reform" bill that was the latest in a series of attempts by the "rulers" of the United States to convince the sovereign people of our nation that we had nothing to fear from endless border incursions, repeated amnesties for illegal immigrants, and a blatant disregard for the well-being of American citizens when compared to the needs of foreign workers and of the U.S. companies that wanted to hire them at low wages. As you read through the essays of the first three volumes of the "Heartland Diaries," you will discover that the border scam run by U.S. politicians is one of the two predominant themes that form the basis of the title and the argument of "Why We Needed Trump." The second, of course, is nationalism versus globalism, and the dilemma of how to fight a global war on terror while at the same time ensuring that we put our national interests first. Between these two major themes, Bush was only half right, as his instinctive protection of the American people was compromised by his willingness to surrender to a global world view that actually made America weaker.

I didn't know we needed Donald Trump when I wrote most of these essays, but I knew we needed someone who was not part of the Establishment, not afraid to try new ideas, and not worried about what people said about him. Trump met the bill, but whether President Trump will succeed at accomplishing what I and others hoped for when we imagined a national savior — well, that remains to be seen. I could still write another volume in this series entitled "Why Trump Failed Us" or just as possibly "Why We Failed Trump." Only time will tell.

In the meantime, I hope you enjoy the first three volumes of the "Heartland Diaries," focused on the campaigns and presidencies of George Bush, Barack Obama and Donald Trump, but including lots of side trips to visit the major personalities and issues that have informed our national debate during the first two decades of the 21st century. Future volumes will cover topics ranging from the history of the Progressive Movement to the dangerous role of the national media in misleading the American public. For additional reading, you can visit me at www.HeartlandDiaryUSA or follow me on Facebook @HeartlandDiaryUSA or on Twitter @HeartlandDiary.

— **Frank Miele**
November 2018
Frank@HeartlandDiaryUSA.com

PROLOGUE

The rest of the story ...

Sept. 27, 2009

Sometimes people ask me why I insist on writing column after column about Barack Obama, or before him George W. Bush, when I am just a small-town editor.

The answer is simple.

Because I care about what happens to this country.

If you know of anything more important to write about than the takeover of health care under Obama or the attempted surrender of sovereignty under Bush, let me know what it is. Oh yeah, the war in Iraq and the war in Afghanistan. You are right. Those are important, too.

More important, for instance, than the city council's vote on whether or not to establish "light pollution" guidelines. More important than whether a new library is built in Kalispell. More important even than my opinion about the rivalry between Flathead and Glacier high schools.

All of those have been suggested as topics for my column, and they are all worthy of discussion. In fact, you can often read the Inter Lake's opinion on such local topics in our editorials.

But this column represents my personal interests and expresses my personal opinions. Therefore, I can write about anything, within reason, that touches my fancy. Sometimes that means I do write about personal topics such as my wedding day, my children's accomplishments, or a favorite artist such as Bob Dylan. But even then, I try to strike some universal chord in an effort not to be too provincial.

It was not always so. In fact, when this column started five years ago, I had a tendency to write about either the newspaper itself or my family and my personal observations on a weekly basis. This resulted in some heartfelt columns such as several I wrote in honor of my mother, who had died in 2003 of

Creutzfeld-Jakob disease (the human version of mad cow disease). I even won a first-place for column-writing that first year, so I might well have kept on in that vein till this day

But then something happened.

A reader called.

He told me he thought I was a good writer, but he wanted to know why I was wasting his time.

"What's that?" I asked.

"Don't you know what's going on?" he answered. "Don't you read the newspapers?"

"Well, as a matter of fact I do," I insisted proudly.

"With everything going on — with what's happening in Washington and Iraq and the economy — why are you writing about the Seahawks?"

Or maybe it was "Why are you writing about fry bread?" or "Why are you writing about the cold weather?" I confess I no longer remember the topic that had struck my reader as so insultingly trivial in an era when momentous decisions are being made every day.

But I remember what he concluded with: "Why don't you write about something that matters? Don't waste my time."

Phew!

I don't mind telling you, that was food for thought

At first, I demurred. I told the guy that he didn't want to read my opinion. I was just a small-town editor from Montana. If he wanted to know about political issues in Washington, D.C., he could read lots of columnists from Washington or New York. But he told me he wanted to know what I think.

"I don't buy those papers from New York," he said. "I buy the Inter Lake. I want to know what people in Montana think about the things the people in Washington are doing!"

It was kind of my equivalent of one of those town-hall meetings where plain, everyday citizens are confronting their senators and representatives and demanding answers. "Why don't you vote for something that matters?" they could be shouting. "Don't waste our time."

And you know what? I have no idea if my caller was liberal or conservative, Democrat or Republican. He was just someone who saw big things happening all around him, and wanted confirmation from me, his local newspaper editor, that I "got it."

Again, it reminds me of those folks in the town-hall meetings who are demanding answers from their government today and insist that they are non-partisan, even though many of them might vote for Republicans. Their anger doesn't have anything to do with PARTY; it has everything to do with COUNTRY.

Do you get it? I do.

And if anyone thinks I write these columns to advance the interest of a political party, they don't know me. My purpose in writing passionately about big issues is not to satisfy any politician; it is to satisfy one reader who picked up the phone and told me he expected me to do better.

Like it or not, now you know the rest of the story.

Part 1: Bush's Global Failure: Half Right

What's a border for?

April 24 2005

The power of an idea can be staggering, even world-changing.

Thus, we saw the central idea of Jesus — to love one another — defeat the greatest empire the world has ever seen, Rome and all its glory. Thus did the notions of a failed young German artist — Adolf Hitler — turn Europe into a charnel house that devoured more than 50 million lives. Thus did Gutenberg's idea of a printing press convert us in a few short hundred years from superstitious barbarians who knew nothing for sure into supercilious post-moderns who are sure they know everything.

Yes, indeed. Ideas have a power that often confounds presidents, armies and even the tide of history.

Take the words of Thomas Paine. His "Common Sense" provided the impetus for a ragtag group of philosophic revolutionaries to thumb their nose at the king of England — yes, THAT king of England, the most powerful man in the world — and unleash a movement that extends from Philadelphia in 1776 to Baghdad in 2005.

In the past few weeks, another such movement has been born quietly. It is the subject of bemused scorn by the major media and the D.C. establishment, but that does not mean it should be taken lightly. One thing that history proves is that entrenched power never recognizes the incipient power of a new idea until being hit between the eyes by it. Call it the David and Goliath principle.

What is this new idea that could change the world?

How about this? Let's protect our investment in this great country of ours by making sure that new shareholders pay for their share of the American dream instead of stealing it. That means legal immigrants, who follow the rules and prove themselves to be of worthy character, will always be welcome in the United States, but cheaters (those who enter by fraud and deception) will not.

Like all great ideas, it is a simple one. Perhaps it is not even new, but for the past 30 years at least, it has been untried. The great border between Mexico and the United States has not been a barrier at all, but rather a mile marker for Mexican workers on their way to Los Angeles or Tucson or San Antonio. And make no mistake about it — they do not just work. They also tax the social welfare system, burden our schools and clog up our jails. And then to reward them for their perfidy, every 20 years or so, a new American president decides to make them legal residents by drawing on that deep reservoir of affection America has for all immigrants.

It isn't right. And more and more Americans have been getting tired of it, especially since 9/11 when it became clear that our national defense is partly wrapped up in keeping a closer watch on who is entering our country and what they are doing here.

Now, that growing concern has turned into a grass-roots movement which has the potential to change our national policy, and thus the course of history.

Indeed, for the past couple of weeks, the Minuteman Project has been showing the way to a new paradigm of national self-defense. It turns out that a few hundred retired plumbers, beauticians and truck drivers know more about protecting our national treasure — literally the wealth of our economy and of our traditions — than do all the politicians in Washington.

About 650 of them so far, working in shifts, have patrolled 27 miles of the U.S.-Mexican border in Arizona for the sole purpose of assisting the overburdened Border Patrol. About 10,000 more have volunteered to be part of the project in the future.

It probably is not the most logical way to protect the border, but logic has left us with no protection at all, so it was time for an idea to come from the people. It's our country, after all, and we ought to be willing to defend it. Just as no one would welcome an intruder into his home to eat the family food and sleep in the family bed, so too must we be willing — and wise enough — to say that immigrants are always welcome in our country IF... and only if... they knock on the door first, introduce themselves, and prove themselves to be our friends.

Maybe volunteers aren't the most reliable long-term solution to policing the border, but here's an idea: How about the National Guard? Isn't service on our own border just as important as service in Iraq? It would be much less dangerous for the young men and women, and it gives residents of border towns something they haven't had in a long time: peace of mind.

FILIBUSTER? OR JUST BLUSTER?

May 15, 2005

Everything starts with an ideal. At least, so says Plato.

Then from the reflection of that ideal, we get reality, which is — shall we say? — somewhat less than ideal.

Thus we have, for instance, the ideal of strength... and the reality of steroids. The ideal of beauty... and the caricature of botox. The ideal of godliness... and the travesty of pedophile priests.

It's not a pretty thing, this reality, and maybe we should not get too used to it. There is a tendency to settle for things the way they are, on the assumption that the more things change, the worse they get. But it is certainly possible we are not doomed to a downhill spiral after all. Maybe we are just habituated to mediocrity; maybe we have the capacity to stretch back toward that original ideal and make a turn for the better.

Or maybe not.

Take democracy.

Against all expectations, It works. But in a very real sense it has never worked better that the moment some dreamer thought of it. It inevitably gets people killed when its revolution is worked on a new populace at the expense of some despot or oligarchy. And then it inevitably declines into a sort of free-for-all that is best typified by the ongoing food fight also known as the Japanese Diet.

But the sloppiness of democracy is not just found in foreign climes. One need look no further than the U.S. Congress to realize that it really is a kind of miracle that democracy works at all. The House, for instance, always seems to bring forward its most raptorian members for leadership. This month it is Tom DeLay. Next month it may be the Tasmanian Devil. Ayaaah, what's up, doc?

And what about the Senate? You remember the greatest deliberative body in the world, don't you? All right, here is a case where the ideal is long forgotten, and what we have left over is Harry Reid, the Democratic minority leader from Nevada who just called President Bush a "loser," and our very own Republican Sen. Conrad Burns, who has called various people various things at various times, but no longer does so in public.

If you want a specific example of how the ideal quickly transforms into the less-than ideal, you have no better example available than the Senate filibuster — the traditional ability of one senator to hold the other 99 hostage.

Despite the charm of the old film "Mr. Smith Goes to Washington," however, don't be fooled into thinking the filibuster is some noble institution that is used exclusively by good men for good causes. It is no more than a legislative tool and is thus used by legislators for legislative purposes, and reflects nothing more than the self-interest of politics. For every Jimmy Stewart who has used the filibuster to advance the cause of freedom, there has been a Jim Crow who has stood up as the standard-bearer of oppression.

But the filibuster still had an important purpose. It ensured that the minority had a way to make sure other senators, and ultimately the public, were aware of all sides of an argument before a vote was taken. That meant anyone who believed he was right — even a pompous racist buffoon of the 1950s — could try to prove it, thus ensuring that even a minority of one could be heard.

Today, however, the filibuster has nothing to do with being heard. That's the job of cable TV and the Internet. What we are left with instead is obstructionism. Democratic senators are currently using the threat of filibuster to hold up some of President Bush's judicial appointments who would otherwise be expected to win the simple majority needed for confirmation. And it really is just the threat of filibuster that matters, because in today's less-than-ideal Senate, you don't actually have to get up and talk on the floor of the Senate to hold a filibuster. You just need to send a note to the Speaker of the House and let him know you are filibustering.

Then the Speaker waives the formality of actually engaging in the filibuster and simply puts a hold on whatever legislation is opposed. Thus the filibuster has gone from a tool of rhetorical art to a tool of power politics. Senators no longer need to get sleepy and hoarse from their filibuster; in fact, they can be catching a nap in their limousines on the way to lunch with a fat cat or two, and it still counts as a filibuster.

So much for the ideal.

This is how democracy works in 2005, and you'd better get used to it. Or should you? Maybe we should expect better of our legislators. Maybe we should demand better from them.

Democratic senators are acting offended now because their Republican colleagues are threatening to take away their opportunity to filibuster on judicial nominees. Notice, I did not say their right. It should be clear that the filibuster is merely a rule of the Senate, and has no constitutional status. It is not a gift of God, but a gift of the Senate Rules Committee.

Republicans don't propose doing away with the filibuster altogether, just restricting it to the business of legislation rather than the confirmation process. They say the president has a right to an up or down vote on his judges. And of course they are right, but so too does the "minority of one" have a right to make its case before the public.

Instead of throwing away the filibuster in these cases, why not stretch back toward the ideal and make a filibuster a filibuster again? If some well-to-do senator wants to give up his black-tie speaking engagements and chi-chi soirees in order to stand up in the Senate for 48 hours or 72 hours and say what he really thinks, then I am all in favor of that.

But I have a feeling what would happen instead is that the president's nominees would be quickly and quietly appointed, and the great Senate of the United States would get back to its main business — talking around the issues.

SLOW DEATH FOR THE U.S.?

August 7, 2005

So what do the following people have in common?

Bruno Lopez-Cruz, Juan Carlos Estrada-Medina, Jose Arias-Valadez, Antonio Muzaleno-Cruz, Juan Manuel Ibarra-Lopez, Andres Barragan-Lopez, Antonio Rodriguez-Soriano, Eduardo Garcia-Parilla, Israel Cruz-Zayas, Ose Ramon Beltran-Medrano, and Felix Anselmo Lizardi-Lopez.

Give yourself credit if you noticed they all have Spanish-sounding names, and put down an A-plus if you noticed they all have hyphenated last names.

But that's just a coincidence. The real common thread is that these are all illegal immigrants to the United States who have either been charged, pleaded guilty or been sentenced in the last month to crimes in the United States.

And don't make the mistake of thinking this is some problem far away from us in Arizona or Texas or even Washington. These were all criminal cases that U.S. Attorney

Bill Mercer brought before one of the federal judges right here in Montana.

That's right. Here in remote Montana, at the northern edge of the country, illegal immigration from the southern border is just as significant a problem as it is in the rest of the country.

Day after day, week after week, month after month, I watch as the Department of Justice issues one press release after another showing that illegal aliens have been caught and prosecuted in Montana for crimes that range from drug dealing to using phony immigration documents to just plain-old illegal re-entry after being deported. It doesn't matter to me if they come from Canada or Mexico, but the Spanish-sounding names make it easy to track these criminals and see a dangerous pattern emerging.

And the situation is only worse in other parts of the country. The U.S. bureaucracy is being clogged up with foreign nationals who are taking advantage of our generosity. It's not just the court system where we are spending billions of dollars on illegal aliens. It's also the education system, the welfare system — you name it.

Please don't be cowed by the people who try to make you feel like a racist or xenophobe because you are worried about illegal immigration. It is your obligation to defend your country, and defense should begin at the borders. That's a no-brainer. In fact, it's one of those truths we hold to be self-evident, as Thomas Jefferson phrased it in the Declaration of Independence.

But apparently some people don't think our "independence" should extend to Mexico. Indeed, the virtual open border policy allows as many as 10,000 illegals to cross into the country each day, so we are anything but independent. Rather, we are intertwined, and the climbing vine of 20 million illegal aliens is weaving in and out of our economy, threatening to put a stranglehold on our lifeblood.

If this continues, you don't have to be a statistical wiz to figure out that our way of life itself will eventually collapse. One of the most significant problems with the illegal immigrant population is that it has absolutely no incentive to assimilate into our American culture. Indeed, many of these illegals are loyal to their home country, not to ours, and they would rather spread their language, customs and values here than learn the ones that have made us the greatest country in the world.

I guess we are supposed to shut up and keep quiet about this problem because some rich people in California like having cheap nannies and gardeners, but frankly I don't give a damn.

It's time to stand up for our country, our culture and our way of life. To paraphrase Patrick Henry, "Give us a secure border or give us a slow death." The choice is ours — today, right now — and if we don't demand the first, we deserve the latter.

HOW TO STOP THE FLOOD OF ILLEGALS

August 21, 2005

Bill Mercer is the guy with his finger in the dike.

He's the U.S attorney for Montana, and in the past five years he's seen a big increase in the number of illegal immigrants — mostly from Mexico — being charged with crimes in the state.

Just look at the numbers from the last two years. In 2004, there were 51 illegal alien defendants charged in Montana's federal courts with either immigration violations or more serious crimes such as drug trafficking. So far in 2005, there have been the same number of defendants charged — 51. In just seven months.

That's right, if prosecutions continue at the same pace for the rest of the year, we are on track to see a 63 percent increase in prosecutions in just one year.

We can partly thank Mercer for that. The U.S. attorney doesn't think it can be seen as any kind of success to merely turn illegal aliens over to the immigration service and have them deported.

"Relatively early in my term, it occurred to me that if we looked at people being deported rather than being charged with a serious crime, it would be a very bad deterrence policy."

Of course, that's just what we see in a lot of other jurisdictions. The Border Patrol has a kind of revolving-door policy for illegal aliens. They catch them and send them back to Mexico over and over again until eventually they don't catch them, at which time the population of the United States has just increased by one.

Mercer is more interested in increasing the population of U.S. prisons with illegal aliens, and he's doing what he can to put them there.

That's why Mercer and his staff now are prosecuting all illegal immigrants captured on a return trip to the United States with a felony. If they want to visit our country so bad, they can have an all-expenses paid stay in a federal penitentiary for two years.

That's the typical penalty for illegal re-entry after deportation.

Unfortunately, as I said, Mercer is just like the little Dutch boy with his finger in the dike. Leaks in our border protection policy have sprung up in so many places that Mercer's small attempt to restore respect for American law is almost invisible in the bigger picture.

Remember, we are talking about as many as 25 million illegal immigrants living in our country, committing crimes, attending schools, using public facilities such as libraries, sapping dollars out of the health-care system, forcing communities to invest in bilingualism, and just generally taking advantage of the American people's generosity.

You can't even hope to estimate the cost to our country of this slow invasion. It's far away in the billions of dollars though, and it pervades every sector of our lives. The Justice Department is just one place where it's easy to see.

By one report, the percentage of non-citizens in our federal prisons is now as much as 35 percent of the total federal prison population. What are they there for? You guessed it. Most of them are illegal aliens busted for drug crimes.

That's the case in Montana, too, on a smaller scale. Mercer didn't have the numbers available, but he said that it was his sense that "if you looked at the arrests over the past five years, you would find a disproportionate number of illegal aliens represented in the number of people convicted of drug trafficking" in Montana.

Indeed, based on the current caseload, illegal immigrants represent nearly 20 percent of all the prosecutions in federal courts in Montana. That is a staggering number when you remember how far we are from Mexico.

So what's the answer?

We can't just count on Bill Mercer to solve the problem for us. This is a nationwide emergency, and the sooner ordinary Americans such as you and I decide to get involved, the sooner the problem will get fixed.

Remember, we still outnumber the illegal aliens by about 10 to 1, and we've each got 10 fingers. Takes my advice, folks, and put your fingers in the dike. If we all do our part, we have a chance.

Otherwise, the flood that is coming will overwhelm me, you, our schools, our prisons, our economy, our children, and our grandchildren.

9/11: A SOMBER REASSESSMENT OF OUR RESPONSE

Sept 11, 2005

Exactly four years ago today, as I was contemplating what the Inter Lake's Sept. 12, 2001, front page would declare a "Day of Horror," I sat down to write an editorial that took stock of the deadliest attack ever on America.

We did not know much yet — just the scope of the wickedness which had been done, and the depth of the heroism which had been exhibited by many of those who lost their lives.

In a sense, we were innocent. We had no idea that the war on terrorism had begun — or that the war would make adversaries of not just al-Qaida and the United States, but of the right and the left.

That day four years ago was a day for tears and a day for prayers. It was hardly a day for analysis or expectations or understanding. There was no perspective yet — just the painful open wound that we all shared.

Naively, perhaps, I assumed then that our country would be drawn closer together, that our citizens would rally behind one cause — the cause of righteousness — just as we had done 60 years before when the Japanese bombed Pearl Harbor.

I wrote that "we all need to come together as a nation in prayer. Our strength does not just come from weaponry but from our traditions and our faith. As those have always sustained us in the past, they will once again be the rock on which we stand — and prevail."

Today, I'm not sure those words still ring true.

Another line from my editorial of Sept. 12, 2001, perhaps explains why. I wrote then that the terrorists' attacks "will forever change our country in ways we do not yet begin to understand."

We have indeed been changed, and not just superficially — not because we have to stand in line longer at airports and not because the government has the power to tap your cell phone if you are a suspected terrorist.

Yes, today we have a Patriot Act to increase police powers, but that is not a fundamental change. Similar measures have been used during other periods of our history, and we have survived them all. I'm certainly not a big fan of curtailing civil liberties, but if we are going to curtail them for anyone I would hope it is for people suspected of plotting to blow up their neighbors.

It seems to me there should be less worrying about the rights of librarians to protect their patrons' privacy and more concern about how to make sure our libraries are not being used as training grounds for al-Qaida.

Maybe the people who are more afraid of the American government than Osama bin Laden know what they are talking about. There are such people, and sometimes when they appear on TV, with their outrage at President Bush for trying "to rid the world of evil," I feel like I am trapped in a dream.

People like Michael Moore, Howard Dean, George Soros, the senators from California and New York, and many of the people who write impassioned letters to the Inter Lake week in and week out seem like they are from another planet sometimes.

That would at least be an explanation for why they don't understand the concept of evil. Maybe there is some planet somewhere that is like the world of the Teletubbies, where people roll and bounce and giggle all day under a smiling baby-faced sun, and where no harm is done to anyone ever.

That's at least as good an explanation as the real one — that Americans no longer have a common vision, that we are at risk of being torn asunder, and that our country has fallen into peril because we are afraid to defend ourselves.

A huge gulf has opened between President Bush and his supporters and those who not only oppose him, but oppose his goal of making the world safe for democracy. Such people don't seem to think any cause is worth dying for.

I wish they would tell that to the children of the firemen who died going up, not down, the stairwells of the World Trade Center. I wish they would tell that to the widows of the heroes of Flight 93 who fought their hijackers and may have saved the White House from destruction. I wish they would tell that to the veterans of Iwo Jima and the Battle of the Bulge who watched their friends torn up by bullets and bombs in World War II.

America has always depended on the sacrifices of its citizens to win and ensure our freedom. It was thus so in 1776, and it was thus so when Ronald Reagan fought the Soviet empire to a standstill without firing a shot.

But now, we are told, all that has changed. We are instead today supposed to use negotiation and reason to convince the bad people that they have gone astray. We are supposed to protect our American way of life with kind words and donations to good causes. We are supposed to think that Osama bin Laden will develop a newfound respect for our country if we just get out of Iraq and go home. We are supposed to think we are to blame for all the trouble around the world — all the war, the hunger, the hurricanes. You name it.

And if it wasn't the fault of all of us, then it was at least the fault of "Bush and Cheney," those two demigods who wreak havoc everywhere they go.

Trouble is, some people actually believe that.

And if enough Americans hate America — their own country, their own government, their own values — then it's no longer certain that we will once again prevail.

That's why I no longer have confidence in the American people to persevere in the war on terror, and why I can no longer stand behind the editorial we ran on Sept. 13, 2001, when I wrote: "Our leadership has come together to meet a common enemy."

Today those words are entirely laughable.

It turns out that on Sept. 11 our leadership came together only long enough to choose up weapons, march off 10 paces, and turn to fire at each other in an ugly, embarrassing, heart-wrenching duel that leaves all true Americans — those who celebrate our culture and our values — wounded and dispirited.

TIME TO TAKE A STAND? OR TIME TO STAND STILL?

September 18, 2005

A few people took exception to my argument last week that our country is weakened by a widening polarity between right and left.

They don't disagree with the premise, but they have a rebuttal: George Bush made them do it.

It must be convenient to have a scapegoat to blame everything on. It worked for the Republicans in the '90s when they could blame all the moral woes of our country on the personal failings of one man — Bill Clinton.

Likewise, today's Democrats — with their increasingly petulant rhetoric — have determined that the precise start of the decline and fall of Western civilization was the moment when the Supreme Court "appointed" (or "anointed" or "affirmed" — take your pick) George W. Bush as winner of the 2000 presidential election.

This remarkable episode in U.S. history should have redounded credit and glory upon our ingenious Constitution. Whether you agreed with the decision of the court or not, the constitutional process had worked to bring us through a monumental crisis without bloodshed.

But for a large portion of our population, the court's ruling was a license to hate. They don't hate the government, I am told; they hate the "administration." They don't hate the Constitution; they hate the way it was hijacked. They don't hate George Bush — oh wait, yes they do hate George Bush.

And if you remember, that was exactly the mean state of politics in our country four years ago when a collection of evil men from overseas spit in our face, cursed us to their god, and crashed planes full of precious lives into buildings full of yet more precious lives and announced to the world that they had declared war on our way of life — on our freedom, on our tolerance, on our generosity.

And for a brief — very brief, as it turned out — moment, it seemed as though Americans would put their self-interest behind and unite for the common good, that we would stand tall behind not just a president but a commander-in-chief, and that we would confront evil confidently, just as another generation did when confronted with the menace of Nazism and imperial Japan.

But that was not to be the case.

President Bush provided moral leadership and set before the nation a hard path of necessity: Just a few days after we were attacked, he told us the war against terrorism would be "a lengthy campaign unlike any other we have ever seen. ... And we will pursue nations that provide aid or safe haven to terrorists. Every nation in every region now has a decision to make: Either you are with us or you are with the terrorists."

He never said the war to defeat the Taliban in Afghanistan would be the end of the struggle. He never said we were going to settle for the head of Osama bin Laden. And despite the complaints of those who oppose the war in Iraq, he never said we were only going to fight those with a direct tie to the 9/11 attacks.

He said, in fact, that we were about to embark on "civilization's fight" for "progress and pluralism, tolerance and freedom." He told us repeatedly that America could no longer wait for terrorists to kill first, and then be hunted down later. It was time to take a stand.

And for that brief moment at the end of 2001, it did seem as though America had rediscovered its greatness, that we would again be the champion of freedom, that we would make sacrifices and suffer for the greater good.

But when the president proved true to his word and proposed a war in Iraq, suddenly "civilization's fight" seemed not so important to many of our citizens. Suddenly the price of gasoline was more important than the price of freedom. Suddenly President Bush was once again "the Supreme Court's president" instead of the legitimate leader of the free world.

Or maybe it was not so sudden after all.

Do you remember a couple of months ago when it was Karl Rove's turn to be the scapegoat du jour for the Democratic Party? He had the audacity in June to suggest that liberals weren't just against the war in Iraq but were indeed dangerously soft on national security issues in general.

"Conservatives," he said, "saw the savagery of the 9/11 attacks and prepared for war; liberals saw the savagery of the 9/11 attacks and wanted to prepare indictments and offer therapy and understanding for our attackers. ... Conservatives saw what happened to us on 9/11 and said: 'We will defeat our enemies.' Liberals saw what happened to us and said, 'We must understand our enemies.'"

Rove's speech to the Conservative Party in New York brought down the wrath of the Democratic Party's apparatchiks in government and the media, and Rove was branded a vicious liar. It was repeatedly said that he had made up his allegations without evidence, and that Democrats were strong supporters of a military response after 9/11.

Maybe so, but the evidence that Rove was correct about liberal thinking in general is not hard to find. It is recorded in every newspaper that prints letters to the editor, including the Daily Inter Lake.

Listen to some of these comments sent to the Inter Lake in the days and weeks immediately following the Sept. 11 attacks, recorded verbatim as I received them. Then go ahead and send an apology to Karl Rove for the lies said about him.

Sept. 13: "Retaliation, retribution yes but not if it involves the loss of more Innocent Lives; American or Foreign."

Hey, doesn't that pretty much rule out the idea of a just war? If the good guys are not allowed to die for their cause, then how exactly are they supposed to wage their war in defense of freedom?

Sept. 16: "Fear exists due to the anticipated acts of vengeance and retribution, that is being spoken by President Bush and apparently supported by his fellow politicians in Washington. ... If our country takes military action against others, how is that going to replace all that we have lost? Might not this action add to the hatred that was the cause of this tragedy?"

Maybe I missed something, but since when was retaliation supposed to make people love us? And when are we going to take the terrorists at their word, and get it through our heads that they aim to destroy us and everything we stand for.

Sept. 20: "While we are all shocked by the terrorist destruction of last Tuesday, we must carefully consider our response. Will violence truly solve anything? Or will it just demonstrate a neanderthal knee-jerk response from an immature nation? ... I pray rather for an awakened conscience among my American compatriots, that we may not ignore poverty, death & destruction in the rest of the world."

You mean the way we lousy Americans usually ignore poverty, death & destruction? By spending billions of dollars to eradicate them?

Sept. 20: "Yes, the American military can shower devastation on Afghanistan in response to the terrorist attacks of Sept. 11. But what would this accomplish? ... Instead of weaponry and ground troops, let's transport relief supplies to Afghanistan. Picture our military aircraft dropping crates containing items such as agricultural implements, schoolbooks, iodine tablets, shoes, antibiotics, rice, radios, batteries, solar panels, art supplies, bicycles ... whatever the hard-hit people of that country most need and want."

Yeah, I'm picturing our planes dropping art supplies on Afghanistan... and I'm picturing the Taliban dropping our planes out of the sky with anti-aircraft missiles.

Oct. 2: "If we retaliate militarily, logic dictates that we will only make the situation worse. No matter what resources we use, there is no way we can eradicate every last fanatic... Maybe first we should take a step back. Maybe we should ask ourselves why we are hated so bitterly, and what did we do to create such a terrible desire for revenge?"

If we don't retaliate militarily, logic dictates the bad guys are going to keep blowing up our buildings and killing our people. Maybe we should just not worry about whether people hate us or not, and do what is right. If good thoughts were enough to defeat evil, then Tibet would be free now, right?

Oct. 3: "These terrorists are not 'evil.' They are misinformed about America."

Poor Karl Rove. You'd have thought that the liberals who could forgive the people who killed 3,000 on Sept. 11 would have found it in their hearts to forgive him, too. But do you remember any Democrats getting on TV and saying, "Karl Rove is not 'evil.' He is just misinformed about liberals."

Didn't think so. And you never will.

Because what we call political discourse in the 21st century is actually political dissonance. It's all about making noise in order to confuse voters. It's about name-calling and race-baiting. It's about blame and poll numbers and self-interest. It's full of what Macbeth — when confronting his ghosts of greed and political ambition — called "sound and fury," and it ultimately will lead us to the same dark grave where he and all others go who delude themselves that their selfishness is actually sacrifice.

'CONSCIENCE DOTH MAKE COWARDS ...'

December 11, 2005

"The idea that the United States is going to win the war in Iraq is just plain wrong."

With those words, Howard Dean, the head of the Democratic Party, told the world which side he is on in the war against terror. He told the terrorists in Iraq that they can win the war, and he told the soldiers from the small towns and great cities of America that they can't.

And Dean is not alone. Far from it.

Sen. John Kerry, the Democratic nominee for president in 2004, said on "Face the Nation," that "...there is no reason... that young American soldiers need to be going into the homes of Iraqis in the dead of night, terrorizing kids and children, you know, women..."

Rep. John Murtha, in his widely publicized speech of Nov. 17, said this:

"I believe before the Iraqi elections, scheduled for mid December, the Iraqi people and the emerging government must be put on notice that the United States will immediately redeploy. All of Iraq must know that Iraq is free. Free from United States occupation."

Murtha of course is an honorable man; so are they all — all honorable men. But when they doubt American strength; when they question American decency; when they challenge American motives, then they stick a dagger in the heart of the national interest just as surely as "honorable" Brutus stuck a knife into his friend Julius Caesar.

Can this really be happening?

I thought for sure that when Islamic terrorists attacked our nation and killed nearly 3,000 people, there would not be any debate about the appropriate response. I thought we would all agree that we would do what must be done, and that in Churchill's words we would "never, never, never, never ... never give in."

This, after all, was the equivalent of Pearl Harbor — an attack by an ambitious, imperious enemy on our homeland — and it could only be met with the same fury, determination and single-mindedness that was seen in the war mobilization that occurred after Dec. 7, 1941.

Or so I thought.

Instead, it turned out that our enemy knew us better than we knew ourselves. Or maybe they had read Sun Tzu on "The Art of War," where it is written: "When you engage in actual fighting, if victory is long in coming, then men's weapons will grow dull and their ardor will be damped."

There is no better description I can think of for the collapse of will power and spirit in the American population as a whole while fighting what amounts to a skirmish. Yes, we have been in Iraq for two years, and that might be considered a fairly long time to be fighting; yes, there have been real deaths of real people — regrettable deaths — but the fact of the matter is we are not really "fighting" a war. We are using our nation's tremendous resources to out-wait and out-think an opponent that has the advantage of being small and mobile. Such a war is never easy, as the British learned when fighting the French and Indian War in the American colonies, for instance. But it can be won, as evidenced by the fact that we are today speaking English and not French. There will certainly be casualties in such a war, but they are much, much less than you would find in trench warfare, air raids, or nuclear confrontation. Nonetheless, some Americans —serious, thoughtful Americans — have concluded that even the death of 2,000 soldiers is too high a price to pay to avenge the deaths of the 3,000 killed on Sept. 11, 2001 — and to prevent a similar attack from happening again.

How could that be?

How could even 10 times 2,000 deaths be too much to pay for the cause of democracy and freedom? Should we not be willing to pay the same price to save civilization from being held hostage by madmen that are parents and grandparents paid?

Thank goodness Americans were not so fearful in 1862 when the Battle of Shiloh was fought during the Civil War. It is recorded that 3,477 men died in that one battle alone. There must have been many unhappy mothers and many who wondered if the prize was worth the price. But yet the Union forces fought on, and the cause of righteousness prevailed.

So too have there been other battles, other deaths and other questions.

In World War I, the Battle of the Somme cost over a million lives. On the first day alone, more than 19,000 British soldiers were cut down. It was a horrible price to pay, but only a down payment. By the end of the battle there were more than 400,000 dead from Britain and its kingdom. But British historian Sir James Edmonds wrote of that battle, "It is not too much to claim that the foundations of the final victory on the Western Front were laid by the Somme offensive of 1916."

Brave soldiers fighting for what they believe to be right — for what they know to be right — that is the only bulwark between civilization and the myriad dark forces that would destroy it on the altars of personality, religion, or terror.

Look at the lengthy battle the Soviet Union waged to defend itself against Hitler's aggression. That struggle cost the Russians anywhere from 8.5 million to 15 million lives. Do not ask the Russian people if they think it was worth it! They paid the price they had to pay, and they did not even have democracy or freedom as their prize — just the assurance that they were more right than Hitler.

We must be clear. The issue is not whether any one of us supports war in the abstract. The issue is whether or not the alternative to war would be a better world or a worse one. No sane person endorses war as a desirable course of action. Every death of a human being is a horrible loss, and war is all about death. I know that, and so does President Bush. Do not presume that either he or I do not care about life. We do, but we care about what makes life worth living, too, and so we stand for a principle.

Would you prefer to live in a world where the Confederacy had prevailed and where the Union was dissolved? Would you prefer to live in a world where either the Ottoman Empire or the Nazi scourge had conquered all of Europe and done away with Western civilization? Would you prefer to live in a world where the British crown had stamped out rebellion — and the seeds of American democracy — in the summer of 1776? Any of those things could easily have happened — and might have — if the few resolute warriors on the front lines had not been buoyed by the prayerful determination to prevail of their leaders and their people.

Today, it is certain that there is prayerful determination to prevail among our enemies. But it is less and less certain that any such determination exists here in America — "the land of the free and the home of the brave." Indeed, all evidence suggests that what we have here is not a determination to prevail, but rather a determination to fail.

Call it "cut and run." Call it "strategic withdrawal." "Call it "appeasement." But whatever you call it, be fully aware that it is surrender. And be prepared to live in a world where democracy and freedom do not have the upper hand, where the flame of righteousness flickers close to extinction.

Shakespeare had Hamlet say, "Conscience doth make cowards of us all," and perhaps that is where we Americans have come. We have a conscience about torture. We have a conscience about secret prisons. We have a conscience about putting underwear on the heads of prisoners who would cut our heads off. We have a conscience...

> And thus the native hue of resolution
> Is sicklied o'er with the pale cast of thought;
> And enterprises of great pith and moment,
> With this regard, their currents turn awry,
> And lose the name of action.

Leave it to Shakespeare to say with a few words that which I have struggled to say with hundreds.

I said earlier that we were out-waiting and out-thinking our opponent in Iraq. But maybe not. Maybe our opponent is out-waiting and out-thinking us. And if he is, then heaven help us.

PASS THE PEACE, BUT DON'T PASS BY

December 25, 2005

This Christmas, as we celebrate the possibility of "Peace on Earth," it would not hurt to consider how peace happens, and what kind of peace is worth having.

In many churches this morning, congregants will stop to shake hands or hug or kiss in a gesture of "passing the peace" of the Lord to one another.

Unfortunately, gestures of peace often fall short of the real thing, as it is easier to shake a hand than to shake a grudge. And even a semblance of peace may turn out to be something far different, as our honest hope for peace sometimes leads us to close our eyes to potential danger. The little lambs are fine on their own, but put one wolf in sheep's clothing among them, and the peace is broken along with bones and blood vessels.

So sometimes peace is a one-way street to violence.

What about the peace that was painted with clown-bright colors on the faces of Hitler, Hirohito and Mussolini before World War II? A smile and a handshake and a treaty or two for good measure. That precious peace of the 1930s cost the world an estimated 62 million lives.

There was a peace of sorts, too, in the old Soviet Union, where for decades a spirit of obedience and oppression was employed by the state to keep down the people. That is a glum sort of peace, a dark peace that wears down men's souls and gives them no hope.

It was that kind of peace which prevailed in Saddam's Iraq, too — the kind of peace that comes when you keep your mouth shut and your eyes down. Of course, it was not so pleasant if you were a Kurd or a Shiite or if you were a woman or a proponent of freedom, but otherwise it was a peaceful place, kept so by a vigilant army and police force that was ready to stamp out any kind of opposition.

Today, Iraq has a different kind of peace. It is not so certain as the peace of Saddam, with its dictatorial certainty and glum acceptance of jackbooted thugs. This new peace is still occasionally interrupted by gunfire and explosions, by death and despair, but it also has something that you didn't see much of in the old Soviet Union or Saddam's Iraq — freedom — and it is hard to imagine a peace worth having without freedom to nurture it.

When 11 million Iraqis went to vote this month, they knew they were at risk to be the innocent victim of a car bomb or an improvised explosive device or a suicide bomber strapped with plastic explosives. They knew that their future was uncertain and risky, but they didn't let any of that stand in their way. This was no longer Saddam's Iraq; it was their Iraq. It was their future. It was their freedom. And it was worth dying for.

President Bush sent America to war in Iraq more than two years ago for just such a cause. It is no accident that the American operation in Iraq is known as Operation Iraqi Freedom. That — freedom — ultimately is what brings about peace — lasting, meaningful peace and not the sham sort that is celebrated by despots.

Yes, there was a lot of talk preceding the war about weapons of mass destruction, and about how dangerous Saddam was to the world. Those weapons were never found. But the fact of the matter is that Saddam was always more dangerous to his own people than to the rest of us, and we could have just ignored his oppression and brutality as we have done in many other cases. Certainly the French and Germans did not think we had to spend any time worrying about the Iraqi people. Those countries had lucrative contracts with Saddam, and there was no reason to stir the pot. Let sleeping dogs lie, they said.

But what if the dog is really a wolf? And what if the wolf has its teeth firmly planted in the shank of a sheep? Do you just avert your eyes and pretend you don't see? The wolf wants nothing but peace with you ("let's just be friends") but what kind of peace is it for the sheep being torn asunder?

The Iraqis had been abused and wounded by Saddam for years, and had been essentially left half-dead like the traveler in the parable of the Good Samaritan told by Jesus. In this version of the story, Saddam and his henchmen were the thieves who stole the precious garments of freedom and dignity from the Iraqi people and left them stripped and wounded.

Many nations saw what happened, but they did not all react the same way. The Germans and the French were like the priest and the Levite who saw the wounded traveler and "passed by on the other side." In the parable, those two did not think it was any of their business to take care of the injured man, just as today so many still turn their heads away from oppression and call it an "internal problem."

George Bush and the United States, however, did something remarkable. Along with Great Britain, they stopped and had compassion for the suffering of the Iraqi people and they spent their treasure on helping to put the victims on their feet and in good health. They did not do so for oil; they did not do so for Halliburton. They did so because it was the right thing to do.

"Peace on Earth; good will toward men," the angels said when they announced the birth of Jesus. But that peace did not come then and there. Rather bloodshed came, as Herod ordered the deaths of countless children to protect himself from the prophesied reign of the Christ. And more death has followed through the years.

We must conclude therefore that "Peace on Earth," while desired by both man and the angels, is not easy or cheap. You don't get it handed to you on the proverbial silver platter. You have to pay for it. Sometimes you have to fight for it — and for the freedom that makes it worth having.

And that's why — on this Christmas Day — thousands of Americans are living, fighting and dying in a desert country not far from where Jesus walked.

Peace on Earth?

Not yet, not as long as there are wolves among us, not as long as thieves lay in wait to plunder and destroy.

But as long as the Good Samaritan stops to help the innocent victim — as long as some remember what it means to be a good neighbor — then there is hope.

God bless our country for having the courage to not "pass by on the other side."

MAKING THE COUNTRY SAFE FOR TERRORISTS

January 1, 2006

On the one hand we are told that this can't be a real war because the president has not asked us to make any sacrifices.

On the other hand, we are told that the president can go to hell for asking us to make a sacrifice.

And what is the sacrifice?

Nothing less than giving up our God-given right to commit terrorism in private, without any government busybodies looking over our shoulder.

Huh?

That's right, the Democratic leadership (with an assist from the New York Times) has got a new complaint about the Bush administration. It seems the president is trying to prevent terrorist attacks against this country by listening to phone calls to and from suspected al-Qaida operatives overseas.

This apparently has some Democrats worried. After all, you never know who they will come for when they round up the friends of al-Qaida. It could be your Aunt Essie. You know how she always has those hush-hush conversations with that fellow over there in Afghanistan.

Puh-lease.

The fact of the matter is that your Aunt Essie has nothing to worry about, and neither does the Democratic leadership — unless any of them is on the phone with Osama bin Laden or one of his minions. Harry Reid and Howard Dean and Aunt Essie can make all the phone calls they want about how to bake Christmas cookies or how to block the latest energy bill — or even about how to impeach President Bush — and no one cares. Heck, we can see all of that on the 6 o'clock news anyway.

But as soon as they or anyone else picks up the phone and dials the number of a known terrorist, then watch out — because the president will not just listen to your phone call; he will do whatever it takes to preserve and protect this great country of ours. That's his job.

Except he won't be allowed to do it if the Democrats and other complainers have their way.

Sen. Russ Feingold of Wisconsin is typical: "This administration is playing fast and loose with the law in national security. The issue here is whether the president of the United States is putting himself above the law, and I believe he has done so." It seems that Russ and the other Democrats are worried about the Fourth Amendment rights of the terrorists.

Don't get me wrong. I love the Constitution as much as anyone, but like Lincoln I wonder what good the Constitution will do us if the country is destroyed or we are dead.

Just for the record, let's take a look at the Fourth Amendment that supposedly prevents the president from listening to phone calls in an effort to stop someone from blowing up the Brooklyn Bridge or dropping nerve gas into a subway tunnel.

Here it is:

"The right of the people to be secure in their persons, houses, papers, and effects, against unreasonable searches and seizures, shall not be violated, and no Warrants shall issue, but upon probable cause, supported by Oath or affirmation, and particularly describing the place to be searched, and the persons or things to be seized."

There are two things I want to call your attention to. First, the Amendment protects us against "unreasonable" searches and seizures. I submit that only a fool would consider it unreasonable to try to prevent a terrorist attack through the unobtrusive means of a wiretap. The courts may say differently, but as Mr. Dickens had a character in one of his novels remark, "The law is a ass."

Nonetheless, it should be noted that this matter of executive authority in wiretaps involving national security — especially in time of war — is far from settled law, and the president may be able to convince a court that he is constitutionally entitled to act as he has done — especially in time of war. There are certainly many precedents from the Clinton years and earlier that bolster the president's case, and no president would be wise to surrender power to either the legislative or judiciary branch if it will detract from his function as commander-in-chief.

The point isn't whether or not President Bush could have gotten permission from a court for these wiretaps; he almost certainly could. The point is exigency and expediency and secrecy. What is gained by allowing the president to act in his capacity as commander-in-chief to protect us from intended attack is that we don't have to read about the "secret" investigations in the New York Times or see them on the CBS News. Go to a court for permission to track down a terrorist, and the next thing you know an ACLU lawyer will be on TV explaining that his terrorist client has a constitutional right to make all the bombs he wants as long as he does so in the privacy of his home.

But don't get me started about the ACLU.

The second thing I would call your attention to is the explicit purpose of the Fourth Amendment. NOT its mechanism — the prohibition of unreasonable searches — but rather its underlying PURPOSE, namely to protect "the right of the people to be secure in their persons, houses, papers and effects."

I submit for your consideration the notion that the right of the people to be secure in their persons and houses includes an expectation that we will be safe from being blown to bits by insane foreign terrorists with nuclear suitcase bombs. That being so, then maybe we can stop trying to make the country safe for terrorists, and start making it safe for ourselves.

Just an idea.

Of course, it is an idea that will have me branded as a dangerous radical, a subversive destroyer of civil liberties, and a fool.

That's all right.

As soon as the New York Times or those other defenders of freedom present one shred of evidence that the Bush administration and the National Security Agency have used their eavesdropping program to put people in jail for simple criminal offenses or to settle scores with political enemies, then sign me up for the impeachment campaign. Heck, I will even storm the White House.

But there has been no evidence of wiretap abuses.

All the president's critics can do is speculate about how the president's wiretaps MIGHT someday present a danger to average folks IF he or some future president turns out to be a RAVING MADMAN!

Meanwhile, while these partisan pit bulls are trying to destroy the president, the real enemies of our country are slowly, steadily at work planning their next mission of terror in our homeland. I'm sure they must be happy to know that they have friends in Congress. Maybe they will even take the Capitol building off their list of potential targets.

One thing is certain though. When the next attack comes, as it surely will, the president's critics will be the loudest voices whining: How could this have happened? Why didn't we take more steps to protect ourselves? Where was the president?

But before that day comes, there is one question the president's critics should ask themselves: If you could have prevented the 9/11 terror attacks with a warrantless wiretap, would you have done so?

Answer yes, and you should be wise enough to shut up about the president's so-called abuse of power. Answer no, and

you have proven yourself to be a damned fool — and a
dangerous one.

But no one could possibly answer no, could they?

REAGAN, BUSH AND PERCEPTION

January 15, 2006

Recently, PBS aired a documentary on "American
Experience" that assessed the legacy of Ronald Reagan. Since I
have previously criticized PBS for its often partisan reporting, I
felt it was appropriate to take time to acknowledge that this
two-part program (called simply "Reagan") was an honest,
inspiring portrait of the most important presidency of the past
60 years.

But more than the program itself, I wanted to reflect on
Reagan and what we learn about leadership by studying his
example. Once again, and perhaps more clearly than ever, I was
impressed by Reagan's persistence of vision. He truly was one
of the few giant figures on the political landscape in the second
half of the 20th century, possibly because of his advanced age,
which meant that in some measure he was a carryover from the
earlier era when politicians stood for principles instead of for
the camera (ironic, in light of Ronnie's Hollywood background).

When Reagan was first elected, I was a youngish hippie
type, 25 years old, smart as hell, and condescending to a fault
(oh wait a minute, that goes without saying when it comes to
condescension, doesn't it?). I had no use for Reagan's policies at
the time, being convinced that he would lead us into war (His
1984 joke: "My fellow Americans, I am pleased to tell you today
that I've signed legislation that will outlaw Russia forever. We
begin bombing in five minutes.") and of course I bought into
the common liberal notion that the man was an intellectual
lightweight who was being led by the nose a la Bonzo the
trained monkey.

But nonetheless, I had a hard time disliking the man, and I slowly learned to respect his gift for communicating his vision with humor, strength, self-deprecation and assuredness. When in the year or so after he left office, the Berlin Wall came down, and eventually the Soviet Union collapsed, I decided it was time for me to reassess his policies as well. You could not mistake the glad tidings of freedom for anything else, and no one else had cared enough about those unfortunates behind the Iron Curtain to do anything about freeing them (the pope being an exception, but of course he spoke as a victim of the Iron Curtain himself, one who through fate and fortune had gotten over the wall). Gorbachev also was a lucky ally in the transformation of the "evil empire," but again, without Reagan's much maligned and deeply doubted policies, there would have been no "necessity" for the fall of the empire. It "might" have happened, but it would have been luck and happenstance, whereas under Reagan's watch, it happened because he WILLED it to happen.

That is the difference between a leader of the early 20th century and one of the late 20th century or early 21st. Nowadays, we are not used to strong-willed leaders, and they frighten us a little bit (read a whole lot). But yet still on occasion a phantom memory of the impulse to leadership will make us feel a twitch like the poor fellow who has had his leg amputated but still needs to scratch. It is that belief in leadership, I think, which has given us the presidency of George W. Bush, and perhaps the modern fear of leadership which has resulted in Bush being subject to the same kind of attacks that were used against Reagan.

The parallels between Bush and Reagan have been noted before, but I thought they were quite clear after seeing the biography of Reagan on PBS, and what was most striking was how badly maligned Reagan was during his own presidency for the same supposed flaws that are imputed to President Bush.

Indeed, I believe that if you compare the reactions of the liberal media elite (to borrow a phrase from author Bernard Goldberg) to Reagan and Bush, you will find almost no difference. In each case, there is a persistent campaign to portray the president as a moron who can't think on his own

(Ronnie had his Nancy, and W has his Cheney), but who at the same time aspires to dictatorial power (Iran-Contragate and torture-spygate).

Unfortunately, we can't skip ahead 20 or 25 years to see how incipient history will be judging George W., but it would certainly not surprise me if something happened the year after his term ends that proves him to have been a visionary, too, just as the Berlin Wall validated all of Reagan's "right-wing kook" ideas. It turns out that right-wing kooks can actually free men and women from political enslavement while feel-good kumbayah-singers can do nothing more than try to convince us that if we change our way of thinking (and give up our dependence on violence, blah blah blah) it won't hurt so bad when we all get blown up by terrorists, communists or whomever.

But I digress.

The question is whether we can learn from our history of being wrong in our judgments of great historical figures (and here we have to include Lincoln, Churchill and many others) and step back from our tendency to be tendentious in our thinking. I suppose a lot of us never do acknowledge our mistaken judgments, but they pile up behind us like pedestrians behind the car of a blind driver nonetheless. It would seem prudent, therefore, for citizens to occasionally give their leaders a benefit of the doubt. Just how exactly do we think a whiny Greek chorus of one-liners and insults is going to change history, after all? The only change in history that all the histrionic critics of Reagan brought about is that now there is a big asterisk after their names that says, "Reagan was right, and they were wrong."

I understood that unconsciously, I suppose, whenever I cheered one of Reagan's great speeches exhorting the world to heed its better angels or when I let him bring me to tears during his tribute to the Challenger astronauts. No, I didn't understand the president's war in El Salvador and Nicaragua. No, I didn't understand the need for a Space Defense Initiative. No I didn't understand the need for tax cuts. But I did have a recognition of

the genius of the American people, and I realized that Reagan
was our leader, for better or worse.

I also had to acknowledge that those were difficult times
with no easy answers, and that either fate or heaven had thrust
this former actor into the halls of power. And I had to
acknowledge that he was likable, kind, and genuine, no matter
how much I disliked his policies. And now 25 years later, we can
read the letters and other writings of Reagan and see that he
was not a moron, he was not a stooge, but rather a man of
consistent character and deep thought who left us a much
better legacy than we deserved.

Prudence would seem to encourage anyone with a serious
interest in politics today to likewise find a little middle ground
in their critical assessment of George W. Bush. Otherwise, you
may find yourself on the ash heap of history along with all the
brilliant liberal thinkers who congratulated themselves in 1980
on their good luck that the Republicans had nominated a "true
believer" who would never waiver and thus could not maneuver
in the modern political arena where vacillation is considered
the best defense against the lions or opportunity and insult.
What these great thinkers had not counted on, was that a
certain heroic stature was still possible to a man or woman who
adopted a fighting posture instead of running for cover.

George Bush is not quite as determined as Reagan,
probably, but he still shows a fortitude that sets him far apart
from other modern politicians (Clinton being the exemplar)
who say what they think we want to hear, and adjust or
moderate when they get wind of any opposition. And yes, he has
his weaknesses such as overspending, but this too is a similarity
with Reagan who decided to overspend on defense because he
knew he could and he knew the Soviet Union could not. So we
built up the national debt, and built down the international
armory, not a bad tradeoff.

Bush's war against terror is a riskier proposition probably,
partly because he is the Paul Revere in that war, unlike
President Reagan, who was George Washington at Yorktown. It
is relatively easy to accept the sword of surrender from your
enemy. It is harder by far to be the first in line to shout "the

British are coming" since lots of people would rather not fight the British ("They never bothered me or my family!") or anyone else. Bush, with just as much urgency as Revere, is riding his horse at full gallop to sound the alarm. Some along the road take up their arms and follow him, but many others just retreat into their comfortable houses, pull back the shutters, lock the doors and feel safe.

That is where we are as a nation now, divided in the early years of the war on terror between those who seek the comfort of what was and those who spurn that comfort in order to ensure any kind of a future at all. It is profoundly worrisome to look where Bush is pointing. If there is any chance to see the shadow of a peace-loving Islamic terrorist in that fog ahead of us, then by God someone will see that peaceful terrorist and try to get us to shake his hand. Meanwhile, the president's vision of a murderous brutal enemy does not waiver, and he is either right or wrong, but like Reagan he will not be deterred.

IRAQ AND IRAN AND CONSENSUS

January 22, 2006

When you read what our nation's leaders have been saying about Iran's continuing effort to develop nuclear weapons, you have to think there is a pretty good chance that our war in Iraq could soon shift east to Tehran.

Here is a sampling:

• "Launching some missile strikes into Iran is not the optimal position for us to be in. On the other hand, having a radical Muslim theocracy in possession of nuclear weapons is worse."

• "A nuclear-armed Iran is an unacceptable risk to us and our allies."

• "We cannot take any option off the table in sending a clear message to the current leadership of Iran that they will not be permitted to acquire nuclear weapons."

• "The president always has the right and always has had the right for pre-emptive strike."

No one likes the prospect of another front in the war on terror, but Iran has thumbed its nose at the international community and insisted on the right to carry out its nuclear program without oversight, which means ensuring the opportunity to create enriched uranium for use in nuclear bombs.

And an Iran with the capacity to deliver nuclear bombs through either its missiles or its terrorist friends is enough to make even the most devout atheist wake up with visions of Armageddon dancing through his head.

So it's easy to see why President Bush might be considering a military option against Iran.

Nonetheless, in order to expand the war on terror to yet another country, the president would need a national consensus, wouldn't he? And getting the Democratic Party to support military action against Iran would be impossible, wouldn't it?

Maybe not.

You see, all those quotes at the beginning of this column are not from members of the Bush administration as you might have suspected, but from Democratic sources.

The attribution for the four quotes is as follows: Sen. Barack Obama, D.-Ill.; the national platform of the Democratic Party in 2004; Sen. Hillary Clinton, D-N.Y.; and Sen. John Kerry, D-Mass., the party's presidential candidate in 2004.

So it's obvious that there already is an emerging consensus about the necessity for action if Iran turns belligerent.

The problem, of course, will be maintaining national unity if such a war goes from theoretical to actual. We all saw what happened when President Bush took our country to war against Iraq. Almost everyone, including most Democratic leaders, was on the record supporting the invasion as an appropriate response to Saddam Hussein's stonewalling tactics as the world tried to find out about his weaponry programs.

But then a few days after we were in Baghdad, the united front collapsed and Democrats started looking for political

opportunities in the chaos of battle. They even had the audacity
to claim they were misled into war, even though Democrats like
Kerry, Clinton (senator and ex-president both) and Sen. Joe
Biden were among the biggest supporters of taking out Saddam.

Could that happen again?

Probably not, and here's why.

You probably recall many of President Bush's critics
complaining that the war in Iraq was "the wrong war in the
wrong place at the wrong time." A lot of them went so far as to
say that the war was just about oil, not about terrorism or
security. Why, they asked, didn't we fight even more dangerous
countries such as Iran and North Korea — countries that
already had or were developing nuclear technology?

The implication was that as long as there was a real threat
to world peace and national security, such as a nuclear Iran,
then Democrats would be happy to join the fight.

Well, Kerry, Clinton and the gang may just get their wish
for a "just" war.

Iran's new president, Mahmoud Ahmadinejad, has taken
the gloves off. No more Mr. Nice Iran! This guy went to the
Osama bin Laden School of Charm and Bombmaking, and he is
clearly looking for an invitation to be Saddam's dance partner
the next time the band strikes up the "Paranoia Polka."

For instance, in October, Ahmadinejad declared that the
state of Israel should be "wiped off the map." He later revised
that statement somewhat to allow that he could support
relocation of Israel to somewhere in Eastern Europe, where (by
the way) he also doesn't think a Holocaust ever took place.

In addition, he has announced that, "The skirmishes in the
occupied land are part of a war of destiny ... a historic war
between the oppressor [Christians] and the world of Islam" and
he has said that he is awaiting the return of the messianic Shiite
"Twelfth Imam" to rescue the world from "terrible and
unprecedented calamities and misfortunes" (remember
Armageddon?) and to establish Islam throughout the world.

The fact that this man rules a large and powerful country is
worrisome in itself, but not unique. We certainly can't fight
wars with all the irrational loudmouths who run countries. But

what makes the chance of war with Iran more likely is the combination of Ahmadinejad's inflammatory rhetoric with a nascent nuclear weapons program (remember the bombmaking school?) that has the capacity to not just inflame but to incinerate.

So as the war in Iraq winds down and the Iraqis go about their business of setting up a constitutional democracy, the war on terror may very well have to turn its sights to Iran. After all, a world where rogue nations possess atomic weapons is a world with no security at all.

Who knows? If such a "just" war becomes necessary, perhaps the United States could even count on support from its allies.

Surely, with Iran arming missiles to destroy Israel and concealing nuclear reactors in hardened bunkers, the civilized world would have to come together in one united front to demand that Ahmadinejad and his cleric cronies give up their bombs or become the victims of ours.

Don't believe it?

Well, we started with quotes from Democrats, so let's end with a quote from a Frenchman:

"Everyone recognizes that Iran ... [has] a right to peacefully use nuclear energy. But it is imperative for the international community to ensure that the commitments reached for everyone's security are respected. [The Iranians] would be committing a grave error if they do not grasp the hand that we are extending to them." —Jacques Chirac, president of France.

Considering the stakes, Germany, France, the Soviet Union and other countries may very well join with us and Great Britain to build an international coalition to prevent Iran from following through on its nuclear threats.

Heck, if the Democrats and Republicans can come together to agree to use America's military might in defense of our national security, then anything is possible, right?

WITH FRIENDS LIKE THESE ...

January 29, 2006

Think of it this way:

You are in the middle of a no-holds-barred fight with this crazy dude who broke into your home hollering and screaming about injustice and Satan and the fact that he would be happy to die just as long as he takes you with him. He used to be a friend of yours a long time ago, or at least an acquaintance, and you did some business with him once. But then he started telling everyone how horrible you were, spreading malicious lies about you and threatening to kill you and your family.

He even tried to do it one time, several years before, when he attacked you in an underground garage with no warning. He scratched you up pretty bad, but fortunately the gun he had with him misfired, so you got away relatively intact. That time, he turned and ran, and you wrote him off as a coward.

But this time, he came to kill you, your wife, your kids. He has already kicked in your wife's teeth and gouged out your eye. You know he fights dirty, but you don't care. You just want to settle the score, get revenge and protect your family from this madman. The children are safe now, but what if he gets past you?

So you start fighting back just as hard and as mean as the bad guy. You bite his ear off and try to gouge out his eye, too. He's starting to look like a bloody mess, and you think he just might be about to say uncle when your neighbor knocks on the door to see what's going on.

You and your neighbor have not always seen things eye to eye, which is why there is a fence that runs between your yards, but fences make good neighbors is what they say. So you figure the many years of car-pooling kids, block parties and polite howdies at the end of the driveway when you pick up your mail are finally going to pay off.

Thank God for neighbors, you think.

Come on in, you holler while the bad dude is sticking his fingers up your nostrils to try to rip your nose off your face. You figure your neighbor will jump right in and throw a few punches at the crazy dude, or at the very least pick up the phone and call 911.

But 911 apparently never even occurs to the guy, and instead of throwing punches he just says kind of sheepishly that it doesn't seem like a fair fight.

"What!" you shout back. "Of course it's not a fair fight. This maniac broke in here and he's hyped up on some kind of unholy drug that makes him think he is invincible and immortal and he's ripping my nose off and all I want to know is WHEN THE HELL ARE YOU GOING TO HELP?"

"Well, not so fast. Of course, I'm going to help," says the neighbor. "I'm against maniacs as much as you are, but I just want to make sure I know all the facts. After all, maybe this guy has good reason to hate you. I don't know, and I'm not saying he does necessarily, but I probably need to at least take a little closer look to assess the situation."

And with that, your neighbor climbs up on your back and throws you off balance and reaches around your neck and starts to shut down your windpipe with his locked arms and just about then the maniac is picking up a dining room chair and rushing across the room at you like a medieval knight trying to run the king through with his own sword.

Fortunately you manage to swing around in the nick of time, and instead of impaling you, the crazy dude actually hits your neighbor a glancing blow, scratching him along the arm before hitting the wall and breaking the chair into pieces.

"Hey, why'd you do that?" asks your neighbor, and when you don't say anything back, he lifts one of his arms from around your neck and grabs ahold of a hunk of hair and pulls back on your scalp like a hooded al-Qaida murderer holding up the sawed-off head of an American hostage in Iraq, and it hurts like hell.

"I'm talking to you," he says. "Next time that guy attacks, be more careful or I'll knock you down myself," and now you are starting to get worried that you have two madmen in the house instead of just one. The difference is that the one is trying to kill you outright, and the other is trying to kill you by helping you.

"Look," you say. "Let's just take care of this maniac, and then we can settle our problems."

But your neighbor is having a hard time seeing how the maniac is really a threat to him, especially in his weakened condition, and so he is thinking maybe it is time to declare a truce and clean up the place and get back to normal, but then the maniac pulls out a gun and starts pointing it at your head, only now your neighbor's head is right behind your head, and if he shoots you he shoots both of you, and so your neighbor yanks your head one last time, calls you an incompetent jerk, and says with more than a hint of derision, "What will it take to get you to do something about that maniac who's trying to kill us?"

•••

Or think of it like this:

When the hell are the Democrats going to get off the president's back and and let him do what he was elected to do — protect America from the terrorists who want to kill us all?

SHIPPING IS GLOBAL, BUT NATIONAL SECURITY IS NOT

February 26, 2006

Have you heard the one about the Trojan horse?

Maybe President Bush and his advisers had better bone up on their ancient history, because those who forget ancient history are apparently doomed to repeat it — or maybe become it.

Here's the scenario:

You are fighting a war on terrorism. That war focuses on Mideastern fundamentalists because they have shown a particular inclination and determination to bring death and destruction to your shores. In order to prevent terrorism you have instituted new security measures across the board, ranging from new restrictions on airline boardings to warrantless wiretaps to a color-coded alert system that tells us just how scared to be (green means "sleep tight"; red means "your worst nightmare").

In addition, you have waged war against the terrorists in the Middle East and elsewhere to try to root them out. Naturally this has stirred them up like hornets whose nest was poked through with a stick. Everyone understands that retaliation by the terrorists is just a matter of time. But meanwhile life goes on, and there is a steady stream of trade between nations that must continue unabated. Although your ports are where you are most vulnerable to penetration by terrorists, you understand that the ports cannot be closed. They must continue to operate efficiently in order to maintain the economy even while security measures are being taken.

So in order to keep those cargo containers moving, you have hired a couple of smart hornets from the Mideast to run the ports and have assured everyone that these particular hornets don't sting. Besides, even if they did sting, they have been "thoroughly vetted," so they won't sting too bad.

Can anyone say Threat Level Red?

Not President Bush.

He and a surprising number of other people are saying we should be glad that a pending sale will put the United Arab Emirates in charge of major shipping operations in New York, New Jersey, Baltimore, New Orleans, Miami and Philadelphia. Shipping is a global operation after all.

Maybe so, but national security is not.

And the idea of putting our ports of entry into the hands of a foreign government, any foreign government, is absurd. And when that foreign government has ties to al-Qaida and the Taliban, the terrorists who we are at war with, then it is beyond absurd. It is downright criminal.

The company that will run the port terminals, Dubai Ports World, is owned by the government of Dubai, one of the seven emirates that form the United Arab Emirates. Two of the September 11 hijackers came from the United Arab Emirates and hijacker money was also laundered through the country. Emirate royalty used to like to take their private jets over to Afghanistan in the good old days of the Taliban theocracy and go hunting with their pal, Osama bin Laden.

So if anyone thought I was a lackey of the "imperial" Bush presidency, forget about it. I am a lackey of American survival, and I will support any steps that will allow us to take another step forward into the blackness of eternity with our tiny beacon of liberty held high.

That means on most national security issues, I stand with the president. But when the president drinks too much chamomile tea and starts drifting off to lotus land, I do my best to slap him back to sanity just like Odysseus had to do when his men fell victim to the narcotic of apathy in the Greek myth.

Hey, Mr. President, WAKE UP!

You just put Iran in charge of our nuclear program!

You just put Mexico in charge of border security!

You just put the hornets in charge of the insect repellent! ARE YOU KIDDING?

I bet the hornets are yucking it up pretty good right about now. I mean they don't have to do anything stupid. There's no need to call attention to themselves by blowing up a bomb in the port, for goodness' sake. They just bide their time, do their job and keep out of trouble. In five or 10 years, they will have lulled us into a false sense of security, and then they can strike.

Kind of funny really that they can get rich by running our biggest ports at the same time they are plotting where and when to sting us to do the most damage.

I know, I know. The president says these are good Arabs, thoroughly vetted. Nothing to fear from them.

And maybe the president is right about the sheiks and crown princes. They probably keep their hands clean. They probably do just want to make more money so they can privately enjoy more of the decadent pleasures of the West which they publicly condemn.

But if we are worried about sleeper cells of terrorists in the United States, why are we not terrified of sleeper cells of terrorists in Dubai? How hard would it be for al-Qaida to infiltrate Dubai Ports World with any one of the hundreds of university-educated time bombs they have recruited over the past 20 years? As a matter of fact they could pack Dubai Ports World full of walking time bombs and we would be none the wiser.

Which brings us back to that other story from Homer's "Odyssey," the story of how Odysseus and his men fooled the poor gullible people of Troy into opening their impenetrable fortress to the giant horse of wood called by Homer a "thing of guile" and known to history as the Trojan horse.

Consider the cry of a patriot of Troy, as recounted in another version of the story in Virgil's "Aeneid," as he warns his people not to accept the gift of the Greeks into their citadel:

O wretched countrymen! What fury reigns?

What more than madness has possess'd your brains?

His warning goes unheeded, and in a drunken celebration at their victory of the Greeks, the Trojans are slaughtered and their city destroyed by those who hid patiently within the wooden horse.

Just as Troy, we too have been given a warning. The cry has gone up loud and clear before the gates have fallen open and the Trojan horse taken into our midst. Despite the protests of President Bush and Rush Limbaugh and a host of other "globalists," it would plainly take a madman to even consider the idea of allowing Arabs to run the ports where we are most vulnerable.

The argument made by Bush is that Dubai Ports World would not be responsible for security at the port; they would just be handling the day-to-day oversight of ships entering and departing the port and leaving behind or picking up thousands of cargo containers a day.

Turns out the Coast Guard would actually be in charge of security, along with Customs. So that should make you feel safer, just like you would feel safer that the Nuclear Regulatory Commisson was keeping an eye on the security of our nuclear energy programs after we turned operational control over to Iran. No chance Iran would want to sneak a little plutonium out of the country, right?

And absolutely no reason to think that Arabs who pal around with bin Laden would have any reason to smuggle a container or two of chemicals or biological agents into the United States when the Coast Guard was busy chasing Cuban refugees one day.

Heck no.

The good news, if you an optimist, is that this story has brought to light a horror story of huge proportions. It turns out that 30 percent of America's ports are already controlled by foreign-based companies. APL Limited, for instance, which is controlled by the government of Singapore, operates port terminals in Los Angeles, Oakland, Seattle and Alaska.

What were we thinking?

All those deals need to be reconsidered, along with this one. It is absolutely unacceptable that national security should be considered of secondary importance to the globalization of the shipping economy.

Everyone needs to speak up loud and clear and get the president to see the error of his ways. Otherwise, when the history of this country is written, it will end with a gagline just as Troy's did:

"Beware of Greeks bearing gifts."

THE GOOD, THE BAD AND THE BORDER

May 7, 2006

Sometimes borders are a good thing.

There is a border between right and wrong, for instance, but that is a hard one for some people to see. They say there is no border, but what they really mean is that they feel free to cross between right and wrong as they see fit and don't want anyone to tell them to "get back to where you once belonged," as the Beatles told Jojo.

There is a border between you and the rest of the world, too. It's called skin, and it holds you in. Most people find it to be modestly (or immodestly, according to taste) useful and prefer not to see it breached. When stuff on the inside crosses that border, it is called bleeding. When stuff on the outside crosses the border, it is called being shot or stabbed. In either case, you should rush yourself to a hospital.

There is a border between the inside of a jet plane and the outside. It comes in particularly handy at 32,000 feet. Breaching is not recommended at any speed.

There is a border between the United States and Mexico, too — oh wait, that's not a border; it's a joke. In fact, the thing between Mexico and the United States is more accurately referred to as the world's largest unguarded port of entry.

That was established once and for all last week when a million or more illegal immigrants from Mexico and a few other countries rallied in the United States of America for their God-given right to American citizenship. Say huh? When did American citizenship become a human right? Oh that's an easy one — it happened when we decided not to enforce our border security. You can't expect to have anything precious left in your treasury when you throw open the doors, send the guards home and invite passers-by in to spend the night. At that point, what's yours is theirs, and not much you can do about it unless you have mastered the magic trick of closing the barn door once the horse is gone.

What is astounding is not that the passers-by want to take your precious pearl of citizenship with them. What is astounding is that so many Americans don't mind being robbed — apparently on the theory that we are all God's children, or maybe just because we are the softest touches on the planet. "What's yours is yours, and what's mine is yours, too."

I suppose at this point I could simply go off on a rant. How dare they! What is wrong with those idiots in Washington! Build the wall! Call in the national guard! Send the employers who are hiring illegal workers to jail! Then let's see how long the illegal immigration problem remains.

But why bother? Everyone who is concerned about the future of the United States of America already knows what needs to be done, and everyone who likes the idea of amnesty for illegal aliens has already sold out the country anyway. Globalization good for America? Yeah, I suppose so — if we aspire to be an outlying province of China. Hitler had a globalization program, too. It was called Deutschland Uber Alles, which roughly translated from the German means, "It's my world, you can cry if you want to."

But there's no use crying over spilt milk is what we are told.

So we had better stop worrying about the good old days when "the common welfare" stopped at the border. That is passe. Nowadays, Americans have a responsibility to share everything with the rest of the world. First we give them our jobs, then we give them our standard of living, and when we have nothing else left to give, we just give up.

It reminds me of the story in the Bible of Jacob and Esau. The elder brother Esau was a mighty hunter, but one day when he was hungry he sold his birthright to his brother for "a mess of pottage" — a bowl of lentils.

That's kind of the position we are in, too. The immigrants are telling us they have something we want — cheap labor — and if we don't want big problems, we had better give them what they want: our birthright of citizenship. Esau decided he didn't want to be troubled with finding a solution to his problem of hunger, so he gave away everything for next to nothing. "Behold, I am at the point to die: and what profit shall this birthright do to me?" So he took the easy way out, but he had a lifetime to regret it.

You hear the same kind of thinking in this country. People have surrendered to the problem of illegal immigration. "What can we do?" people ask plaintively. "Send them all back?" Well, no, probably not, but if we make sure they can't get jobs or government services, they will probably tend to migrate in the opposite direction on their own. That's one of the nice things about an open border. It works both ways.

But let's be realistic. There is almost no chance our government will take any action at all. Like Esau, our president and legislators are "faint." They will take the bread and lentils and rise up and go their way, having given away everything for next to nothing.

So we had better start to assess what we have left and make plans to live in the new world without borders. There are some advantages, after all. It would eliminate the need for passports, for one thing. No need to get the paperwork stamped anymore since you are a "citizen" as soon as you cross the former invisible line that was a border. (By the way, does an invisible line become visible when it becomes former?)

But really, what are you a citizen of anyway? I mean since there are no borders anymore, then we don't really have countries anymore, do we? It's all just one big happy family where you do your thing and I do mine.

But how exactly does anything get done when there are no governments? Or is there just one big government for all of us? And if the majority of the world's population lives under some sort of dictatorship already, then won't the populations that favor dictatorship persuade the rest of us — like the Borg in "Star Trek" — that "resistance is futile." Isn't it inevitable that one-world government will eventually go the way of all governments and become uncaring, corrupt and deadly? And when the one-world government goes bad in a world where there are no borders, where exactly do we go for help?

Borders? We don't need no stinking borders! Just buy your ticket to the dark ages and hold on. It's a helluva ride.

HELP US PROTECT THE NEIGHBORHOOD!

May 21, 2006

Suppose you knew that your neighbor was a drug dealer. A nice guy otherwise, but still a drug dealer.

Then suppose that you noticed the police had been driving by your neighbor's house regularly, sometimes parking out front in unmarked cars and just generally keeping an eye on the property. Suppose you even saw someone tampering with the phone line going into your neighbor's house and you suspected that the police had tapped his phone.

Now, as a good citizen, what should you do? Tip off your drug-dealer neighbor that the police are on to him? Or stay out of the way and let the police do their job?

Hmmmm. Not really much of a choice, is it? The police win that one hands-down almost every time, unless you are a customer of the drug dealer or he has paid you off.

I mean, if you want a safe neighborhood, you really have to give the police the opportunity to do their job and catch the bad guys in action, don't you? It would be crazy to tip off the drug dealer, wouldn't it? After all, are you more concerned about the rights of drug dealers to be safe and secure in their homes or more concerned about the rights of you and your family to be safe and secure from illegal activity in your neighborhood?

About the only valid reason why you WOULD tip off the next-door neighbor is because you were SURE he wasn't a drug dealer and you wanted to let him know he was wrongly suspected. But in this case, that doesn't apply. We have already established that he is a drug dealer and that you know he is (which raises some interesting questions about why you didn't do anything about him previously, but your personal responsibility is not the issue here).

So the only possible explanation for why you would tip him off is because you want to disrupt the police from doing their job. Assuming you are a law-abiding citizen, then the only reason why you would want to disrupt the police is because you have concerns that the same kind of surveillance they are using on the drug dealer might be used against you, too.

But where did your concerns come from? Fear of government in general? Fear of the police? Is there any reason to think you are really in danger of an intrusive police presence? Or are you just paranoid? Have the police ever once in your entire life tried to spy on you while you were not doing something illegal? If they did, wouldn't they be subject to arrest?

And how exactly do you decide to give your hypothetical fear of the police maybe someday spying on little old innocent you more weight than the police being able to do their job and arrest the drug dealer who is trying to kill your children?

Oh dear, hard questions.

But at least it is all hypothetical.

Al least, for you and me it is hypothetical. For the New York Times and USA Today, it is just a story where the names were changed to protect the ... innocent?

Change the drug dealer to al-Qaida. Change the police to the National Security Agency. Change the concerned neighbor to the New York Times.

And now you get the picture.

What appears to have taken over the country is a mass hysteria based on the premise that our own government is intent on herding us like cattle and that they are just using terrorism as an excuse to turn the United States into a police state.

It's an entertaining story, but it bears about as much resemblance to truth as "The Da Vinci Code" does to the Bible.

Yet Americans seem to be giving just as much credence to the "all we have to fear is our own government" crowd as they are giving to the Dan Brown novel about conspiracies within the church.

Which just encourages the national media to dig deeper into national security secrets for the purpose of providing front-page fodder. (Perhaps the Times should change its slogan to "All the news that helps al-Qaida we print.") And, meanwhile, every time they print these secrets, they lessen our confidence in our security as well as inevitably lessening our real security.

Which means they are increasing the likelihood of a second major terrorist attack on our soil. And when that happens, ironically, the government probably will take steps to limit our civil liberties. It's kind of like taking a loaded gun away from a baby. As much as you want the baby to enjoy his Second Amendment right to bear arms, sometimes it just isn't prudent.

Maybe it's like that with the First Amendment, too. The courts have long since established that the right of free speech shall be infringed when it causes harm to the general public, as in shouting "Fire" in a crowded theater where no fire exists.

That being the case, perhaps at some point we must consider whether the free press is doing harm to the general public when it runs front page stories with headlines like this: "Another top-secret program to protect us all from terrorists is revealed to the terrorists by the New York Times."

You know what I'm talking about: The president has acknowledged that he authorized warrantless wiretaps on phone calls involving suspected terrorists, as long as one of the calling parties was outside the country. The government also has acknowledged that it has been collecting domestic phone records in order to collate a database which can be used to track calling patterns that may lead from one known terrorist to another and thus help to foil an attack on our country.

The New York Times and later USA Today revealed the nature of those top-secret programs, thus helping to foil the government's efforts to protect us.

As informed citizens, we should be grateful for information, but we must make reasonable choices about what information is appropriate for the public (including the enemy public) to know. Rather than just giving the New York Times a free pass to publish whatever it sees fit, ask yourself what you would do if YOU were put in charge of vital national security secrets. Would you reveal them because you could? Or would you keep them secret because it makes us all safer?

I suspect that almost everyone in the country would be a good steward of the secrets if they were personally in charge of them. But there is unfortunately a different standard applied to people who ferret out the secrets on their own. It seems that if a secret is "leaked" to the press, then it is no longer considered a secret. Rather than being a matter of national security; it has become a matter of career advancement. The more damage you do to national security, the more likely you are to win a Pulitzer Prize.

Perhaps, the old master spy Allen Dulles summed up the danger best 40 years ago when he was writing about keeping one step ahead of the Soviet Union:

"What a government, or the press, tells the people it also automatically tells its foes... In my own experience ... I always considered, first, how the operation could be kept secret from the opponent and, second, how it could be kept from the press."

He concludes his 1965 book, "The Craft of Intelligence" with a warning that is just as appropriate now as it was then.

"The last thing we can afford to do today is to put our intelligence in chains. Its protective and informative role is indispensable in an era of unique and continuing danger."

The enemy has changed; the danger has not.

'CULTURE OF CORRUPTION'? OR JUST PLAIN DUMB?

May 28, 2006

A few months ago I made a case for heeding the plain language of the U.S. Constitution instead of allowing courts and special interests to insert their wish list of rights, duties, obligations and cotton candy into the document.

That's because I have a very high regard for the Constitution — and the framers who gave it to us — and a very low regard for the average politician's ability to avoid the siren call of self-interest.

Last week, we got a stunning reminder of just how easy it is to hijack the Constitution for political purposes, and we have been granted once more an opportunity to demand that the government obey the simple language of the Constitution instead of stretching it like silly putty to meet the needs of expediency. The Constitution is flexible, but it should not be elastic.

But don't tell that to the leaders of Congress.

When the FBI raided the congressional offices of William Jefferson, a Louisiana Democrat who is under investigation for allegedly accepting bribes, it was as if the Romans were once again entering the Holy of Holies at King Solomon's Temple in Jerusalem. The outraged leaders of the Capitol stood aghast as their "privileges" were trampled by the executive branch.

Former House speaker Newt Gingrich called the raid "the most blatant violation of the constitutional separation of powers in my lifetime."

The current speaker, Dennis Hastert, R-Ill., said, "Insofar as I am aware, since the founding of our republic 219 years ago, the Justice Department has never found it necessary to do what it did Saturday night, crossing this separation of powers line, in order to successfully prosecute corruption by members of Congress."

That all sounds good. Anybody with a fifth-grade education knows that separation of powers is a fundamental cornerstone of our form of government.

But based on the statements made so far, you have to wonder whether our leaders of Congress, past and present, ever got past fifth grade at all.

First of all, to keep it simple enough for even congresspeople to understand, separation of powers works like this: The legislative branch makes the laws, the judicial branch interprets them, the executive branch enforces them.

But as of last week, it got changed to this: The legislative branch makes the laws, interprets them, and tells the executive branch not to enforce them if a member of Congress got his hand caught in the cookie jar.

Montesquieu, no doubt, is turning over in his moldy grave. It was that French political philosopher who developed the modern theory of separation of powers, and the accompanying theory of checks and balances.

The idea wasn't to create a Congress with the powers of a monarchy, but rather to create a government where each branch could limit the powers of the other two branches. Thus, Congress must submit to the legitimate powers of the executive branch and the judiciary — not hold itself above the law.

The separation of powers, after all, is not a shield for wrong-doing. In fact, it is the very opposite. It is a guarantee of the ability to hold wrong-doers accountable.

President Nixon learned to his chagrin that just being president did not mean he could avoid the subpoena power of the courts. His aides and deputies learned that being part of the executive branch did not mean they could stay out of jail. President Clinton learned that he could not lie to a court and then tell the Congress it was none of their business.

In these cases, senators and representatives have powerfully orated on the sanctity of our system, where no man is above the law. They have warned presidents to behave or be chastised.

But now these same senators, in defense of a scoundrel, have rewritten the Constitution to protect one of their own. Instead of standing with the American people in favor of integrity and decency, the leaders of Congress have tried to mislead the public into granting them rights which they have never had before, and never should have

Don't take my word for it. Read the Constitution for yourself. Print out a copy from the Internet (www.usconstitution.net/const.txt is one of many sites where it may be downloaded) and take it with you wherever you go. Read it every minute from now until the day you die, and you will never find one word that exempts members of Congress from the principle that no man is above the law.

Here's what you will actually find — the plain language of Article 1, Section 6:

"The senators and representatives ... shall in all cases, except treason, felony and breach of the peace, be privileged from arrest during their attendance at the session of their respective houses, and in going to and returning from the same; and for any speech or debate in either house, they shall not be questioned in any other place."

That, in sum, is the entire privilege granted to members of Congress in protection against an overzealous executive branch.

Please note that there is no wholesale exclusion of searches and seizures of documents in congressional offices. Please note also that it is entirely permissible for the FBI to enter the Capitol and actually arrest a senator on the floor of the Senate if he is charged with a felony. Please note also that bribery is a felony.

So Rep. William Jefferson can be arrested by the executive branch on the floor of the House for bribery, but — according to

Hastert and Gingrich — his offices cannot be searched with a duly sworn and executed search warrant, even when he refused to honor a prior grand jury subpoena for the same documents.

Huh? How so?

The shaky underpinnings of the argument hinge on that "speech and debate" clause of the Constitution. It seems that those who are trying to make Congress safe for bribery think that documents prepared in the line of duty by a congressman or his staff must be protected from prying eyes, even if the eyes have a warrant.

But the plain language of the Constitution doesn't say that. It says that a congressman may say anything he wants in official speech and debate and shall not be charged with any crime as a result, nor even be questioned about it. That is a fundamental doctrine of fair and open debate and guarantees that Congress shall not be intimidated by the executive with the threat of arrest for simply arguing against a presidential policy. The framers were brilliant to include that passage, and did so because of their experience with a crown that did not respect open legislative debate.

It is the invisible asterisk in Article 1, Section 6, which concerns me. Because it must be in the emanations of the invisible writing next to that invisible asterisk where the congressional leaders have found their penumbral protection from legal investigation of criminal wrongdoing.

Since the ink is invisible, we will have to ask Hastert and Gingrich whether members of Congress may hide evidence of all crimes in their offices or just crimes done on the job. Does the protection extend to evidence against members of their family? What about their friends? Is it possible that congressmen can start making a little extra money on the side legally by advertising their services as hiders of evidence? After all, if the FBI is forbidden to search on Capitol Hill no matter what crime is committed, then why not turn that to advantage. Heck, it may ultimately make bribery old-fashioned and irrelevant. Skilling and Lay probably would have paid big-time to get all the Enron corporate records safely shoved into congressional offices.

Thanks to a little invisible ink in the Constitution and the ever-increasing gullibility of the American public, this could actually be the best scam since diplomatic immunity!

IT'S TIME TO SEND A MESSAGE

June 4, 2006

Let's TP the U.S. Capitol — and maybe the White House, too.

No, that's not TP as in toilet paper. The old college prank of festooning a frat house with toilet paper might be appropriate symbolically, but it would also be disrespectful, and that is not the goal in this case.

We need something grander than a sophomoric prank to protest the inattention of Congress and the president to the sovereign powers of the American people. We need to get a message to the politicians in Washington that they do not own the country; they just run it — for us. We the American people are the shareholders, and just as a company's shareholders need to be consulted before a merger is approved, so too must the American people be consulted before a virtual merger with Mexico is approved.

Make no mistake about it. The Kennedy-McCain immigration bill is just that — a merger with Mexico — and while it is easy to see the benefits for Mexico, it is harder to see what the American people gain by having their sovereignty diluted by between 10 million and 100 million new citizens over the next 20 years.

While it is easy to see the benefits for the illegal immigrants, who have put their self-interest ahead of the common good, it is harder to find any benefit at all for the American people, who must defend the common good against all manifestations of self-interest.

I won't try to enumerate all the wrongs of the Kennedy-McCain-Bush approach to immigration, but suffice it to say that among the most egregious offenses are that it rewards illegal behavior with citizenship, makes a mockery of homeland security, formalizes the creation of an underclass of "guest workers" who will multiply in number but never be assimilated into the American culture, and saddles the American taxpayers with billions of dollars in costs for health care and other social services.

In addition, and perhaps most importantly, it rips at the heart of the unity of the American people, which is best summarized in our motto E Pluribus Unum — "Out of many we are One." Immigration is a beautiful thing that has strengthened America by bringing many different strains of thought and belief together, but we must not lose sight of the "together" part. If we lose that, then we may as well change our motto to E Pluribus Chaos — "Out of many, we enter the Abyss."

But yet the Senate tells us that we must accept this "solution" to the illegal immigration problem. We are told that there is no other answer, because the problem is too big for a real solution. We are told that we must be humane to the illegal immigrants because they are just acting for the good of their families.

But let's get one thing straight — we are not treating Mexicans like "second-class citizens" when we tell them they are not welcome here; we are treating them like non-citizens — which is what they are. Anyone who can't tell the difference between a citizen and a non-citizen needs a civics lesson, and probably should not be allowed to serve in the Congress or White House either.

I think most Americans know that, and I think most of us — despite whatever poll you read — believe that citizenship in this country is our greatest earthly asset. It should not be traded lightly, and it should not be given away.

Which is why I say, "Let's TP the U.S. Capitol — and maybe the White House, too."

We need a symbol that reaches to the heart of American freedom and identity. A symbol that tells the powers that be,

"We won't take it any more." A symbol of grass-roots resistance to imperious foolishness.

We need, in short, a new Tea Party.

The Boston Tea Party is the famous incident in Boston Harbor that was staged by Samuel Adams on Dec. 16, 1773. On that night, dozens of colonists dressed as Indians boarded three ships, seized the tea cargo on board and dumped it into the harbor. This was no mere act of vandalism, but rather a message to Parliament and the crown that they could not take advantage of Americans. The British had concocted several taxes on the colonists, but the Americans were refusing to pay them on the grounds that they had no representation in Parliament and therefore did not recognize its authority.

Thus, the tea went into Boston Harbor, and this simple act of resistance helped to motivate the colonists to stand up for themselves and for self-government.

Today, we see a similar movement that has sprung up, which also takes its name from the Revolutionary War era. The original Minutemen was that ragtag bunch of foot soldiers who responded first to the threat of attack in the 18th century colonies. It is the Minutemen who fought the first battle of the War of Independence at Lexington and Concord in 1775.

That is proper inspiration for the modern Minutemen, who are regular U.S. citizens who have banded together to protect the border with Mexico from the daily onslaught of smugglers and illegals.

It was just over a year ago that I wrote a column about the Minuteman Project. I said then that "the power of an idea can be staggering, even world-changing," and proposed that the idea of a secure border might be just such an idea.

Today, we see that those volunteers who wanted to bring attention to illegal immigration have succeeded admirably, but we must be sure that the politicians do not get their wish to sweep the issue back under the rug.

That is why average citizens such as you and me need to get together and do something. The Boston Tea Party involved only 150 men, but it helped to change the world forever with a symbol of opposition to tyranny.

Today, we need a Tea Party (or TP) of our own, with which we can send the president and Congress a message they can't misunderstand. We need a simple symbol of our opposition to illegal immigration, and of our opposition to a government that is more concerned with expedience than with excellence.

Fortunately, you and I don't have to come up with that symbol ourselves. It already exists. It's called the Send-A-Brick Project (www.send-a-brick.com) and it has as one of its slogans, "Since you have trouble building a wall, here's a start."

Indeed, it's quite a start. All over the country, advocates of real border security are sending bricks — one at a time — to their senators and representatives on Capitol Hill. So far, an estimated 10,000 bricks have been delivered, and each one is earmarked — to use a favorite congressional term — for a fence to be built on the border with Mexico.

This is a real grass-roots rebellion, and only started in April, but it has already had an effect. In fact, last week, the New York Times even took notice of the campaign, quoting a congressional aide as saying, "Given the approval ratings of Congress these days, I guess we should all be grateful the bricks are coming through the mail, not the window."

This may be just one more skirmish in the war on foolishness, but the Boston Tea Party was only a "skirmish," and it continues to inspire us today, more than 230 years later.

So pick up a pen, or send a brick. But do something, for your country's sake.

If our forefathers had not had the temerity to stand up for themselves against the powers that be in England, we would all still be singing "God Save the Queen" today instead of "My County 'Tis of Thee."

If we could tell the king of England what we thought of him 230 years ago, then we should be able to tell the president of the United States the same thing.

Send a brick to send a message. Let the Tea Party begin.

A 'DECLARATION OF INTERDEPENDENCE'

June 11, 2006

I once believed that the United States was sovereign — you know, that we could make our own laws and govern ourselves — but I have gotten over that misguided foolishness, thanks to the illegal immigration debate.

Turns out that we can make as many laws as we want, but all people (or at least Mexicans) are endowed with certain inalienable rights, and among these are U.S. citizenship and the pursuit of a better-paying job.

Since these are inalienable rights, we can't make laws that tell people (or at least Mexicans) who have entered our country without permission that they are criminals and must go home. After all, they just want jobs and U.S. citizenship same as you and me, so what's wrong with that?

I'm glad some kind-hearted people have set me straight on this, because I don't want to offend anyone. I am glad to know that foreigners (or at least Mexicans) don't need permission to enter the country because it clarifies some of the fine points of immigration for me.

But I do have a suggestion.

I noticed when I looked at a map recently that there is an interesting phenomenon that has not been reported too much — borders have TWO sides.

Which means they can be crossed from south to north, but they can also be crossed from north to south.

This is really good news for American citizens. No longer do we have to settle for a couple of weeks every few years at Puerto Vallarta or Cancun.* We can just pack up our bags and move down there. We can hire crews of cheap Mexican labor and build condos up and down the coast. This will help the Mexican economy and will also be good for us because we need places to live (we are human after all!).

The Mexican government may not like it because they have laws that govern immigration, but we are pretty sure those laws don't apply to us. After all, we hold certain truths to be self-evident — that all people (or at least Americans) are endowed by their Creator with certain inalienable rights, and that among

these are Mexican citizenship and the pursuit of a happy life on
the beach. Viva Mexico! (But don't forget your U.S. flags as we
will be needing them for our protests against anyone who tries
to evict us from our new condos!)

This may sound crazy to you, but I'm pretty sure it will
work. I mean, after all, the people who support Mexicans
coming to the United States illegally will surely come to our
defense when we start driving our Hummers into the desert and
head for the Gulf Coast, right? No one could possibly be so
hypocritical as to say that it's OK to cross the border in one
direction, but not in the other direction, right?

But honestly, I think there may be some other good
opportunities here that we haven't yet fully realized. I mean,
after all, we do have 300 million people in our country, legal
and otherwise. That makes us the third most populous country
in the world. Surely there are many smaller countries around
the world where we could quickly become the majority should
we find a way to sneak across (I mean proudly cross) the
border.

We could start small with countries like Palau (where there
are about 20,000 people) or the Cayman Islands (where there
are 45,000 people). With no concerns about immigration rules,
we could probably build up majority rule in those countries over
a three-day weekend. I'm not sure about Palau, but I know it
would be profitable to get control of the treasury in the Cayman
Islands. We could vote ourselves "earned income tax credits"
when we got there. As for Palau, we get a tropical paradise, so it
is probably worth having even if there isn't much money in the
treasury.

Later on, we could aim a little higher. I think even a country
as big as Switzerland might be do-able. They've got about 7.5
million people, but probably lots of those are children. I'm
thinking if we could get 2 million voting-age Americans to make
a run across the border, we could all have a numbered bank
account by nightfall.

I know, I know. It's crazy. I mean if any group of people
from any country could cross the border into any other country
and declare themselves citizens (or even rulers), then it would

have happened long ago. Heck, the Goths would have conquered Rome, the Mongol hordes would have spread across Eastern Europe, and the Spanish armada would have been able to settle far away countries like Chile and Nicaragua.

But this is something quite different. We are not talking about Hitler sending his Blitzkrieg of tank troops and infantry across the border into Czechoslovakia or Poland. No one could possibly approve of that, right? Well, maybe we will give him Poland, and Czechoslovakia, but if he dares to cross the border into France we are going to be really mad (but we will wait a few years to do anything about it — because it is France, after all).

But that is ancient history. This is the dawn of a new era. Without borders there will never again be need of an army to invade another country. This will be economically advantageous, of course, as armies are quite expensive to feed, house and shower, but it will also be less bloody. There is no need to get in these silly wars anymore, now that we have been informed that borders are meaningless.

From now on, like-minded people will simply migrate to whatever country they want to inhabit (which sounds much more polite than "take over," don't you think?) and they will wait for the natives to throw up their hands and say, "There's too many of them. What can we do?" Then the newcomers will inform the old-timers, politely but firmly, "Nothing. You are stuck with us."

Which brings up the next question: What do we in the United States do when China — with its 1.3 billion people — decides to "inhabit" the United States. Oh well, let's cross that bridge when we come to it.

In the meantime, on to Palau!

*For the record, I have never been to Puerto Vallarta or Cancun, so please don't write to me to tell me I am a wealthy, money-hungry Republican who wants to colonize Mexico for use as my personal villa. Although I do want to colonize Mexico for my personal use as a villa**, I am neither wealthy, money-hungry nor a Republican.*

**This part about colonizing Mexico is satire. Please do not send me a politically correct letter to inform me that colonialism is an anachronistic, racist, imperialist policy of exploiting peoples of color. Folks, can't we all just get along?_

MORE ON 'MERGER': THREE NATIONS UNDER GOD?

July 2, 2006

One of the good things about writing an opinion column is that you hear back from readers with their opinions, too.

Sometimes they will write about their own philosophy of life, their belief system, or their heartfelt concerns. Other times, they will encourage me to read a particular writer or look into a particular subject. That means I am constantly being challenged to absorb new information and points of view.

While on occasion these friendly suggestions are meant to re-educate me ("War is bad, peace is good," in case you didn't know) — more often they are legitimate invitations to learn about some aspect of the world that might be an interesting topic for this column.

Such was the case in recent weeks after I wrote several columns on the topic of illegal immigration. In one of those columns I referred to the McCain-Kennedy-Bush "reform" plan as a proposed "merger" with Mexico, and lamented that the "shareholders" of the United States had not been consulted about the merger.

I chose the language intentionally to dramatize the point that U.S. sovereignty was on the verge of being given away, but I thought the idea of a merger was a colorful exaggeration that would be useful to make my point. Now I find out, thanks to the help of several readers, that it was no exaggeration at all, and that the McCain-Kennedy reform plan is not the starting point for the merger, but just one more steppingstone in a path being built for several years.

It has the sound of a global thriller, right? People in high places plotting to advance their own self-interest while the little people go about their business oblivious to the great forces at work all around them. But of course that is not just the stuff of Tom Clancy novels; it's the way the world really works.

In this case, we have the presidents of the United States and Mexico and the former prime minister of Canada meeting at the president's ranch at Crawford, Texas, on March 23, 2005. On that day, President Bush, Canadian Prime Minister Paul Martin and Mexican President Vicente Fox announced the establishment of the "Security and Prosperity Partnership of North America."

It has all the makings of a treaty. It is in fact an agreement between three countries to regulate trade, health care, emergency management and the environment. Yet it has not been presented to the Senate for ratification, nor have the people of the Unites States been consulted. Instead, the "partnership" was born full-grown out of that Texas summit like Athena springing from the head of Zeus in battle gear.

The name itself, Security and Prosperity Partnership of North America, sounds suspiciously like the announcement of a merger, doesn't it? But you don't have to take my word for it. You can visit the official Web site at www.spp.gov or read about it by doing a Google search for "North American Union."

You won't find any explicit acknowledgment that the ultimate goal is to combine these three nations into a sort of North American version of the European Union, but the signs are all there. And if you need any proof that the U.S. government would be willing to cede part of its powers to a foreign government, you just need to look closely at the Senate/Bush amnesty plan for illegal immigrants, which is basically a federally funded bailout plan for the Mexican economy.

So what's the problem with helping Mexico and Canada? Probably nothing in itself. The United States has been helping other countries for the past hundred years, but this goes beyond helping a neighbor.

We need to recognize the impulse to globalization that has taken hold in the past 20 years, and understand who that helps and hurts. It was the first President Bush who announced the coming of the "New World Order" after the collapse of the Soviet Union, and it wasn't long afterwards that the European Union started to come into shape, forcing the ancient states of Europe to give up their monetary independence and inevitably enmeshing them into one superstate.

Such growth toward globalization may be a healthy instinct in some respects. If it works, it could lessen the chance of war and increase cooperation among all peoples. But the downside is that it results in a hybridization and flattening of all human experience. Eventually it could lead to a world where there is no room left for freedom such as the world of "1984." If the American experiment in liberty is considered expendable in the interests of helping to feed hungry mouths elsewhere in the world, then we are all in trouble.

No one can prove such a plan exists, but there is plenty of evidence that there is a government-sponsored effort under way to change forever the relationship between Mexico, the United States and Canada. It is spelled out in detail on the federal government's own Web sites. In addition, there is the 2005 report of the quasi-private Council on Foreign Relations, which proposes "the creation by 2010 of a North American community to enhance security, prosperity, and opportunity."

To me, that idea of a "North American community" sounds like a European Union for North America. In fact, it sounds like a new country. As the Council on Foreign Relations task force wrote: "Its boundaries will be defined by a common external tariff and an outer security perimeter within which the movement of people, products, and capital will be legal, orderly, and safe."

Forget about amnesty for illegal immigrants. That is the least of our problems. This plan calls for the legal and orderly "movement of people" across our former borders as a matter of economic necessity. It says that by 2010 the three nations should "lay the groundwork for the freer flow of people within North America."

If and when that happens, it will be hard to recognize where the United States ends and Mexico begins, but one thing is sure: It will be the beginning of the end for the United States of America as we know it.

SWEET LAND OF LIBERTY ...
BELIEVE IT OR NOT

July 16, 2006

I am always bemused by people who are concerned about the loss of civil liberties in our fair republic as we fight the war on terrorism.

There is no doubt — and I would challenge you to prove otherwise — that we live in a place and time where individual liberties and civil liberties are more extensive and more valued than they have ever been before on the face of the earth.

And yet a huge number of people take the time each day to complain about how dangerous the Bush administration is, or to worry about the "all-out assault" on our civil liberties.

What these people mainly seem concerned about is that the federal government is actually taking steps to try to protect us from additional attacks by al-Qaida or other terrorist organizations. Now, I'm not sure how many of these "civil libertarians" would have allowed the September 11 attacks to go forward as planned if the alternative had been to do warrantless wiretaps on phones being used by Osama bin Laden's lieutenants, but I for one think you surrender your civil rights when you swear allegiance to a holy cause of murder and plot to kill people in an act of war.

Most of the civil liberties crowd say they aren't trying to protect the terrorists; they just don't want the government spies to accidentally get a look at some phone record of theirs while they are hunting down the killers.

Say what?

Perhaps the songwriter got it wrong. Perhaps "freedom's just another word for nothing's more important than me" or "freedom's just another word for too selfish to care."

In fact, freedom is the "absence of restraints upon our ability to think and act." That's the definition used at Wikipedia, the online encyclopedia, and it's a pretty straightforward one, which I think we can all agree upon.

The good news for all us freedom-loving Americans is that we have almost no restraints upon our ability to think and act. Of course, that is sometimes bad news, too, considering how poorly some of us think, and how rudely some of us act.

But from a purely practical basis of daily living, almost every one of us goes about our business with absolutely no restrictions on the choices we make. Indeed, I would challenge you to explain one civil liberty that you personally have lost as a result of the war on terror being fought to protect you and your family from being blown up.

You are free to travel throughout our country without interference. You are free to read anything you want. You are free to call the president of the United States the liar-in-chief without being rounded up the next day and shot, as would happen in many other countries. You are free to be an atheist, a Satanist or a Scientologist and no one can do anything about it except laugh at you. You are free to laugh at anyone you want, including the pope, the president or your neighbor who stockpiles guns. You are free to stockpile guns, as long as they are legal guns.

Of course, you are not free to break the law, but that is true anywhere where there is rule of law, and here in America, the scope of legal restrictions on our freedom is greatly limited by the Constitution. Indeed, our valuation of civil liberties is so extensive that we are willing to let child killers walk free because they did not get their Miranda rights, for God's sake.

All in all, I can't think of anywhere else I would have more freedom to do and say whatever I want.

Which makes me wonder what parallel universe people are living in when they complain about the loss of their civil liberties under the Bush administration.

Just what exactly are they talking about? Oh yes, they want to live in absolute certainty that their phone call records will not be seen by anyone other than the phone company. They don't like the idea that government agents trying to track down terrorist activity might get a look at the phone call they made to their mistress, or their bookie, or their hit man. But let's face it, the federal government has absolutely no reason to hunt down criminals through phone-call records, and even if they did so, the courts would throw out the charges in a heartbeat. Thus, there is no true infringement of a liberty involved unless you are a terrorist.

Besides, when you make a phone call, you are already giving the phone company access to that information. If the phone company chooses to keep track of calls made to terrorists or pornographers or hit men and turn that information over to the government, there would be nothing you could do about it. You made the phone call, but the phone company owns the information about the phone call. If they think you are breaking a law, they have just as much right to call the police with a tip as you do if you see a marijuana plant growing in your neighbor's cellar.

No one's freedom gives them the right to break the law. The right to be secure in your own house does not mean you have the right to do anything you want while you are there. You have no right to do illegal drugs in the privacy of your own home (at least not yet) and you have no right to violate national security laws just because you are a reporter shielded by the First Amendment (at least you should not).

But, of course, because we are a freedom-loving people we have made it as difficult as possible for the government to wield its power against individuals. The government needs to have probable cause before searching a home or issuing an arrest warrant. Those civil liberties have not been diminished one bit for the average American, and unless you are chatting with terrorists on the Internet or by telephone, then you will almost certainly not hear from the FBI or the National Security Agency.

You still have exactly the same freedoms and civil liberties today that you had six years ago. And truth be told, you have many more civil liberties today than you would have had 100 years ago. At that time, if you sold pictures of naked women you could be sent to jail; today you can become a rich celebrity. At that time, if you were to criticize the government of the United States you could be arrested for sedition; today you can become a media darling. At that time, if you were to perform an abortion, you could be arrested and sent to jail; today you can become a rich doctor.

I guess some people just don't know enough to be grateful for living at a time when they have VIRTUALLY NO RESTRICTIONS on how they go about their lives at church, in their homes, on their computers, and on the road from sea to shining sea. They don't see it that way. They figure if the government is trying to track down terrorists by looking at library records, then by God, it is a personal infringement of their civil liberties.

Sorry, but no, it isn't. When the terrorists blow up the library with you and your family in it, however; yeah, that is an infringement.

I don't expect some people to see the difference.

WHO NEEDS SAFETY
WHEN YOU'VE GOT RIGHTS?

August 6, 2006

I've written columns about football before. I've written columns about terrorism before. And I've written columns about civil liberties before.

But I wish I didn't have to write a column about how good old American civil liberties are making football stadiums safe for terrorism.

I suppose, to be accurate, I should say that civil liberties are not the culprit, but rather the American Civil Liberties Union, that bastion of ensuring individual "freedom" to do whatever

you want, whenever you want, no matter who it hurts —
freedom at all costs even if it kills us, you might say.

Last week, a federal district judge in Florida agreed with the
ACLU lawyers that "pat-down" searches of football fans
entering NFL stadiums are unconstitutional and unreasonable.

The argument is that the government is violating citizens'
Fourth Amendment rights by trying to make sure they are not
carrying explosives into the stadium. Forget about the fact that
the policy was instituted by the NFL, not Homeland Security.
Forget about the fact that the Tampa Sports Authority — the
defendant in the lawsuit — is to "the government" what Play-
doh is to "fine art." Forget about the fact that terrorists have
made no secret of the fact that they will hit any facility where
people congregate because their goal is to kill as many innocent
people at once as possible.

Forget all that.

All that matters is that Gordon Johnson, a civics teacher in
Tampa, is oblivious to the fact that we as a civilization are
engaged in a war of survival with a competing civilization that
has pledged to destroy us. All that matters is that Mr. Johnson
is sensitive about having another human being touch his
midsection for a millisecond — more sensitive about that
apparently than the prospect of having himself or hundreds of
other people blown apart by plastic explosives.

All that matters is that a federal judge has decided there is
no "substantial and real risk" of terrorists killing people at
football stadiums. Thus, there can be no pat-down searches,
and thus the chance of "substantial and real risk" to those
attending NFL games has increased exponentially.

So what exactly are we dealing with?

Here is what you need to know:

• "The right of the people to be secure in their persons,
houses, papers, and effects, against unreasonable searches and
seizures, shall not be violated, and no Warrants shall issue, but
upon probable cause, supported by oath or affirmation, and
particularly describing the place to be searched, and the
persons or things to be seized."

That's the Fourth Amendment to the U.S. Constitution.

- "The ruling to kill the Americans and their allies — civilians and military — is an individual duty for every Muslim who can do it in any country in which it is possible to do it, in order to liberate the al-Aqsa Mosque [in Jerusalem] and the holy mosque [in Mecca] from their grip, and in order for their armies to move out of all the lands of Islam, defeated and unable to threaten any Muslim. This is in accordance with the words of Almighty Allah, 'and fight the pagans all together as they fight you all together,' and 'fight them until there is no more tumult or oppression, and there prevail justice and faith in Allah.'"

That's an excerpt from the Feb. 23, 1998, Fatwa of Osama bin-Laden declaring war on the United States and its people.

- "Are you ready for some terrorism?"

That's my proposal for the new slogan of the National Football League, thanks to Judge James Whittemore's ruling that the Fourth Amendment prohibition against unreasonable (emphasis mine) searches ensures that terrorists should have a right to walk into American football stadiums and blow them up. The good judge has declared that it is not reasonable to expect a sworn enemy of the United States to try to kill our innocent civilians just because they have said they will do so. It would only be reasonable — and thus appropriate to do pat-down searches — if the terrorists were stupid enough to announce in advance that they are coming to a particular stadium on a particular day.

Bottom line?

If Osama bin Laden and his band of unmerry men were looking for the Achilles' heel of this nation, they may have just found it. You know the old Greek myth about the warrior Achilles, right? He was invulnerable to attack except on one heel where his mother had held him when she dipped him into the river Styx as an infant.

So, too, is the United States invulnerable in many respects. We have the most powerful military in the world, the most energetic economy, and the most vital form of government. But it would seem from our recent experience that this nation also suffers from a fatal weakness — the belief that we must protect the rights of every individual at all times and in all circumstances, even to the detriment of the nation as a whole.

This is a noble failing, certainly — very much the stuff of myth — but a failing nonetheless. If we are more concerned about the propriety of a middle-aged man having his butt touched for a split second during a search for strapped-on explosives than we are about the possibility of an America-hating suicide bomber killing several hundred people in Rows JJ through XX, then we certainly cannot expect to defeat a determined enemy.

And yes, we have a determined enemy.

• "If avenging the killing of our people is terrorism, then history should be a witness that we are terrorists. Yes, we kill their innocents and this is legal religiously and logically."

That's from Osama bin Laden's videotaped confession (released in November 2001) of responsibility for the attack on the World Trade Center.

Enough said.

Are you ready for some football?

DO WE SOLVE OUR PROBLEMS OR JUST TALK ABOUT THEM?

August 27, 2006

Call me crazy, but every once in a while, I actually start to think we have turned the corner and will solve a problem instead of just talking about it.

It happened in 2001 when the American public united for one brief moment to defend our way of life and our liberty against a continuing and growing threat from Islamic terrorists and the nations that sponsor them.

It happened in 2005 when President Bush threatened to fix the Social Security mess in time for me to have a retirement income when I retire in 15 or 20 years.

It happened earlier this year when it seemed like the message had finally gotten out that illegal immigration was not only draining our resources, but had the potential to forever change our nation and culture.

For a while, when I get optimistic, I feel as though I am part of that great American experiment in democracy that was started in the parlors and on the battlefields of Massachusetts in 1775. A group of people banded together then out of common interest and stood their ground against a common enemy. They did not fear death; they did not fear slander; they did not fear imprisonment. They also did not fear to kill. They did not fear to speak their minds. And they did not hesitate to take any means necessary to vanquish their enemy.

They thought victory was not only possible, but necessary, and they did everything in their power to achieve it.

About the time I remember this, alas, is when I become most pessimistic about our own times, and our ability to confront our own enemies and solve our own problems.

Take, for instance, the problem of illegal immigration.

This week, there is a hearing in Montana on border security and illegal immigration. It is hosted by Rep. Denny Rehberg and will be held Monday from 1 to 3 p.m. at the Bedford Building, 223 S. Second St., in Hamilton. The hearing is part of a 12-state tour by various House members to "evaluate options" for improving border security.

At first glance, it certainly looks like cause for optimism that Congress is still actively seeking a solution to the problem of illegal immigration, instead of pretending it doesn't exist. There are many Montanans who would like to speak out on this issue, and be heard by their elected leaders, but optimism in this case must be tempered by an honest assessment of the facts.

Fact 1: The hearing is only scheduled to last two hours.

Fact 2: The witness list includes five people, including the regional forester, two local law enforcement officers, and two people who work for Immigration and Customs and the Border Patrol, and they will all speak extensively.

Fact 3: The public will barely get a word in edgewise.

I know several local residents and readers of this column who will be in attendance at the hearing, and perhaps they will report back to me that I was wrong, but I don't think the hearing is really intended to "take the temperature" of local residents to find out what they want their government to do.

Indeed, this particular hearing seems to be aimed more at winning pork and jobs for the Montana border communities than helping to protect us from the flow of illegal immigration where the real problem exists in the south.

Rehberg's press release said: "This is an opportunity to show my colleagues that the southern border isn't the only border we need to worry about. Montanans deserve the opportunity to have their voices heard on what has become one of the most important issues facing our country. I expect this hearing will highlight the need to secure the U.S./Canada border. It's no secret that illegal activity can take place along the northern border, too."

That's right. Illegal activity can take place anywhere, and we should always work to circumvent it. But worrying about border security with Canada while our nation is being repopulated from Mexico is like giving an alcoholic massage therapy to solve his problem because chemical-dependency treatment was just too expensive or too horrible to contemplate.

With any luck, those in attendance will have a chance to tell Rep. Rehberg that Montanans are worried about border security for the same reason that people in Arizona and Texas are concerned — because they don't want millions of illegal immigrants streaming across the border every year. It is a national emergency, not a local one, and the long-term issue of border security in the north should not be used to deflect attention from the immediate problem we face.

But deflection is part of the standard political playbook these days, isn't it?

It seems that in the 21st century, our solution to everything is to put together a blue-ribbon committee to study the problem, and the only thing necessary is for the government to stall long enough for the problem to seem unimportant compared to such monumental issues as who killed JonBenet

Ramsey, is Tom Cruise an idiot, and what is the etymology of the imaginary word "macaca."

Perhaps some evil mastermind planned this massive diversion of our attention to the mundane, the trivial and the obscure, or perhaps it just a natural result of people having too much time on their hands and too much information. The brain is a curious organ which can turn a series of random numbers into a sudoku puzzle and a series of random occurrences into a one-size-fits-all conspiracy theory to explain why our life sucks.

But another thing I have also noticed is that the optimist in me always returns no matter how many times he has been forced to turn tail and take cover. I always start out with the assumption that a wrong can be righted, no matter how many times I have been proven wrong in the past.

I consider this a corollary of Jesus' commandment to Peter when asked if he should forgive a transgressor as much as seven times, and Jesus said, "I don't tell you until seven times, but until 70 times seven," which was Jesus' way of saying there is no end to forgiveness.

I don't think there is an end to optimism either. It is a bottomless well, and a positive attitude is absolutely essential to problem solving. However many times we meet with failure on our daily journey, we must resolve to meet with success the next day. The alternative is defeat — what the allegorist John Bunyan called "the slough of despond," a pit of despair from which it is impossible to see a way out.

Therefore, I contend that it is possible to win the war on terror, to stop the invasion of illegal aliens across our borders, and to even — what the heck! — save Social Security without just borrowing more money from our grandchildren.

But every victory begins with a single step in the right direction. That single step is always the same — belief in the possibility of victory. When we say that the terrorists can't be stopped, they have won. When we say that we can't build a wall across our border that will protect our sovereignty, then the invaders who don't care about our sovereignty have won. When we accede to the impossibility of making Social Security solvent, then the phony manipulating politicians have won.

Don't give up.

Don't surrender to despair.

Don't listen to people who tell you it can't be done.

United we stand; divided we fall. This is our country; those are our choices. If we keep at it — this hard work of democracy — we may even survive as a nation long enough to once again see our government pay attention to "we the people."

But don't call me crazy; call me an optimist._

A HARD DAY TO FORGET, BUT DO WE REMEMBER?

September 10, 2006

I remember.

I was awake with the children on a morning not too different from this. The details may be faulty, but the feelings linger — the dread, the hopelessness, the anguish.

As I recall it, I had gotten downstairs a little before 7 a.m. in my effort to get the day started on a reasonable schedule. I was settling the children in to have breakfast, and then get them to their school and day care on time, and I turned the television on as usual to keep them entertained while I muddled through the chores.

Fortunately, the TV was set to NBC from the night before, not the Disney Channel, so I knew right away that something was wrong. My recollection is that the "Today" show was on, and it wasn't yet 7 o'clock. I felt puzzled — thought that perhaps I had overslept, and got a bit disoriented. The "Today" show should not have been on yet.

Then I heard the tone of voice of Matt Lauer and his co-hosts, and I stopped what I was doing long enough to see the pictures — inexplicable pictures of flames shooting out of the side of one of the World Trade Center towers.

My first thought was, "My God, those crazy terrorists really did it!" But then Lauer (or whoever it was) was saying there were reports that a small plane of some kind had hit the tower, and perhaps it had been off course for some reason.

But all you had to do was look at the pictures to know that wasn't true. It was a beautiful fall day in New York, marred only by the black smoke billowing out of what I would later learn was the North Tower. There was no way anyone had accidentally hit that tower on that clear crisp day.

I thought about the time I had gone to New York with my friend Mike, and we had traveled up the elevator in World Trade Center 2 to the observation deck on the 110th floor of the South Tower. It was amazing how long the elevator ride lasted, and even standing back from the edge I felt a little queasy being so high above the skyline of Manhattan. Five years ago, when people starting jumping out of the top floors of both towers, I cried to think about the fear that had driven them to such desperation. It was unimaginable, but so was everything on that day.

I began to wail out loud, and my children grew frightened, for me, for themselves. They understood even less than I did, just 6 and 2 years old at the time. So I hugged them and told them some bad people had flown a plane into the building and that a lot of people were going to die. There was no way to hide it. I knew what was going to happen immediately. The gaping hole in the side of the building would weaken the structure considerably, and the fire burning inside would eat away at the girders and beams until they were so weak they could not sustain the millions of pounds of concrete above them.

It was just a matter of time. As soon as that building started to buckle, it was all going to come down, and there had to be thousands of people inside. Thousands of victims.

Lauer was still talking, and whoever else was with him that day, and they were trying to make it seem ordinary somehow, but it wasn't. It was the most un-ordinary thing I have ever seen, like waking up and finding yourself in a painting by Salvador Dali. There was no place for fireballs in skyscrapers in New York, and no room for planes drilling into them either.

I was trying to think about how to wake up my wife and tell her what had happened, but I was stuck to the TV. I needed to see it for myself, the whole damn thing. I couldn't move. It was what Joseph Conrad calls the fascination of the abomination. I couldn't believe Lauer couldn't (or wouldn't) bring himself to say it — THEY did this! Those damn crazy Islamic terrorists! What the hell is wrong with them! What part of human is missing in them?

But then everything took a turn for the worse, and Lauer got it — along with everybody else. The still lingering innocence of that insanely surreal day was shattered once and for all when something, some plane, some death thing, hit the South Tower, and flame exploded out the other side. Oh my God, for a minute, they got it. They understood that we were under attack, and that people were dying. People were dead, instantly if they were lucky, or almost instantly when the fireball rose up through the tower, or waiting to be dead, if they were unlucky enough to be trapped on those upper floors. Damn it.

"Damn it," I told the kids. "Those crazy bastards. They really did it."

And then I went to wake up my wife, who is now no longer my wife but who on that day was the only person I could count on, and who I didn't want to hurt too bad, but who I knew could not be allowed to sleep any longer while those people were burning alive, as if it were just another day.

"Honey, I've got bad news."

How do you begin to tell someone this story? "Something horrible has happened. Somebody flew a plane into the World Trade Center, and they thought it was maybe just an accident, but now somebody just hit the other tower, and it's bad. It's those crazy Islamic bastards. They've gone and done it now. Oh God, baby, they're all gonna die, all those people."

And then I was crying again. Not for the last time that day, and not for the last time in this life when I think about what happened to 3,000 souls on that day. And it just kept getting worse. The Pentagon was hit. A plane crashed in Pennsylvania, maybe on its way to the White House. Heroes were made that day, and heroes were killed. When the first tower came down, I got on my knees and prayed: "Dear Jesus, oh dear Jesus, please

God, help those people, help their souls" because I knew that was all that was left to help.

And meanwhile life went on. I had to go to work, to tell the story, to cry secretly in my office at the Inter Lake, where we put out the only special edition in at least the last 38 years since President Kennedy was assassinated. That day, we in the newsroom were the same as everyone else in the country. Throughout the day, we shuffled like robots, went to the television set again and again, like supplicants in search of grace and understanding. But there was no grace. There was no understanding.

By that time, both the towers were down, and there was no hope either.

Survivors? How could there be? Answers? How could there be?

I knew that we were at war, and I thought about my 6-year-old son, and I wondered what would become of him. This would be a long war. He might die in that war, but I thought about those people who died in the towers and I knew there were worse ways to die than fighting a war to protect your country and your way of life.

But meanwhile, he had to go to first grade. He had to get his shoes on, and eat his breakfast and go to school. He had a long way to go before he needed to worry about war. But the rest of us would worry right away. We had to try to make sense of what had happened. We had to determine once and for all that we would never again be attacked in such a way, and we needed to tell the world that we would not be quiet victims. We had to unite, and stand united, and prevail. We had to, or we would die.

I remember the words: United we stand! Never forget!

But that was then. That was five years ago. And five years later, we are starting to think that forever is a pretty long time. We are starting to think maybe we should get back to life as normal. As if there were a normal to get back to.

People are tired of war. I understand that. They wish it would all end. An understandable emotion. Perhaps they've even begun to forget that which we said we would never forget.

Dear God, I wish it were not so. I wish there were some way to bring back the grief, and the anger. I wish we had not skipped to acceptance quite so easily, as if Matt Lauer had been right all along, and it really was just an ordinary thing.

It was NOT ordinary. It was not acceptable.

But today, we act like nothing ever really happened. Most of us will commemorate 9/11 on the fifth anniversary tomorrow, because it is expected, and because we remember that once it meant something to us, but we don't seem to know what it means. We don't seem to have learned its lessons yet.

We act as if it was a fluke — as if the Islamic terrorists have somehow learned their lesson, and will never do anything so stupid again. Or that they have repented, and will be our friends if we just shake their hands and make nice.

Make nice? Good God, what is wrong with us?

I never imagined five years ago when I watched nearly 3,000 people being incinerated and pulverized that their lives would mean so little to those who came after them. But it may be true. It is hard to believe that their sacrifice has been forgotten so quickly, but that may be the case. We don't debate how to defeat our enemy anymore, but whether we even have an enemy, and if so, why he doesn't like us much. What did we do wrong?

Last week, I watched one of those endless cable TV debates about what is the matter with George Bush, and I was shocked to learn from one of those commentators that Bush was backing a lost cause — that Americans won't take the threat of Islamofascism seriously until there is "another Pearl Harbor."

Another Pearl Harbor? We need another Pearl Harbor to wake us up to Islamofascism? Another Pearl Harbor? What in God's name do we need another Pearl Harbor for when we have September 11?

What we don't need — what we shouldn't need! what all decency proclaims against! — is another September 11. But we will have it, someday, because we demand it, and it may wake us up, or it may not. Sometimes the slumber of lethargy is too hard to wake from.

But I am just a voice crying in the wilderness, and the wilderness is growing thicker, and the light of civilization is growing dimmer.

Another Pearl Harbor?

No, we don't need another Pearl Harbor. What we need is another MacArthur, or another Eisenhower, or another FDR. We need another Churchill to stand strong with us, and declare with those stalwart words of his that ring through the halls of time from one war to another: "Never give in, never give in, never, never, never, never... — in nothing, great or small, large or petty — never give in except to convictions of honor and good sense. Never yield to force; never give in..."

I remember.

Do you?

WILL WE FIGHT TERRORISM OR NOT?

September 17, 2006

Thank God for Jack Bauer.

The fictional hero of the television series "24" may be the only true defense we have against terrorism in this country. We just have to hope and pray that Osama and the other cave-dwelling Muslim terror rats get Fox on their satellite service.

If they do, and they watch counter-terrorism agent Bauer interrogating murderous vermin using any means necessary, they may actually start to worry that the American people have the will and strength to defend themselves against any enemy using whatever means is necessary.

On the other hand, if they are watching cable TV news, we are doomed because they will discover that we are quivering neurotic feel-good do-nothing pansies who would rather make friends with terrorists than make them talk.

Never mind the 3,000 dead Americans from September 11. Or worse yet, never mind the 3 million dead Americans the first time we don't stop Jihad Jim from blowing up his nuke bomb in the middle of Manhattan.

All that matters — if you get your world view from the politically correct folks at CNN, FNC and MSNBC — is acting by the "rules" and behaving yourself like proper gentlemen. It kind of reminds me of the battles between France and England in the 17th century where the commanders would enjoy a tea behind the lines while sending their troops forward in neat, orderly rows to "engage" the enemy and die.

That gentlemanly form of slaughter worked fine until one side decided not to play by the rules. But the bloody French and Indian War on our own continent established that one man playing by his own rules could kill a dozen playing by gentlemen's rules. Within a few years, the British had learned their lesson and stopped marching men to their deaths.

Nowadays, we have one side that doesn't play by any rules — the terrorists whose only goal is to kill as many of us as possible — and one side which still thinks it is more important HOW you fight the war than whether you WIN it. Yeah, that's us, the guys with the sign on our back that says, "Blow Me Up!"

How could this be? Are we so morally clouded that we honestly do not recognize the difference between a U.S. victory and an al-Qaida victory in the War on Terror? Do we really think we will win the world's accolades because we are "nice" to our enemy while he cuts our heads off?

Unfortunately, many of our most influential citizens do think that way. Rosie O'Donnell does. Keith Olbermann of MSNBC does. David Gregory of NBC does. Howard Dean does. So if the terrorists are watching cable news or talk shows, they are probably not at all worried about being caught by us.

And this week, the terrorists found out that many U.S. senators are trying to protect terrorists from the indignity of being interrogated (in the unlikely event that the under-manned American military or the depredated U.S. intelligence agencies should get ahold of them in the first place).

John McCain, Lindsey Graham, John Warner and Susan Collins are four Republican senators who decided to put international law (and feel-good moral superiority) above

American law and down-home, no-terror-tolerated homeland security. As leaders of the Senate Armed Services Committee, they teamed up with Democrats to try to stop the CIA and other agencies from interrogating terrorists. Oh sure, we can still bribe them to talk, and we can feed them three-course dinners to fatten them up, so that they may decide to spill the beans while smoking cigars over snifters full of brandy afterwards.

But heaven forbid we dunk these vermin in water and try to scare them into talking about where the next bomb attack is planned! That would be an "outrage upon human dignity."

Thanks a lot, Sen. McCain. I mean, thanks a lot for looking out for the human rights of Osama bin Laden. We wouldn't want to upset the world's top terror madman in the unlikely event that we captured him — we wouldn't want to deprive him of sleep by playing heavy metal music! We wouldn't want him to get the idea that we were so dedicated to our own survival that we would sink to that level!

The "outrage upon human dignity" line comes from so-called Common Article 3 of the Geneva Convention of 1949 where civilized nations came together to try to prevent war crimes and atrocities in future conflicts. That noble goal is obviously very dear to the people of the United States, and anyone who does not think so is a fool.

But the Geneva Conventions and other international treaties should not be used for something other than what they were intended — which for the most part is to establish civilized rules for the treatment of uniformed soldiers in armed combat. They were not meant to be loopholes to permit murderers to go unpunished. And they were not meant as a way to ensure that future murders could go forward as intended by the bad guys.

In fact, they were not even intended to be applied to a war like the current War on Terror — at least not in the way that the Gang of Four on the Armed Services Committee would have you believe.

First of all, the Geneva Conventions apply only to signatories of the treaties. Article 2 of the 1949 treaty says plainly that the provisions apply only when two or more of the "High Contracting Parties" are in conflict against each other. So far as I know al-Qaidastan is not a nation yet, and even if it were, I don't think President Osama would sign a document that would forbid al-Qaida from torturing women and children or cutting heads off of innocent American contractors like Nick Berg.

So the Geneva Conventions don't even apply.

But let's say that they did, as former Secretary of State Colin Powell and McCain's Gang of Four claim. If that were true, then Common Article 3 would have to apply in our dealings with Osama, wouldn't it?

Uh, no. Actually just the opposite if anyone were to read the actual document instead of listening to the talking heads on cable TV. Article 3 applies specifically to "armed conflict not of international character occurring in the territory of one of the High Contracting Parties."

Can you think of a more international war than the War on Terror?

Article 3 is relevant only in internal wars, civil wars or rebellions — not the kind of conflict which we are engaged in now, a conflict of civilizations that stretches from a field in Pennsylvania to the caves of Afghanistan.

So Article 3 is only a club used by anti-American forces to try to sway worldwide public opinion against us as we work to defend ourselves from a brutal enemy. Congress and the president should in reality not be wasting our time with such a debate in the first place, but since they are, let's consider the crux of the argument — whether or not the United States has a right to define "outrages upon personal dignity."

As used in the document, the phrase merely encompasses "humiliating and degrading treatment." Since this is vague and unclear, the president has asked that the language be amplified with America's understanding of what kind of treatment of terror prisoners is "humiliating and degrading." Thus everyone will know what can and can't be done.

Short of that definition being put into place, the military has informed the president that interrogation of prisoners of war will need to cease immediately because of the risk to military personnel of being put on trial for war crimes.

Well, Sen. McCain, what say you? To paraphrase Sen. Kerry's infamous quote of the 2004 campaign, were you "for" the war on terror before you were "against" it? You can't have it both ways. You are either in favor of interrogating terrorists, or you are against it.

And don't try to confuse the issue by saying that if America uses waterboarding on its prisoners, then the same thing may happen to our soldiers when they are captured. Our soldiers would be relieved and delighted to know that if they were captured in Iraq, the worst that would happen to them is they would be dunked in water until they were coughing and frightened and paralyzed with fear. Instead, they face mutilation, burning, electrification and beheading. I'll say it once again — al-Qaida does not honor the Geneva Conventions. Period.

Which brings us back to Jack Bauer.

He doesn't follow the Geneva Conventions either. If he catches a terrorist, and he thinks there is even a chance the guy will be able to provide information that will save innocent American lives, he doesn't mess around by calling Sen. McCain for permission to interrogate — he shoots the terrorist in the leg. After that "warning shot," he puts the gun to the terrorist's head. Every once in a while the gun goes off. Usually, Bauer feels bad about it, but not as bad as the terrorist.

And you know what? Bauer usually wins. Maybe HE will run for president in 2008. We could sure use him._

AN EPISTLE ON FEAR

October 1, 2006

> *"Be not afraid." —Jesus of Nazareth, circa 33 A.D.*
> *"Be afraid, be very afraid." —Hollywood screenwriter*
> *("The Fly," 1986)*

I suppose somewhere between those poles — between divine intervention and Hollywood melodrama — is the appropriate reaction to everyday life with its many challenges.

We should begin by saying — any rational conversation on the subject should begin by saying — fear is neither good nor bad in itself, but rather an emotional reaction to a sense of danger.

Fear thus motivates us to stay away from poisonous snakes, for instance. No one argues against fear in such a case, as everyone knows that self-preservation is a healthy instinct. But fear also motivates people like Howard Hughes to lock themselves up in their room for years at a time and not come out because of a nameless unspoken dread which is not pinned to any real threat. In this case, we can all likewise agree that fear is unhealthy.

The question that should arise therefore in any discussion of fear is not whether fear is good or bad, but whether the threat behind the fear is real or unreal. If we can make that one simple adjustment in our approach to fear, then perhaps we can have a civil debate about our future as a nation and a culture.

For one thing, it would do away with such witticisms as this:

• "When all else fails, start fear mongering." —Think Progress blog.

• "When it comes to scaring the American people, the Bush administration is in a league of its own — the fear-mongering equivalent of the 1927 New York Yankees, the Steel Curtain Pittsburgh Steelers, or the Showtime era Lakers of Magic, Kareem, and James Worthy. Everywhere you turn, there is another Alarmist All-Star." —Arianna Huffington blog.

• "Reject fear — dump Bush." —Bumper sticker.

The implied argument of all such polemic is that "fear is bad," and we have already established that no one can make such a claim and hope to be taken seriously as a proponent of logic and reason.

Indeed, fear cannot be rejected anymore than death can. They are facts of life — somewhat unpleasant, but undeniable. The value of such arguments as "Reject fear" can best be exemplified by substituting another unpleasant fact of life in the slogan, and seeing how effective it is. Let's try this one: "Reject beheading — dump al-Qaida." It's got a nice ring to it, but the problem is that it doesn't make beheading go away. So, in this case, "Rejecting beheading" simply means denying reality.

In the case of "Reject fear," it means denying ourselves the ability to rationally look at a threat and determine whether it is a valid danger or an imaginary one. Fear is not the enemy; it is instead a reaction to an enemy, whether real or perceived. What we must do, therefore, is look at the enemy and determine how dangerous it really is.

For the Bush administration, the enemy is worldwide terrorism and Islamic fundamentalism. The evidence that it is real, pervasive, persistent and deadly is overwhelming. Before Sept. 11, 2001, however, that evidence was largely being ignored. Both President Clinton and President Bush "rejected fear," and that is what empowered our enemy to hit us hard. After Sept. 11, President Bush said we would never make the same mistake again, and that we would increase our vigilance and determination and would take seriously the threats of terrorists like Osama bin Laden.

Most people would agree that ramping up the fear after such an attack was a good idea because it would make us safer. So, this is another subtlety of fear which is ignored by the liberals who misinterpret Roosevelt's dictum that "All we have to fear is fear itself." Fear can either leave us paralyzed or it can energize us to take action. Roosevelt believed in taking bold action and getting things done. Fortunately, that was the course we as a nation took after 9/11. We went on the offensive against terrorism and determined to make ourselves safer.

But even that cannot be accepted by some. As you no doubt realize, many Americans are more afraid of their government than anything else. They believe that President Bush and his minions engineered the attacks on the World Trade Center and other U.S. facilities in order to begin their nefarious takeover of the United States. To these folks, "Big Brother is already in the building," and George W. Bush is the big bad wolf who huffed and puffed and blew our Constitution down.

This theory, however, is not considered to be fear-mongering by its proponents. Instead, they think they are saving the country from Bush and his bogeymen. One of the main advocates of this theory is radio host Alex Jones, who makes a living off of accusing the U.S. government of complicity in a variety of crimes. But if you listen to him carefully between his rants against the government's alleged mind-control experiments, super secret surveillance of you and me, and black ops by the Bushies including blowing up the Pentagon, you will hear him tell his listeners in all seriousness, "Just say no to fear."

If you do not see the irony of this statement, then all hope is lost.

The problem is that we do live in an age of fear. You can't "say no" to fear without putting your head in the sand. There is plenty to be afraid of, inside government and out of it. I am afraid of President Bush's apparent intention to promote a North American Union that would join the United States with Canada and Mexico in a de facto superstate. I am afraid of the crush of illegal immigrants to our country who will forever change the values and culture of our nation. I am afraid of an asteroid blinking out 99 percent of human life on the planet when it hits our pebble in the sky sometime in the next 10,000 years.

Yes, there is plenty to be afraid of. I admit I am even afraid of terrorists launching a strike against our country that will leave millions dead when a nuclear bomb is exploded. Heck, I was even afraid of that before the head of al-Qaida in Iraq sent out a global recruitment message last week for nuclear engineers to join the jihad against the United States and the other "Western dogs."

But what I am not afraid of is being afraid. The only damn fool in a foxhole who isn't afraid is the damn fool. Like it or not, we live in a foxhole. Courage is not the absence of fear; it is action in the face of fear. And combined with determination and the instinct for self-preservation, fear will help us to fight our way out.

Or we could just keep our heads down, smile the blissful smile of the ill-informed, and hope like hell we keep our heads attached when the jihadists launch the next wave of attacks.

A VOTE FOR CHANGE IN BIG SKY COUNTRY

October 15, 2006

(ORIGINAL EDITOR'S NOTE: This week's "2 Cents" column may look familiar to a few readers. A shorter and somewhat nationalized version ran in the Wall Street Journal on Thursday, but the author says he saved the best for his local readers.)

"Are you tired of business as usual in our state and federal government?" asked a letter to the editor in the Daily Inter Lake last weekend. It was written by Joani Young, a Montana grandmother who probably speaks for not just a lot of Montanans but a lot of voters across the board as we approach the mid-term elections.

Young had queried me, as managing editor of the Inter Lake, whether I thought she could make a difference in putting the people back in charge of their government. I told her frankly that it seemed like a long shot. You would need money, I told her — a national leader, a political action committee, a movement — but then I realized I was thinking about "business as usual."

"Go ahead, Joani," I told her. "Send your letter in, and let's see what happens."

"It's in God's hands," she said.

The campaign that drove Joani Young to action to protest the state of American politics was Montana's U.S. Senate race between incumbent Conrad Burns, a three-term Republican from Billings, and Democrat Jon Tester, the president of the state Senate. (The race also includes Libertartian Stan Jones, but few people have noticed.)

Her solution: "None of the above."

The problem: A campaign that has been run from Washington, D.C., which has offended every decent Montanan with its big-city advertising blitz, its finger-pointing, and its name-calling.

This, after all, is Big Sky Country, where there used to be room enough for ideas all across the political spectrum and where a man used to be respected as much for what he didn't say as what he did say. But Big Sky Country has been made smaller and meaner thanks not just to the importance of this election on the future of the U.S. Senate, but thanks also to the tightening web of the Internet and cable news (noose?) on our body politic. The Daily Show and blogs like the Daily Kos have pervaded not just the East and West Coasts with their cynicism, anger and disrespect, but also small-town America.

A few weeks ago, for instance, the high school auditorium in Hamilton, population 4,500, was the scene of an embarrassing scrap that is emblematic of why people like Joani Young, who grew up being taught to respect the political process, have now all but given in to despair. There, a debate between Tester and Burns turned into an unruly shout-down in which an audience packed with Tester supporters heckled and cursed Burns, one even calling him a "psycho."

Sorry, folks, that may be standard fare in New York or San Francisco, but it isn't here in Montana, and most of us are dismayed and disturbed as much by the coarsening influence of the "culture of politics as usual" as by the so-called "culture of corruption."

Of course, Burns has been caught up in the Democrats' national plans to take back the Senate by trying to convince voters of the improbable premise that Republicans have a monopoly on corruption while Democrats sleep with the angels.

Oh wait, sleeping with the angels is another form of corruption, isn't it? And the word from Democrats is that Republicans also have a monopoly on that.

Indeed, Conrad Burns may be the only Republican member of Congress who considers the Mark Foley sex scandal a welcome diversion.

That's because just about the only kind of foolishness Burns hasn't been accused of in the past year of campaigning is fraternizing with congressional pages. To be fair, it's hard to imagine either Burns or his opponent committing the kind of indiscretion Foley is accused of.

In fact, the race between the 71-year-old Burns — who cussses and chews tobacco like the former Marine and livestock auctioneer he is — and Tester, a burly, flat-topped 50-year-old rancher from Big Sandy (population: 700 and change), has all the sex appeal of long johns. When these two guys get together in a room, the temperature falls by five degrees.

The problem for Burns is that he has been living in Washington, D.C., for 18 years, so some of his down-home aw-shucks lovable rascal act is long on rascal and short on lovable. Nationwide, Burns is best known for topping the list of all members of Congress who took money from Disgraced Lobbyist (note capital letters: This is his official title) Jack Abramoff.

It's that "culture of corruption" charge which has made Burns vulnerable even though he is better known round these parts for taking money from Congress than for taking it from lobbyists. In fact, Burns and fellow Sen. Max Baucus, a five-term Democrat, are proud participants in the "culture of pork" and loudly trumpet their accomplishments in winning appropriations for a variety of water projects, highways, research grants and farm subsidies. Around the Inter Lake and other newsrooms in the state, we can measure our representation in D.C. by the number of faxes we get from each member of Congress with an accompanying ka-ching.

Mastery of that kind of practical politics has helped Burns survive one gaffe, blunder and scandal after another which would have rocked a senator from a big media state. Just in the past year, he has reportedly insulted working women and firefighters and implied he may have an illegal immigrant on his home payroll.

Similar missteps in the past had a short shelf life, but today's electorate is not in a forgiving mood, thanks in part to the national media attention which is shining an unwanted spotlight on the race between Burns and Tester, thanks also to the gravity of the challenges facing us.

Tester has capitalized on Burns' blunders to take a 4 to 7 point lead in the latest polls, which means that the national focus on Montana will increase dramatically in the last three weeks of the campaign. It's no secret that control of the Senate could hinge on the outcome of this and a couple of other key races, and money from both national parties and their friends has been pouring into the state.

Money — isn't that what politics is all about? And despite the putative efforts of Sen. John McCain, R-Ariz., to clean the system up a few years ago, isn't it worse than ever?

That's the way it looks to Joani Young and untold millions of other Americans. That's why Joani called me up to ask me if a campaign to vote for "none of the above" would have any effect, and later that day e-mailed me her letter and claimed for herself the power Thomas Jefferson wrote about in the Declaration of Independence, the right to "alter or abolish" a failed government, although in Joani's case she hopes for "a revolution without a shot fired."

So what is the target of Joani's outrage? People who say one thing, and do another, especially politicians "not caring about you and not serving you in whatever way they indicated they wanted to."

It is no accident that the race Young chose to target for her campaign to change American politics was the Senate race between Burns and Tester. After all, these are two politicians who offer hope in their lineage and demeanor for simple, straightforward truth-telling.

If these two can't keep focused on what they want to accomplish for our nation, instead of what's wrong with their opponent — if they can't tell the moneyed powers to take a hike — if they can't put partisan politics aside and do what's good for their state — then what hope is there for real change, for real progress, for solving the real problems we face?

So Joani Young wants to send a message to Washington instead of a senator. Sen. Burns and Sen. Tester, take note. Democratic National Committee, take note. Republican National Committee, take note.

Joani Young of Kalispell has voted: "None of the above."

BORDERLINE INSANITY:
LIES ABOUT THE FENCE

October 29, 2006

On Thursday, President Bush signed into law the so-called Secure Fence Act, which authorizes (but does not fund) 700 miles of double fencing between the United States and Mexico.

An earlier Homeland Security appropriations bill earmarked $1.2 billion for border security, so a down payment on the fence is available, but there is some question as to whether that money will or won't be used for the fence, which would cover approximately one-third of our border with Mexico.

One thing is certain, however: The fence represents a great divide — not between Mexico and the United States, but between those who believe in self-defense and those who don't. Remarkably, there is a question these days as to whether or not it is appropriate to maintain control over who is allowed into one's own country.

The president of Mexico, Vicente Fox, says he doesn't think it is right for the United States to keep Mexicans from entering our country illegally. He feels there is some unspecified human right that allows Mexicans to move north whenever they feel like it, although there is oddly enough no corresponding human right for Americans to move south when the migratory itch hits.

Fox feels there is something unseemly about the idea of a fence. He has called it an "embarrassment," and said it is proof that "the United States does not see immigration as a subject that corresponds to both countries."

Say what?

Apparently it is not an "embarrassment" for the Mexican government to instruct its citizens on how to break U.S. law, as routinely happens. And since when did immigration become an issue of concern to the countries that are losing their citizens? They don't have any say in the matter whatsoever, and never have. The Irish government did not instruct the United States to accept Irish immigrants during the potato famine. The Vietnamese government did not instruct the United States to accept Vietnamese refugees during and after the Vietnam War.

Immigration is a privilege, which means that it must be granted. It is not earned. It is not guaranteed. It is not immutable. Every nation maintains control over who may enter its borders. This is prudent, wise and responsible.

Yet the president-elect of Mexico, Felipe Calderon, says the United States committed a "grave error" in planning to construct a fence, and he was one of many commentators who compared the border fence to the Berlin Wall.

So let's do away with this odious comparison once and for all. It is the most common of several phony arguments against the border fence, most of which rely on emotional rhetoric in a blatant attempt to shame proponents of border security.

But despite the glib analogy, a border fence is simply not the Berlin Wall. There is a fundamental difference between building a wall to keep people out and building a wall to keep people in. If you don't believe me, perhaps you should canvass the inmates at Deer Lodge and the millionaires at Iron Horse.

Likewise, there is a vast difference between the Berlin Wall, which was intended to prevent people from escaping their virtual imprisonment in a dreary economic gulag, and the proposed border fence between Mexico and the United States.

The United States is not building a fence to prevent its people from escaping to freedom, but rather to protect its citizens from a huge economic and political burden which could very well bankrupt us as a nation.

Second phony issue: You can't keep people out with a fence.

Of course, you can't keep people out with a fence! That's because they are PEOPLE — you know, the most intelligent species on the planet, capable of reasoning and skulduggery, and even digging a tunnel.

But hey, you know what? You can't keep bank robbers out of a bank either, but that doesn't mean there is a bank in the world that doesn't have security measures such as steel bars, armor, reinforced concrete and high-tech gadgetry including cameras, motion detectors, heat sensors, and stuff you and I never heard of.

Third phony issue: It's too expensive to build a fence.

Who's kidding who? We can afford to fight a war in Iraq for $400 billion, but we can't afford to build a fence for $5 billion? The richest nation in the world, with the best technology and the greatest workers, can't build a wall that's 1951 miles long? That's pretty pathetic when you recall that the ancient Chinese built a nearly 4,000-mile long wall to protect themselves from northern invaders. I wasn't alive 2,700 years ago when that wall was started, but I doubt there were very many Chinese folks complaining about the emperor's efforts to defend his people from an alien onslaught.

Fourth phony issue: If you are in favor of keeping non-citizens out of the United States, you must be a racist.

Because racism is so widely despised, this argument has replaced patriotism as the last refuge of the scoundrel. Whenever you are about to lose an argument based on the facts, you can quickly accuse your opponent of racism, fold your arms and glower. It doesn't matter what your opponent says; you have won the argument ipso facto. And moreover, you are immune from being accused of "playing the race card." You played the "racist card" and that is apparently a joker in the deck which can trump any other card whatsoever.

The fact is that culture, not race, is an important part of the border dispute. But that is the whole point of borders. They separate different populations which have their own unique identity. If we want to do away with the varieties of human culture through some sort of New World Order homogenization and re-education program, then it would make more sense to do away with the border between the United States and Canada first since we share much more heritage in common with Canada than with Mexico.

But as a student of anthropology, I can tell you that the more homogenized we become, the poorer we become as a people, as a race — the human race — and the less prepared we are to cope with the many varieties of chaos and calamity that have befallen us in the past and will befall us again in the future.

There is also nothing racist about wanting to protect one's own culture. Otherwise the French would be called racists instead of lauded for their jealous husbandry of their considerable cultural treasure. Vive la difference! as they like to say over there.

Indeed liberal-minded proponents of diversity should take note. If you really believe in diversity, if you honestly value variety in human experience, then you should be able to see the importance of a fence. We may inevitably become one big global village, but anyone who has ever lived in a big city like New York can tell you that what makes it exciting and educational and valuable is that it is not all alike. When New York loses its Chinatown and its Little Italy and its Spanish Harlem and its other ethnic neighborhoods, then New York will be poorer.

The same goes for the community of nations — and one nation in particular, one cultural identity we should not allow to perish from this earth, is the American identity, which is the flowering of many traditions into a unique blossom of liberty, tolerance and diversity. If we surrender that identity, if we do not cherish it and protect it with all our might, then not only will we be poorer, but so will the whole world.

OK, DEMOCRATS, NOW WHAT?

November 19, 2006

People who don't know me may assume I have always been a conservative, but nothing could be further from the truth. Indeed, I'm pretty sure I'm not a conservative even today — at least not in the sense most people use the term.

Rather, I'd cautiously classify myself as a pragmatic optimist. I usually look for the best possible outcome of any occurrence, including elections, but don't necessarily expect to see it.

Thus, while I personally would have preferred a Republican victory in the recent congressional elections, I am entirely ready to be proven wrong by the Democrats taking action to save our country from the train wreck that is in progress.

Let's face it, the Republican Congress had a dismal record of inaction, corruption, and overspending. It's hard to see how the Democrats could do much worse.

I guess that is a kind of optimism, but on the other hand I have no reason to expect real solutions to real problems anytime soon. Suppose that Speaker of the House Nancy Pelosi and Senate Majority Leader Harry Reid accomplish some of what they wish to do — increase the minimum wage, decrease deficit spending, improve health-care coverage, even force the president to get our troops out of Iraq. Should that all happen, we would still be the same country, facing the same dilemmas, ignoring the same crises as during the era of the soon to be departed Republican Congress.

It is those crises which concern me — the crisis of declining morality, the crisis of immigration, the crisis of a jihad declared against us by Islamic fascists — and it does not matter to me which political party puts aside expediency and picks up a sword to solve them. The fact of the matter is that our leadership is the only thing between us and total chaos, and if I have to root for the Democrats to come to their senses and save our country, then I will do so, just as I have rooted for President

Bush, even though he has proven himself to be a flawed president.

Did I call myself a pragmatic optimist? Maybe I should change that to prayerful pessimist. I do pray for our country to come to its senses, or for a strong leader to arise who may get us back on track, but the evidence of the past 50 years is that some prayers are not answered, and I would hope we could get a bipartisan AMEN! from the back rows on that one.

Indeed, in a way, I suspect we are better off to have a Democratic Congress in place for a few years, so that the Democratic Party can take part of the blame for the problems the country faces. There's no reason why anyone should think these are Republican problems. Instead, they are problems that have occurred over the past 50 years, as presidents both Republican and Democrat, have dithered.

But some politicians, at least, think they can win and keep power by blaming their opponents for all that is wrong in our country. Lord knows, Rep. Pelosi and Sen. Chuck Schumer and Rep. John Murtha have loved to call President Bush names for the past six years, but now they will have to take responsibility for their own actions — or inaction — as the United States of America collapses into a second-rate power.

Am I too pessimistic? I hope the Democrats prove me wrong. Maybe they can stave off the coming collapse with a well-placed tax-raise here or another government program there. Maybe they can do it by preventing any public acknowledgement of God in the town square.

I'm sure they have a plan.

Otherwise, our children's children will one day be kneeling toward Mecca five times a day and making their goodwill offering in Mexican pesos.

DO YOU REALLY FEEL MORE SECURE AND PROSPEROUS?

January 7, 2007

Psst! Do you want to know a secret?

The Security and Prosperity Partnership of North America is attempting to join the United States with Canada and Mexico in a tri-lateral union that could spell the virtual end to U.S. sovereignty.

"Hey, that's not a secret. I've already heard about that."

You've heard about it, but you've done nothing about it. Possibly you made a joke about it, or laughed about conspiracy theories. Or like the conservative pundit Michael Medved, you've derided the people who talk about it as "lunatics and losers."

The only problem is that the lunatics and losers are only telling you what anyone could find on his own by looking on the Internet or a public library. There is a Security and Prosperity Partnership created by President George Bush and the presidents of Mexico and Canada in 2005. It does aim to promote greater intermingling of government functions in the areas of security and economics between the three nations. The SPP "initiative" was admittedly spurred by the work of the Council on Foreign Relations, which is spelled out in a 2005 report called "Toward a North American Community." That report did propose establishing by 2010 a "North American economic and security community, the boundaries of which would be defined by a common external tariff and an outer security perimeter."

So depending on how you feel about hitching your security and economic future to the Mexican government — that paragon of efficiency, prosperity and human rights — you may or may not be concerned about the Security and Prosperity Partnership of North America.

But one thing you should not do is dismiss the concerns of people about potential loss of U.S. sovereignty as a "paranoid and groundless frenzy," the way Michael Medved did. It's not like people are making up stories about the proposal to create a common currency called the Amero. It's not like people are making up stories about the proposed superhighway corridor between Mexico and Canada that would travel through the American heartland. It's not like people are making up the public discussions of why a North American Union would be a good thing for America and the world.

But it is one of the interesting elements of human psychology that the more people know about something, the less they are worried about it. That is an outcome of the mistaken belief that knowledge is wisdom. People think that if something is not hidden, it is understood. But that is not the case, and never has been.

Have you ever heard of an open secret?

Not the kind of open secret which is a badly kept secret, but the kind where secret information is shared publicly because it will be understood only by those in the know.

The best kept open secret in the world is perhaps the one in the New Testament, where Jesus tells the truth to everyone and then cryptically enjoins them, "He who has ears to hear, let him hear." Of course, other than a few of the deaf people he treats with miracles, everyone around him had ears to hear. But yet Jesus clearly didn't expect his message to be understood except by a very few. "Many are called, but few are chosen."

The difference wasn't in the words of Jesus, but in the discernment of his listeners.

Similarly, many religions throughout the ages have had an exoteric or public message on the one hand, and an esoteric or hidden message on the other. The same is true of many schools of philosophy such as that of the Russian George I. Gurdjieff or the mystery schools of ancient Greece. Modern secret societies such as the Rosicrucians and Masons work under the same principle — their teachings and beliefs are widely disseminated as a kind of lure for potential initiates, but until the initiation is held, the teachings have no power.

Political parties and governments to some extent operate the same way. Although it is routinely said that information is power, very often information lies dormant in the sterile hallways of the bureaucracy until the right person sees it, and seizes on it. Only then can it be used to turn those sterile hallways into the corridors of power.

In our current government, for instance, there is the open secret that love of campaign money is the root of all evil in Congress, but nothing is done to fix the problem. Another open secret with wide implications is the fact that privacy no longer exists in our society, thanks to the digitalization of information. Anyone who wants to know these things only needs to study for about an hour to realize the bad news.

As Sherlock Holmes remarked in "Sign of the Four," "How often have I said to you that when you have eliminated the impossible, whatever remains, however improbable, must be the truth?"

The improbable truth is all around us, but people are afraid to be associated with it. They are afraid that someone like Michael Medved will label them as lunatics. And, if truth be told, there are numerous "open secrets" which are safe from prying eyes because they are just too uncomfortable to ponder. Most people don't want to consider the possibility that members of our own government, even our own presidents, might work to promote agendas that could harm the Constitution or our sovereignty.

So instead of investigating the Security and Prosperity Partnership of North America (www.spp.gov), they just pretend it is a harmless something, a little nothing that will blow away with the wind. Maybe so. We can hope so. We can just pretend it doesn't exist, or tell ourselves that it is a silly feel-good bit of foolishness. Or we could open our eyes and look around, study the matter for ourselves and decide whether we like international alliances to be forged without benefit of treaties or congressional involvement.

Security and prosperity sure sound good, don't they? Much better than the alternative. And there's no chance they put those words on there to fool us, is there? After all, this is 2007, not 1984.

He who has ears to hear, let him hear.

TOLERANCE OF THE INTOLERABLE

January 21, 2007

In mosques all around the world, a crier known as a muezzin calls the faithful to prayer five times a day. He shouts to the four compass points one after the other, "Allah is the greatest... Make haste towards prayer... Make haste towards prayer... Allah is the greatest."

This public display of obdurate virtue is well-known, but it is less well-known what goes on inside the mosques where Muslims gather for their prayers. The Islamic religion has always had an element of secrecy about it, including keeping the holy city of Mecca off limits to anyone except Muslims.

That veil of mystery has been penetrated from time to time by outsiders, including Sir Richard Francis Burton, the great 19th century explorer and author who disguised himself as a Muslim in order to enter the holy city and the Kaaba, the cube-shaped building which is the mystical center of the religion and toward which Muslims pray five times a day no matter where on earth they are located.

In recent years, because of the increase in terrorism led by Muslims worldwide, there has been a growing need for information about the Islamic religion. But most non-Muslims today know just as little about what happens inside a mosque as they did before Burton's pilgrimage and before 9/11.

That lack of knowledge has allowed a public debate to take place about whether Islam is a religion that "teaches the value and the importance of charity, mercy, and peace" (as President Bush described it) or whether it is a religion that teaches domination, destruction and subjugation.

For a variety of reasons — including fear, political correctness and tolerance — most Westerners have been unwilling to make a true and honest inquiry into this question, but this month we may have started to see a few chinks in the wall of silence.

It started in England last week when Channel 4's "Dispatches" news show did a special report called "Undercover Mosque," in which a reporter attended services in mosques that "claim to be dedicated to moderation and dialogue with other faiths." Instead, the reporter found what the show's Website called a "message of religious bigotry and extremism being preached." That included general hatred for non-Muslims and more specifically calls for the overthrow of the British government and democracy.

This weekend, the light continues to shine in dark places as both CNN and Fox are showing documentaries dedicated to unveiling the threat of Islam to our way of life.

Fox News's report, called "Smokescreen: Hezbollah Inside America," tells the story of a Hezbollah cell that operated for several years in Charlotte, N.C., before being broken up a year before 9/11. The connections of this criminal enterprise stretch back to Lebanon and Iran, and though al-Qaida has gotten more publicity, Hezbollah is considered as big a threat to the United States, if not more so.

On CNN, reporter Christiane Amanpour introduces a new show called "Special Investigations Unit," which again focuses on the British Muslim community to illustrate the threat to Western society in a report called appropriately "The War Within." Amanpour apparently links the radicalization of Britain's Muslims to the War in Iraq, which I certainly don't agree with, but even so I am glad to see the word get out that we face an enemy that intends to destroy us.

In a column on the CNN Website, Amanpour wrote, "we found shocking evidence of the bigotry, intolerance and hatred preached by some Muslim fundamentalists in the UK. We met men like Anjem Choudary of the now-banned Al-Mahajiroon extremist group, who denounces democracy and predicts Britain will be ruled by Sharia, Islamic law."

Despite this clear and "shocking" evidence, however, the CNN reporter takes two steps back when she concludes that the violent, intolerant Muslims are a small minority in Britain. She holds out hope that "mainstream Muslims" will reclaim their religion, and speaks of a "deep sense of Islamophobia" on the rise in Britain and across Europe, as if fear of people who want to kill you is somehow a mental illness.

It is this almost pathological tendency toward self-blame which has the capacity to undo us. But the evidence abounds that there are millions of Muslims who intend to destroy our culture or to subjugate it, and no evidence that any substantial number of Muslims intend to do anything to stop them. Indeed, if Muslims speak out against intolerance and oppression of the "infidels" — namely us — then they themselves risk being put to death.

Perhaps, Amanpour should once again read the words of Osama bin Laden:

"This war is fundamentally religious... Those who try to cover this crystal clear fact, which the entire world has admitted, are deceiving the Islamic nation. They are trying to deflect the attention of the Islamic nation from the truth of this conflict... Under no circumstances should we forget this enmity between us and the infidels. For the enmity is based on creed."

Yes, bin Laden blames part of the war on the fact that "you (Americans) attacked us and continue to attack us" in Palestine and Somalia, but much more relevant to the "enmity" that exists between Islam and the Judeo-Christian world are bin Laden's words such as this:

" What are we calling you [Americans] to, and what do we want from you?

"(1) The first thing that we are calling you to is Islam.... and of the discarding of all the opinions, orders, theories and religions which contradict with the religion He [Allah] sent down to His Prophet Muhammad (peace be upon him).

"(2) The second thing we call you to, is to stop your oppression, lies, immorality and debauchery that has spread among you.

"(a) We call you to be a people of manners, principles, honor, and purity; to reject the immoral acts of fornication, homosexuality, intoxicants, gambling, and trading with interest....

"(b) It is saddening to tell you that you are the worst civilization witnessed by the history of mankind:

"(i) You are the nation who, rather than ruling by the Sharia of Allah in its Constitution and laws, choose to invent your own laws as you will and desire. You separate religion from your policies, contradicting the pure nature which affirms Absolute Authority to the Lord and your Creator."

So bin Laden, with the blessings of his mullahs and Islamic teachers, freely admits that he and his kind will not be happy until they have converted the West to Islamic law, Islamic religion and Islamic customs.

The war against terror is not about fighting to prevent a bombing here or there; it is about fighting for survival.

The evidence should be clear to anyone who hears the muezzin's cry. The call to prayer is a call to action, and as long as we in the West continue to ignore the very real, very vocal threat of Islam, then we will continue to be victims of our own good nature.

There is really no secret about the nature of Islam, and these television shows of the last few days don't really teach us anything we didn't know already if we were paying attention.

The question, of course, is whether our love of diversity will continue to be greater than our love of life. If so, it promises to be our ruin. Because however much we Americans pride ourselves on our tolerance — that tolerance will not protect us from zealots; rather it will protect the zealots from us.

SO WHAT'S WORSE? FEAR OR FOOLISHNESS

January 28, 2007

I was upbraided this week, as I have been before, for spreading fear in this column.

To which I plead guilty. But of course I call it spreading awareness.

Cesar Hernandez of Polson wrote a nice letter claiming I was "peddling fear as a course of reaction for [my] unwillingness to look within [myself]." He cited my columns on illegal immigration and the Muslim terror threat and said that I was "inflicting" my readers with a "series of articles on fear immigrants, fear Muslims, fear their religion. Fear, fear, fear!"

Oddly enough, or really not so oddly at all, it was just one sentence later that Cesar pulled his own "fear card" out of his back pocket — "This formula and writing are right out of the extreme right's playbook."

So really what it all comes down to is that Cesar and I are both afraid, but he is afraid of the "extreme right" — of which I am not even a member — and I am afraid of people who strap bombs on themselves and blow up women and children. He is afraid of President Bush; I am afraid of President bin Laden.

The question, as I have written before, isn't whether you should be afraid, but rather what you should be afraid of. I don't mind telling you that I am afraid of what will happen to our country if we continue to allow illegal immigrants to flood across the border from Mexico at the rate of a million or more a year. I don't mind telling you I am afraid of what will happen to our country and our world if we do not have the courage of our convictions, or worse yet, if we have no convictions at all.

Now I have a question for Cesar: Why should I be afraid to say so? Why should I shut up? Why should I keep quiet about my concerns for myself and my children? Why should I be considered an extremist because I love my country and way of life and want to protect them from threats foreign and domestic? Isn't that what good Americans have sworn to do from the day our great country was founded:

"I do solemnly swear that I will support and defend the Constitution of the United States against all enemies foreign and domestic, that I will bear true faith and allegiance to the same, that I take this obligation freely without any mental reservation or purpose of evasion, and that I will well and faithfully discharge the duties of the office on which I am about to enter, so help me God."

Well, my office is a high one indeed — citizen of the United States, and as a citizen of the country that gave us Washington, Jefferson, Lincoln, Roosevelt and Eisenhower, I do so solemnly swear to support and defend the Constitution and the nation of states which it stitched together. I do bear true faith and allegiance not just to the words of the Constitution, but to its ideals, and that means I will not be cowed, bullied or shamed into silence.

There used to be a name for people who hated their culture, their upbringing and their way of life — they were called "antisocial." There is still a word for such people, but now they call them "liberals." At one time, not too long ago, I counted myself among their number, but when you are repeatedly berated as a racist, fear-mongering, right-wing toady by such people, by such "it takes a village to pat yourself on the back" liberals, you eventually decide there might be something better than being a liberal, after all.

If being a liberal means I must be chained to a party line, then I don't want it. If being a liberal means I must be more concerned about defending my enemy's rights than protecting my own children's lives, then I don't want it. If being a liberal means finding fault with everything that makes America great, then I don't want it. If being a liberal means sticking my head in the sand, then I don't want it. You can keep your Charles Lindbergh liberals who pride themselves on "speaking truth to power," but conveniently close their eyes to the truth of Hitler. You can keep your Chuck Hagel liberals who pride themselves on "speaking truth to Bush," but close their eyes to the inconvenient truth of Ahmadinejad.

As for me, I will "speak truth to liberals" until they stop trying to dismantle the foundations of our freedom and our civilization, or until they succeed and throw me in a prison cell. It was the great historian Arnold Toynbee who said

"Civilizations die from suicide, not by murder." That puts it very well, and takes the blame off the Islamists or the Mexicans, and puts it squarely on ourselves. If this country, this civilization is going to perish, then it will be because we sacrificed our values, and laughed at our principles, not because a few thousand terrorists or a few million Mexicans crossed our borders.

Which brings us back to fear.

Isn't "fear" just another name for "understanding consequences"? When you see a child playing with matches, are you afraid because you are a right-wing extremist, or because you understand the potential consequences to your house, your neighborhood or your national forest if the child is not stopped?

Is it fear mongering when the National Park Service hands out those brochures about grizzly bears when you drive into Glacier Park? Or is it merely an attempt to avoid the unpleasant task of scraping up bear scat for signs of human DNA after a couple of campers go missing?

Many of the people who complain most loudly about "fear, fear, fear" being the tactic of the "extreme right" are also the first ones to tell you that we are all going to die a horrible death from global warming. No fear mongering there. Just good, calm rational thinking about how the "extreme right" is trying to kill everyone off, including their own families, for the sake of a little filthy lucre.

What about the liberals' fear of the Forest Service, and its long-standing policies to ensure that America's national forests are utilized as a renewable resource rather than as a source of fuel for forest fires? Is fear OK for liberals, but not the rest of us?

What about the often repeated bromide that the Bush administration failed to sufficiently scare people prior to Hurricane Katrina's devastating arrival on shore in 2005? Is ramping up fear OK for the "extreme right" in some cases, but not in others? Is there a double standard for fear? Will the "extreme left" admit that it is deathly afraid of wiretaps, timber companies, trans fat and Christian values, and hopes to spread that fear from sea to shining sea?

And perhaps most importantly, will the "extreme left" ever take responsibility for its strategy of "deny, defy, decry" as it tries to shut up those of us clamoring to save Western civilization? Will it accept the blame for the fall of Europe to Muslim domination 50 years from now because they pooh-poohed the warnings of people like me as "peddling fear"?

Do they have any idea of what "rough beast," as the poet Yeats said, "slouches toward Bethlehem" to be born? Do they live in this same 21st century as you and me? Do they remember 9/11? Do they remember the Taliban destroying the giant Buddhas of Bamiyan?

Ah yes, that is a story the Islamo-fascists will tell their grandchildren with glee. The two megalithic statues were built on the side of a cliff more than 1,300 years ago and survived intact until the year 2001 when the Islamic Taliban regime in Afghanistan bombarded them with artillery and dynamite for more than a month to dismember them. Why did they do it? Perhaps just to prove their passionate intensity, or just to prove their disdain for all things that are not Islamic. All we know for sure is that a panel of fundamentalist clerics ruled that all statues are idols, so they had to be destroyed regardless of their artistic and historic and cultural importance.

What do you think will happen to Florence when it falls under sharia law? What will happen to the David of Michelangelo? What will happen to Botticelli's "Adoration of the Magi"? What will happen to "Il Duomo" — the domed cathedral at the heart of the great city of the Renaissance? Will they be destroyed piecemeal? Or will the entire city have to be pulverized with an atomic blast? One idol after another, one Christian sculpture, one painting, one church after another? How else could it be cleaned up so that no Muslims are offended? Blow it all up.

Of course, Italy only has about a 1 percent population of Muslims now, but that will change. France already has a population of 10 percent. Many other countries in Europe have between 3 and 6 percent. It doesn't sound too threatening, but the fact of the matter is that in a generation or two, unless something is done to prevent the suicide of the West, these numbers will shift dramatically, and then it may be too late to save the Louvre or the Uffizi Gallery or the Prado. If you do not think so, then you should read the words of the great Italian author Oriana Fallaci in her book "The Rage and the Pride," written as a jeremiad to warn the world after September 11. Look it up for yourself online at http://italian.about.com/library/fallaci/blfallaci1.htm and if you read it with a clear mind you will understand that this is not the time to wonder how we can get along better with our Muslim friends. This is the time to worry about how we can survive our Muslim enemies.

Am I afraid? Of course I am afraid. The question is "Why are you not?"

As Fallaci says in her great book, "Wake up, people, wake up! Intimidated as you are by the fear of going against the mainstream, that is to appear racist (a word inappropriate here because we are not discussing race, but religion), you do not understand or don't want to understand that what is underway here is a Reverse Crusade. ... you don't understand or don't want to understand that what is in motion here is a religious war. A war that they call Jihad. Holy War. A war that is not after the conquest of our territory, perhaps, but certainly aims to conquer our souls. To the disappearance of our freedom and our civilization. To the annihilation of our way of living and of dying, our way of praying or not praying, of our way of eating and drinking and dressing and enjoying ourselves, and informing ourselves...

"You don't understand or don't want to understand that if it is not opposed now, if we don't defend ourselves, if we don't fight, the Jihad will win. It will destroy the world that good or bad we have managed to create, change, make better and render it a little more intelligent, that is less bigoted or not bigoted at all. With that it will destroy our culture, our art, our science, our morality, values, pleasures... Christ! Don't you realize that [all these] Osama Bin Ladens consider themselves authorized to kill you and your children because you drink wine or beer, because you don't wear a long beard or wear a chador, because you go to the theater and the cinema, because you listen to music and sing some songs, because you dance in the discotheques or in your house, because you watch TV, because you wear mini skirts or short pants, because at the beach or pool you're naked or almost naked, because you make it with whom you want, when you want, where you want?

"Don't you care ... even about this, idiots?"

But, of course, Fallaci, knew they don't care — she knew it was a losing battle — but she knew there was no alternative. She grew up as a girl whose family was under the thumb of the Nazis in Florence in World War II. Because her father refused to submit to their fascist regime he was sent to jail, and the young girl learned the importance of resistance and principles.

As Winston Churchill famously said, "If you will not fight for the right when you can easily win without bloodshed; if you will not fight when your victory will be sure and not too costly; you may come to a moment when you will have to fight with all the odds against you and only a small chance of survival. There may even be a worse case; you may have to fight when there is no hope of victory, because it is better to perish than to live as slaves."

From one fear monger to another, right on, Winston, right on!

IS THIS IT?
CONSERVATIVES ARE FROM MARS; LIBERALS ARE FROM VENUS?

February, 4, 2007

One of the reasons we should know that we are in a world of hurt as a nation is that we no longer speak the same language.

No, I am not talking about making English the national language, although if you want to have that debate, I am more than willing to take it on. Nor am I talking about the intrinsic problems created when a large segment of a nation's population refuses to learn the common language such as we have seen recently with many Mexican immigrants, legal and otherwise.

No, what I am talking about is the absolute, unbridgeable linguistic chasm that exists between so-called liberals and so-called conservatives. It's the old "you say puh-tay-to, I say puh-tah-to" problem made famous in the Gershwin love song. It's not that we can't understand each other; it's that we don't like what we are hearing.

This cultural barrier stretches across every important issue in American life, from illegal immigration to education to secularism to mass media to civil liberties, and most importantly — because most divisively — to the war in Iraq, which I guess you could call the hot potato of the language wars.

President Bush, poor man, is expected to bridge the chasm between these two branches of the body politic, and so he has learned to say "puh-tay-tah-to" and "puh-tah-tay-to," which of course pleases no one.

When he says "potato" to a liberal it inevitably comes out sounding like this: "We are going to stay in Iraq because I am a tool of Big Oil and they told me I had better do it or I could wind up like Kennedy with my brains on the windshield, and besides, what does it matter if some more soldiers get killed, we have plenty to spare, and all I am really interested in is spreading American hegemony around the globe so that Wal-Mart can get richer and if you don't believe me, I can tap your phones and read your mail and by the way, the Constitution is just a piece of paper, and by the way when you call me King George III, you better say that with a smile, pardner, cause I may just have a nuc-u-lar bomb in my pocket and if you don't think that's a weapon of mass destruction, think again, buddy."

But when he says "potato" to a conservative, it sounds more like this: "We're gonna win this here war in Iraq because we have to, we have no choice, but I just can't go in there and win the war with weapons because weapons are scary and I don't want to scare anybody because I have to win the hearts and minds of the Iraqi people because they have purple thumbs and if our boys have to get Purple Hearts from going in there and getting shot, then that's OK because that is their job and nobody is going to tell me how to do my job, because I am commander-in-chief and that means I can tell everybody except the generals what to do, and if the generals want more troops they will get them, and if they don't want them, they will get them too, because I am afraid to win the war, but I am afraid to lose the war, too, and I don't want to make anyone mad at me because I am really a nice person and why doesn't anyone love me anymore?"

You say puh-tay-to, and I say puh-tah-to, but when it comes to President Bush, liberals say "demagogic dictator," and conservatives say "wimp."

And because of the huge divergence between the two streams of modern political thought, it is unlikely any other president would fare any better. The "legacy thing" just makes it too hard for a president to act presidential. Can you honestly imagine a contemporary president deciding to drop a nuclear bomb on a major city like Harry Truman did? Even if it were clearly the best military policy, it would be determined to be politically risky, and when the National Intelligence Estimate was leaked by the New York Times there would be a loud national discussion about would we? should we? how could we? blow up hundreds of thousands of innocent people, and then the president would come on TV and announce that "no military option is off the table," but our enemy is the government of Al-Qaidastan not the people of the republic of Al-Qaidastan, and so we will not be blowing up anybody at this time.

On the other hand, if somehow the New York Times did not get its hands on the secret reports and the president actually decided to drop a nuclear bomb in order to demonstrate once and for all the terrible might of the United States, we can pretty much foresee the outcome. No, not submission by the enemy, but rather an impeachment of the president for war crimes. How dare he blow up innocent people? After all, our enemy is the government of Al-Qaidastan not the people of the republic of Al-Qaidastan!

Heck, even by raising the possibility that an American president should consider using an atomic weapon, I will be branded a warmonger and a racist xenophobic troglodyte who wants to kill innocent people. Which makes me wonder what

those same people would call Harry S. Truman. Because if
dropping a nuclear bomb today is a war crime, then dropping
one 62 years ago was also a war crime, and so we lose one more
American hero to political correctness.

Perhaps we should not drop a nuclear bomb today; perhaps
that is too extreme. But if I were president, here is what I would
do — make a public pronouncement on my first day in office
that if any American city were attacked with a weapon of mass
destruction (nuclear, chemical or biological), then the following
cities would be targeted for possible destruction if we
established an Islamic connection to the plot: Tehran,
Damascus, Islamabad, Riyadh, Baghdad, Jakarta. We used to
have a similar policy in regards to the Soviet Union and it safely
delivered us through the dangers of the Cold War. In this case,
there would still be plenty of madmen who would be rushing to
deliver suitcase bombs to San Francisco and New York, but
there would also be hundreds of millions of Muslims suddenly
working with us to find and destroy the terror networks. Cool.

But of course that isn't going to happen.

For some reason which I can't quite fathom, many
Americans seem to be incapable of recognizing the threat we
face from abroad. Perhaps it's because conservatives are from
Mars and liberals are from Venus, as a popular book describes
the language gap between men and women. Mars, in case you
don't recall, was the god of war, and Venus was the goddess of
love. But the fact is that many conservatives practice a religion
that teaches "God is love," and many liberals have served in the
military with distinction and honor.

So the answer must lie elsewhere. Perhaps, it's because we
have convinced ourselves that progress is inevitable, that reason
is universal, and that nightmares only happen in our sleep. But
such a viewpoint would only prove that we ARE sleeping. We
certainly have been blessed in the United States the past 50
years, but let's face it, folks, that's just a very short 50 years in
the big scheme of things. Fifty years of prosperity and freedom
doesn't guarantee anything.

In case you haven't been paying attention, it was just 150
years ago when you could own a human being in the United

States of America — yes, THAT United States of America, the land of the free and home of the brave. It was just 60 years ago when virtually the entire German nation fell into a trance and called an evil madman "The Leader" as it followed him blindly into a war of expansion and empire-building while thousands of its own citizens were being locked up and killed.

Sixty-two million people died in that war, in World War II — yes, 62 million! — compared to the 3,000 plus Americans who have died in the war in Iraq, but if you don't look at history, if you live in a world that begins with the "Today" show and ends with the "Tonight" show, then you don't have to worry about perspective, you don't need to consider consequences or worry about fascist death squads. You just close your eyes and somnambulate from one false syllogism to another: "The war in Iraq is longer than World War II, so it is worse than World War II" (3,000 American deaths compared to 418,000 American deaths). "More Americans have died in fighting since 9/11 than during it, so the war against terror is a foolish mistake" (by which inane logic the 415,000 American deaths that followed the 2,400 deaths during the attack on Pearl Harbor made WWII a horrifically foolish mistake).

But there is no need for opponents of the war against terror to make sense as they clamor with Chamberlain for "peace in our time." They simply need to pander to the selfishness of a largely uneducated citizenry and wait for hedonism to prevail over heroism. It doesn't take long. Heck, it just took 50 years of prosperity and domestic tranquility to turn us into a nation of sleepwalkers who could no more defend ourselves against a serious attack than the French could keep out Hitler's Panzers with their imaginary Maginot line. The only thing most of us are interested in anymore is protecting our own butt; the country can take care of itself.

Oh yes, we can get behind a police action like the first Gulf War, where death looks like a video game from 30,000 feet. We can even get behind a ground war like the Bosnian War if the United Nations or NATO runs it, so we know that we can run for cover at the first sign of danger. Something like the Bosnian War, indeed, allows us to exercise our befuddled belief in the inevitable triumph of good over evil, and of the march of progress.

But the first war in Iraq and the Bosnian War were just little eddies and whirls in the great sea of history. They may have looked like progress up close, but to get the big picture, you need to look at history from a more distant point. Consider, for instance, that the Bosnian War of the 1990s is really just the latest eruption of a war that dates back more than 600 years.

Those who would dismiss the expansionist tendencies of the Islamic civilization should do themselves a favor and read about the Ottoman Empire's war against Europe from the 14th century to the 17th century. I have written previously about Muslim domination of Spain, but it was the Battle of Vienna in 1683 which preserved Western Europe as we know it. Thanks to the Hapsburgs, the army of Kara Mustafa Pasha was turned back, and by the end of the century, the Ottomans had been forced to withdraw from Hungary and Transylvania as well. They didn't withdraw from Bosnia and Herzegovina until 1878, however, and the Muslim influence there remains dominant to this day.

Of course, the United States defended the Muslims in the former Yugoslavia from being massacred because of our respect for human rights and our love of peace, but we should not lose sight of the larger lessons to be learned from history. Bosnia is part of Europe to you and me, but to the Islamic world it is part of the Caliphate, a transboundary, multi-national federation of Islamic states and people who are devoted to the concept of establishing Muhammad's law across the face of the earth. They suffered a setback at the end of the 19th century and the beginning of the 20th, but they are patient, and today they are staging a nice comeback. They see the big picture much more clearly than we do, and they have no reason not to be optimistic about their success in the next 100 years, especially since they are ruthless and we are guileless.

The threat of Koranic law (or sharia) being imposed across the formerly free countries of the world does not even faze most Americans. To raise the specter of such a narrow-minded religious law being applied to nations such as the United States and Great Britain is considered an appeal to fear, a mere rhetorical device that could not possibly reflect a true threat. And so we walk unconcernedly toward our doom.

Women who would basically lose their status as human beings and who would be reduced to chattel under sharia do not seem to be afraid. Homosexuals who would be killed do not care. Adulterers who would be stoned to death do not care. In general, Christians and non-Muslims do not seem to care either, although they would have to accept the rule of Islamic law and pay a tax to their oppressors, or else fight and die. To liberals, this statement of fact is called fear-mongering. To conservatives, it is called a history lesson. But it doesn't matter what you call it because we can't hear each other anyway. Conservatives are from Mars; liberals are from Venus, and there is no love doctor on the "Dr. Phil" show who can tell us why we just can't talk anymore.

You say sha-ree-uh and I say sha-rye-uh; let's call the whole thing off.

BORDERING ON INSANITY

February 11, 2007

The strange case of Ignacio "Nacho" Ramos and Jose Compean deserves your attention. More importantly, it deserves the attention of President Bush.

Ramos and Compean are those two former Border Patrol agents who were convicted of shooting a Mexican drug smuggler as he ran from them in February 2005. The smuggler, Osvaldo Aldrete-Davila, fled back into Mexico, and it was unclear at the time whether he had been hit with a bullet or not, but later it was claimed that a bullet fired by Ramos had hit Aldrete-Davila in the buttocks.

Apparently worried about the consequences of shooting at a suspect, Ramos and Compean collected the spent casings and discarded them. They also may not have reported the incident to their superiors, although this aspect of the case remains in question.

A few weeks later, Aldrete-Davila contacted a friend of the family, Rene Sanchez, who is himself a Border Patrol agent, and he worked through Sanchez to obtain immunity for his testimony against Ramos and Compean.

In other words, the drug smuggler accused the Border Patrol agents of wrongly shooting him, and he convinced a federal prosecutor to go after Ramos and Compean and to leave him alone.

Perhaps if that were the end of the story, we might all just wonder about the ironies of the case, and speculate about whether or not the agents had done anything wrong or not. Typically, law officers are not permitted to shoot at fleeing suspects, except under certain circumstances such as concern for the well-being of others or belief that the suspect had already used deadly force in the commission of a crime.

Because of the uncertainty which that creates in the administration of law, I for one had been prepared to say that I could not resolve whether justice had been done in sending Ramos and Compean to prison. I did not like it certainly, but I was willing to put my faith in the jury's decision.

All that changed last weekend, however, when Ignacio "Nacho" Ramos was brutally attacked in his prison cell by five inmates at the Yazoo City Federal Penitentiary in Mississippi. These inmates had apparently seen a report about Ramos on "America's Most Wanted" earlier that night and had recognized Ramos as a former Border Patrol agent.

The men who attacked him are believed to have been illegal immigrants themselves and they yelled in Spanish "Maten a la migra! Kill the Border Patrol agent!" while they kicked and punched him.

This incident led me and thousands of others to study the facts of the case anew and to conclude that Ramos had been mistreated not just by his fellow inmates, but by the justice system and by the Border Patrol itself, which sent him into battle without giving him the legal tools to defend himself.

Certainly now it is time for all Americans and particularly for President Bush to look at this case with new eyes. The president, of course, has the power to pardon the Border Patrol agents and declare that for their safety, he is freeing them from prison. He has pardoned drug dealers in the past; it seems like now he might want to consider pardoning two men who shot a drug dealer.

Above and beyond concerns for the safety of the two officers, there are numerous doubts about the evidence in the case, and about the handling of the case, which would make it easy for the president to use his constitutional pardon power to free Compean and Ramos.

Here are just a few of the irregularities in the case:

• Aldrete-Davila and his childhood friend Rene Sanchez contradicted each other numerous times in their testimony, including Sanchez's disputed claim that he had not spoken with Aldrete Davila in many years; Aldrete-Davila recalled many contacts.)

• According to a U.S. congressman (Rep. Dana Rohrabacher, R-Calif.), three of the jurors said after the trial that they were leaning toward a not guilty verdict but were told by the jury foreman that the judge wanted them to "go along with majority."

• Another U.S. congressman (Rep. John Culberson, R-Texas) said this week that the Department of Homeland Security has admitted the agency misled Congress when it reported that Ramos and Compean had said they "wanted to shoot some Mexicans." Homeland Security apparently just plain made up the story, which certainly does not instill confidence in the federal government which, through another arm, prosecuted the agents.

• A third U.S. congressman (Rep. Duncan Hunter, R-Calif.) wrote to the director of the federal Bureau of Prisons on the day when Ramos and Compean were incarcerated to "urgently request" that the two agents be segregated from the general prison population for their own safety. Although he says he was assured that the prisoners would be segregated, Ramos was returned to the general population where he was assaulted.

And if you think it is just Republicans raising questions about this trial, you are wrong. Sen. Dianne Feinstein, D-Calif., requested a Senate hearing on the case in August 2006. Here's what she said:

"After reading the August 11th statement of U.S. Attorney Johnny Sutton on the convictions and news reports regarding this case, I have significant concerns that there may have been a serious miscarriage of justice... It appears that the facts do not add up or justify the length of the sentences for these Agents, let alone their conviction on multiple counts."

Certainly, after the beating of Ramos, it is time for all of us to take a look at this case and determine just what kind of country we want — one that goes out of its way to protect drug smugglers or one that goes out of its way to prevent drug smuggling and to prevent illegal immigration. Whether or not, the Border Patrol agents made all the right decisions in this case, they were clearly doing their job and trying to do it well when the incident happened. It is hard to see why they should go to jail, and it is really hard to see why anyone else would ever want to be a Border Patrol agent again.

The prosecution bent over backwards in this case to take the side of the drug smuggler against the Border Patrol agents. But the rest of us have to ask, what good do we think comes from the decision of the prosecutor to grant immunity to a drug smuggler in order to emprison two Border Patrol agents. Deciding to fire the Border Patrol agents would be one thing; even deciding to prosecute them might be acceptable if there were enough evidence independent of the smuggler's testimony. But it is entirely optional whether to grant immunity to known criminals in order to complete a prosecution.

It seems that in this case the prosecutor sided with the devil in order to pull the wings off of two tarnished angels. And they didn't just grant Aldrete-Davila immunity once. He was arrested with another drug load even before the trial began, and yet he was allowed to testify and released back into Mexico again as if nothing had ever happened. The jury never heard anything about it. He had all the rights, and the officers had none. Again, I have to question exactly how this prosecution benefited society.

In the same vein, one must question the Border Patrol's official policy of not pursuing suspects. That's right, according to statements by Assistant U.S. Attorney Debra Kanof during the trial, it's not just incorrect to shoot a fleeing suspect; it's incorrect to even chase him:

"It is a violation of Border Patrol regulations to go after someone who is fleeing," she said. "The Border Patrol pursuit policy prohibits the [vehicular] pursuit of someone."

Well, heck, no wonder the Border Patrol is losing the war against illegal immigration — they are fighting under the same rules of engagement as the U.S. military: "Do whatever is necessary as long as it doesn't make anyone angry or result in bodily harm or loss of civil rights."

Ramos and Campeon may or may not be heroes, but they are certainly not criminals. President Bush needs to pardon them and then he needs to ensure that the Border Patrol has the tools to do its job right in the future.

Border security starts with border sanity.

PRESIDENT BUSH RETURNS HOME — TO MEXICO

March 18, 2007

President Bush's recent trip to Mexico was something of a homecoming for him.

After visiting Brazil, Colombia and other countries in Latin America, Bush made a stop in Mexico, and it must have seemed to him like he had returned to the motherland.

After all, Mexico and Canada are part of the Security and Prosperity Partnership of North America, which the president is promoting as the first step in a virtual merger of our three nations. Besides, as we have heard repeatedly over the last two years, there really is no border between Mexico and the United States.

So when President Bush held a joint news conference with Mexico's President Calderon, it is not surprising that he forgot for a moment — just a moment — that the United States and Mexico are still nominally independent.

Thus, in recounting his work with Calderon, Bush noted that, "We discussed ways to make our nation safer." He immediately corrected himself, and changed it to "both nations safer," but the cat was already out of the bag.

Fact of the matter is, President Bush's entire trip to Mexico was more like a politician's pandering visit to an electoral-rich state than the visit of a head of state to a foreign country. It was evident time after time that President Bush was "sensitive" to the needs and wishes and desires of the Mexican people, but it was not at all clear that he is sensitive to the needs and wishes of the American people.

Indeed, he had the audacity to publicly assure the Mexicans that he was working for them in the immigration battle: "Mr. President, my pledge to you and your government — but, more importantly, the people of Mexico — is I will work as hard as I possibly can to pass comprehensive immigration reform."

Say what? Isn't it a might unseemly for the president of the United States to be making pledges to push the agenda of a foreign government?

But that is just what happened. Our newly "sensitive" President Bush adopted the preferred Mexican code word and repeatedly described illegal immigration as "migration." He made it clear that the United States ought to find a way to accommodate these "migrants," who would not be doing anything wrong at all if it were not for that big, bad border. Remember the mantra: Border bad, migrants good.

What we have now is "a system that encourages people to sneak across the border," said President Bush using doublespeak that would have made another George — George Orwell — proud. Apparently by trying to keep people out, we are encouraging them to come in. Next thing you know, the president will be applying this same logic to his drug policy. No need for laws to prohibit meth and heroin, because then we are just creating "a system that encourages people to sneak needles into their arms." As sensitive people, we should work above all to end the shame for lawbreakers. Why should they have to sneak?

Which brings us to the president's pledge of "comprehensive immigration reform," which he said would "take the pressure off the border." So far as I can tell, I think that means that if we let the Mexicans into our country legally, they won't have to sneak in. Makes sense in a diabolical way.

The president's plan for letting the Mexicans enter our country legally is a "guest worker program," which another columnist rightly called a form of "indentured servitude." Obviously a steady source of cheap labor would be good for American business. The question is whether it would be good for America.

The president apparently sees no other solution. He acknowledges that the America people don't support amnesty and he argues, probably correctly, that there is no practical way to kick out the 12 million illegal Mexican immigrants who are already here. But he doesn't seem to be able to envision the possibility of a solution that is good for the United States and bad for Mexico, such as cracking down on employers and taking away all benefits, education, and housing grants for illegal aliens. The end result would not be "kicking out" Mexicans. They would leave on their own, possibly with a travel subsidy from the U.S. government. But the president is more concerned about the "human rights" of the criminals who are sapping our nation of its strength than about the well-being of our country. It really is as though he sees himself as president of both countries, the United States and Mexico.

"A good migration law will help both economies and will help the security of both countries," he said last week. Recognize the language? More code words to get us ready for the Security and Prosperity Partnership. If it sounds good, it can't feel bad, can it?

The same theme is hammered home in the "Joint U.S.-Mexico Communique issued at the conclusion of the president's visit to Mexico: "In seeking to enhance North American competitiveness based on the twin pillars of security and prosperity, the Presidents [of Mexico and the United States] ... underscored their awareness regarding the need to work together to facilitate the transition to full free trade in such areas as agricultural products."

Full free trade. Nice. That means we can buy all the Mexican products we want that are being manufactured by U.S. companies which moved their facilities south of the border to take advantage of the cheap labor market.

Sending good U.S. jobs to Mexico is part of President Bush's plan for "comprehensive immigration reform." It turns out that if American companies sink billions of dollars into the Mexican economy, there will be more good-paying jobs there and the Mexicans won't be "forced" to "sneak" across the "border" to take "jobs that no one else wants."

Which raises the inevitable question: Once the high-paying U.S. jobs have all been exported to Mexico, and the Mexicans can therefore stay home, who are we going to get to do all the "jobs that no one else wants"?

ILLEGAL IMMIGRATION: ARE WE JUST TOO STUPID TO SOLVE IT?

April 22, 2007

You would think that "immigration reform" would have something to do with immigration, but it really doesn't.

Immigration is the orderly process of entering a foreign country by applying for a visa, meeting certain requirements of residency, waiting in line, and then being invited to cross the border.

Of course, it has not always been that way. I suppose in the 13th century when the Mongols invaded Europe, they might have thought of their sweeping presence as a kind of "immigration" — and who in Austria would have had the temerity to stamp "visa denied" on the broad swords of the khans?

Come to think of it, perhaps immigration these days really isn't all that different from the 13th century — at least that is what you would believe if you listen to President Bush and many leading Democrats talk about "immigration reform."

Although the invasion of the United States by Mexico has been much less violent than the invasion of Europe by the Mongol hordes, it should not be considered any less significant. There are at least 12 million people who have swept across our southern border in the past 20 years, and now they are asking the government of the United States to surrender to them.

"Our numbers are too great for you," they say. "Resistance is futile."

And if you only listened to our nation's leaders you would have to conclude that the illegal immigrants are right — apparently there really is nothing to do but surrender.

It appears we find the task of building a wall across the southern border, or otherwise policing it, to be an insurmountable obstacle. What the Chinese people were able to accomplish more than two thousand years ago when facing their own Mongol invasion, we today can't do. "It's just too hard," we are told. "The border with Mexico is 2,000 miles long and can't possibly be closed." Funny that the Chinese were able to build a wall 4,000 miles long without any of the benefits of modern technology. I guess they were just smarter than us.

Another thing we apparently can't do is police our homeland. We are told that there are just too many illegal aliens already here, and there is nothing we can do about it. Police departments across the country don't even consider being an illegal immigrant to be a crime. It's just a tip o' the hat and "Have a nice day, ma'am," as they send them back into anonymous obscurity.

And then there is the infamous argument of economic necessity — we can't stop illegal immigration, and should actually promote it, because we need the workers. This is the grand doozy of all the foolishness that is spouted on this issue, so let's consider exactly what it tells us.

First, breaking the law is acceptable as long as it is profitable to do so. Farmers say they need pickers. Builders say they need carpenters. Packing plants say they need meat cutters. And the entire economy will grind to a standstill if these companies begin to follow the law and hire only legal residents.

Ridiculous. It's as if no one has ever heard of using your imagination to solve a problem. As long as we have the illegal immigrants doing the job, why should we think of a legal way to fill our worker needs anyway?

Well, let's just imagine that we were serious about not "immigration reform" but rather "illegal immigration solutions." All it takes is two things: A way for employers to verify employment eligibility, so that illegal workers come off the payroll, and a new source of employees to fill the gap.

The first part of that — employment verification — is already being proposed as part of "immigration reform" legislation known as the STRIVE Act of 2007. It is the second part which seems to stymie further discussion, but there are several easy answers.

If employers are really determined to hire Mexican workers, and the U.S. Congress determines that it is in the best interest of the nation to hire more Mexican workers, then the Congress can do what it has always done — increase the quota for legal immigration.

There is no need to reward the lawbreakers who are already in our country because they snuck across the border, as the president proposes. As soon as employment verification is in place, most of those illegal workers will be forced by economic necessity to return to their Mexican homeland anyway. As we are always told, they came here for the jobs. So when the jobs are gone, they will return to Mexico.

Cruel? Unusual? Punishment? How exactly? The nation of the United States has a right to enforce its citizenship and residency rules, and we are under no obligation to provide jobs to people who should not be here in the first place. If you cannot understand that, then you simply don't understand the concept of nationhood.

So let's encourage a reverse migration of illegals to the border where they can sign a form of some sort admitting that they had no right to be in the United States and are leaving of their own free will, and then let's start bringing law-abiding Mexicans in through the front door.

But wait! Perhaps if we took control of our own immigration process instead of leaving it up to the human traffickers and the thuggish coyotes, we might be able to figure out an even more beneficial way to select new citizens for our country than to just invite Mexicans. Mexicans could certainly apply, but why exactly should they get priority? They don't seem particularly inclined to assimilate to our American culture, certainly not to our primary language. English is the second language in their communities, and sometimes not spoken at all. Some of them indeed profess that California, Arizona, New Mexico and Texas are rightly a part of greater Mexico, not really part of the United States at all. Such people might not make good citizens.

So why not open the door a little more broadly. If we have too few citizens in our country to do the jobs that need to be done (a side effect of legal abortion, some claim) then we really ought to have a national policy to address that shortage. Is it possible that Congress could develop a national policy that would work better than the international policy given to us by the coyotes?

Perhaps if we opened up immigration to other nations, we could find people who speak English and would embrace our American culture instead of revile it. There are many citizens of Europe who would welcome the opportunity to move to the New World, just as their cousins did years ago. There are also millions of people in Asia and Africa who would welcome the chance to enjoy the opportunities of American citizenship.

Indeed, perhaps our country could repay a great debt to the continent of Africa by bringing to our shores in this century willingly as many sons and daughters as we stole from there during the many decades of slavery. That might be a true and just reparation our country could make instead of the absurd notion of paying modern African-Americans a settlement to apologize for the great wrong of slavery.

But wait again! That raises one more possibility, apparently not yet gleaned by the great minds who have studied this issue of the economics of illegal immigration. We are told that there is no one to do the jobs that illegal immigrants do. But what about the people in America who have no jobs?

In March of this year, unemployment for the nation as a whole was a very respectable 4.4 percent, but unemployment for blacks was 8.4 percent. Unemployment for blacks in major urban areas is even higher.

So do we just write those American citizens off, and say they don't want to work? Do we let them founder and fail because they live in drug-infested, crime-ridden communities and it is easier to shut them in than to bring them out? Or is it just possible that with a little imagination, with the spirit of American ingenuity, that we could think of some way to solve two problems at once?

Most young black men who are unemployed don't work because they don't have anything to work at. If there really are so many jobs in our country that are fair-paying, non-abusive, and unfilled unless illegal immigrants fill the gap, then I propose a much better solution would be to put our own citizens to work.

This kind of National Economic Security Job Corps would not be modeled on the Depression-era Civilian Conservation Corps or even on the modern-day Job Corps, which is a campus-based job training program for young people ages 16 to 24. What we really need is a way to recruit and transport American workers from where they are to where the jobs are. That would not only benefit employers, it would also benefit whole communities. The government could subsidize training opportunities for the new workers, and possibly even subsidize their housing for the first year in their new location. They could ensure that workers who do not have a high school education get one by making night classes a requirement.

Think of how much better off our country would be if instead of leaving poor blacks to the hopeless cycle of crime and poverty in the ghettoes of our big cities, we were to find a way to give them the same opportunities we afford to illegal immigrants.

Or just think about how hard the whole problem is, and decide to bury your head in the sand again. It's just possible you might meet a member of Congress down there, or two.

LET'S CREATE A SAFE HAVEN FOR TERRORISTS!

April 29, 2007

I have remained silent on the worldwide war against Islamic fascism recently, because, well, frankly, what is the point?

The war is lost, says Senate Majority Leader Harry Reid, and he may be right. In D.C. this year, along with the cherry blossoms, there is the whiff of defeat in the air.

Oh, but wait, he was just talking about the war in Iraq, wasn't he? Certainly he did not mean to suggest that it is the war against Osama bin Laden and al-Qaida and the other Islamic fascists that is lost, does he? That surely would be treasonable.

But yet, have we heard any Democrats talking about how we are going to defeat the worldwide enemy we face? Has there been any discussion of how pulling out of Iraq will benefit our larger war effort against Islamic fascism? Or how we will redouble our efforts against our foe elsewhere?

Sometimes a strategic retreat is necessary in war, but does anyone imagine that Harry Reid will assure the Iraqis the way Gen. MacArthur assured the Filipinos when he was forced to abandon Corregidor? "I shall return!"

Of course not. Because what the Democrats propose is not a strategic retreat; it is simply surrender. The Democratic policy is based on the principle of avoiding death, not of achieving victory, and while no American is happy to see our soldiers perish in battle, military victory is impossible without such casualties. If you are unwilling to incur losses, then you are unwilling to fight. If you are unwilling to fight, then you have signaled your enemy that you are not a serious threat. That is what bin Laden always said about us, and maybe he is right.

It was MacArthur who famously said, "In war, there is no substitute for victory." But today's America seems not to have the taste for victory. Instead, it has acquired a taste for easy living — even our soldiers must be protected and pampered.

So once we conserve our forces by pulling out of Iraq, once we "redeploy" to Okinawa or Antarctica or California, or wherever Rep. John Murtha decides it is safe for our soldiers, what exactly are we going to do with them? Are we paying them merely to defend their home bases? Or are they actually going to be used as intended — to intimidate, to regulate, to force to negotiate, and if necessary to fight to the death.

I haven't yet heard any Democrats talking about where they want to confront the Islamic fascists with these redeployed forces, have you? Oh, that's right, the Democrats don't want to fight; they want to negotiate instead, don't they? Confrontation is immature and dangerous, we are told by the "peace at any price" crowd. So instead of winning the war, like MacArthur would recommend, we are told to ask for help from our biggest enemies — Iran and Syria — so they can take charge of ensuring security in Iraq and let us off the hook. ("Foxes, meet the hens. Hens, meet your doom.")

The Democrats (and their weak-kneed Republican friends) say the war has gone on long enough — the war in Iraq, that is. They say it is longer than World War II, as if that somehow proved something. I often wonder whether the Democrats would be happier if the war in Iraq had been shorter than World War II, but cost us the same number of casualties. Isn't that insane? Should we not be righteously happy that the lengthy war in Iraq has cost the lives of not yet 3,500 soldiers compared to the 407,000 American servicemen killed in

WWII? Isn't it better to have a long war that takes fewer lives than a short war that takes many lives?

You would think so, but yet the Democrats continue to talk about how long the war is, as if there is some statute of limitations on defending your culture, your civilization and your way of life.

Perhaps they did not notice that World War II was a war fought between armies. Such a war is relatively easy, and relatively straightforward, although more deadly. It is not the same thing as a war against terrorists — not even remotely. But when you compare apples to apples, then our record in Iraq is quite admirable. As you remember, we captured Baghdad in about 20 days, with major combat operations declared completed three weeks after that. On the other hand, it took us more than three years to defeat the German army, and nearly four years to defeat the Japanese imperial forces. What happened after we defeated the Iraqi army had no equivalent in either Germany or Japan; thus any comparison is irrelevant.

Have no doubt. We could have shortened this war in Iraq considerably if we were a ruthless uncaring superpower. We could have used nuclear weapons not just to kill, but to crush. Does anybody even remember Hiroshima any more? Does anyone recall the terrible military power that the United States wields? Does anyone doubt that we could level city after city in Iraq with our jets and artillery, our cruise missiles and our other fighting machines?

But we did no such thing. Our goal has NOT been to subdue Iraq these past four years; our goal has NOT been to defeat an army, or even a nation. Instead our goal has been to find a way to bring Iraq into compliance not so much with a U.N. resolution, but with common decency.

If some percentage of the Japanese citizenry and former soldiers had decided to wage a war against our soldiers after their defeat, then that war would have stretched on for many more years, too. But the Japanese did not want war after World War II, after Hiroshima, after Nagasaki. They had seen enough death. They had seen the full power of the U.S. Army, the Air

Force, the Navy and Marines. They had seen death surround them; now they wanted life.

In comparison, the Iraqis saw 20 days of full-scale war, of "shock and awe" as it was called. They saw buildings crushed, but relatively little death compared to what might have been meted out. Then they saw the United States military forces try to become friends of the people of Iraq, and the terrorists in Iraq saw their opening. They knew that the United States would not wage ruthless war against the innocent bystanders of Iraq, so the terrorists decided to do so instead. This produced chaos, hopelessness, paralysis and fear — the four horsemen of the terror apocalypse.

The United States could not stop the killing, because for the most part we were not responsible for the killing. But the United States is held to blame for the killing because it followed our invasion. This is a simple but effective use of the post hoc, ergo propter hoc fallacy, which erroneously claims that because one event is earlier in time, it necessarily caused the second event. Thus al-Qaida has brilliantly been able to kill thousands of people without taking any of the blame. Instead, it all comes back to us.

Al-Qaida is not an enemy to be underestimated. If you do so, then you can be sure that you will wake up someday to discover that another skyscraper has been leveled — or worse, a city. Al-Qaida knows the secret of war. Maybe they paid attention to MacArthur. "There is no substitute for victory." Or maybe they are just smarter than us.

But then, you don't have to be particularly smart to understand this. It is relatively easy to kill people. Someone as stupid as Cho Seung-Hui can do it. All it takes is a gun or some other weapon and a lack of conscience. You just have to care more about a cause than about your humanity.

And so the United States has indeed put its soldiers in harm's way in Iraq. There are indeed evil people who would kill them, just as they will happily kill innocent men, women and children in the streets of Baghdad. Just as they would like to kill men, women and children in the streets or schools or malls of the United States.

But what exactly is the Democratic alternative? We've heard from Harry Reid and other Democrats that they want to withdraw U.S. military forces from Iraq, and let the Iraqis take care of their own problems. We've heard that the conflict in Iraq is nothing but a religious-based civil war which we can't resolve. But no one on the left seems to care that this civil war was started by our enemy intentionally as a tactic to sow doubt and confusion among the American public. No one on the left seems to have the wherewithal to say that we Americans — the spiritual descendants of George Washington and Andrew Jackson and Abraham Lincoln — shall not be manipulated nor moved by the fear tactics of al-Qaida and its deadly allies.

Indeed, they seem to be saying just the opposite. They have passed a funding bill for the war effort which includes language demanding that the troops withdraw whether the mission is accomplished or not. That bill will be vetoed, but that is not the end of the push to surrender. Even worse perhaps is the proposal voiced by Gov. Bill Richardson of New Mexico last week while he was campaigning for president.

Richardson proposed that the Congress should pass a resolution "de-authorizing" the war in Iraq — in other words, revoking the permission granted to the president to go to war in the first place. At first glance this seems like the moral equivalent of the timeline for surrender proposed by Harry Reid, but it is in fact quite different, and much more dangerous.

If the Supreme Court agreed that such a "de-authorization" was valid and binding on the president, it would essentially create a safe haven for terrorists in Iraq that would be almost impenetrable by the U.S. military.

Think of it, such a resolution would essentially create a hideout for al-Qaida and for all other outlaws. The Islamic fascists would know that Congress had given them a free pass. Get to Iraq and you are safe.

And that would literally be true, because unless I miss my guess, no future Congress would ever again authorize a war against Iraq. No matter how unstable the situation got there, no matter whether al-Qaida were able to establish itself as the government of Iraq, we would never again have permission to launch military action against that nation. It's too dangerous, we would hear. They will just blow us up with their improvised explosives. How can we possibly beat such a powerful enemy? "Sorry, but military action in Iraq is 'de-authorized.'"

God forbid that we ever hear such talk. But we will if Bill Richardson gets his way. Then we can all agree with Harry Reid that not just the battle, but the war is lost.

AL-QAIDA CARES WHO WINS IN IRAQ

May 13, 2007

Last week, the American media was blaringly silent on the issue of al-Qaida endorsing the Democratic plan for withdrawal from Iraq.

I suppose it might be seen as vaguely embarrassing to the Democrats — kind of like having Charles Manson endorse someone for president because the candidate is sufficiently soft on crime.

But you would expect the mainstream media, with its vaunted ideals and undying quest for the truth, to have realized the significance of the moment when the Democratic proposal was welcomed by al-Qaida as an acknowledgment of "American failure."

Instead, what you got was an obligatory news story or two about the video being released, and then a deep abiding silence. It's almost as though the media and the Democrats were taking a pre-9/11 approach to the story — If we ignore it, maybe it will go away.

In case you blinked and missed the story altogether, here it is: On May 5, Sheikh Ayman al-Zawahiri, who is the Joseph Goebbels of al-Qaida — devout follower and propagandist of the movement's Hitler, Osama bin Laden — made his latest Internet video pitch for the destruction of America and establishment of a united Islamic empire over much of the world.

Most significant was Zawahiri's assessment of the recent congressional gambit of trying to force President Bush to quit the Iraq war by setting a timetable for withdrawal. Zawahiri welcomed the Democratic bill, which was subsequently vetoed by President Bush, as an acknowledgment by America that it was defeated.

"This bill reflects American failure and frustration," he said, and he lamented that the prospect of American surrender might mean the jihadis would lose their chance to kill thousands of U.S. soldiers.

"... [T]his bill will deprive us of the opportunity to destroy the American forces which we have caught in a historic trap. We ask Allah that they only get out of it after losing two hundred to three hundred thousand killed, in order that we give the spillers of blood in Washington and Europe an unforgettable lesson which will motivate them to review their entire doctrinal and moral system which produced their historic criminal Crusader/Zionist entity."

If you took al-Qaida seriously as a threat, you would have to be a little worried, right?

I mean, this could actually be seen as a threat to attack U.S. soldiers in greater numbers before the Democratic timetable for surrender kicked in, right? Maybe even a threat to use weapons of mass destruction. How, after all, would you kill 200,000 or more troops?

Is it possible that al-Qaida could try something as brazen and daring and deadly as attacking U.S. soldiers in their own bases to maximize casualties?

Nah, that could never happen.

Just the usual Islamic hot air, right?

Except it wasn't hot air when Zawahiri and bin Laden swore to strike a mighty blow against the United States before 9/11, was it?

Even the Democrats seem to understand the danger of al-Qaida in hindsight. After all, they constantly harp on the colossal blunder of George Bush in failing to act swiftly after getting the daily briefing entitled "Bin Ladin Determined to Strike in US" on August 6, 2001, fully a month before the planned al-Qaida attack that took place on September 11.

The top-secret briefing for the president began by noting that bin Laden had publicly said he and his followers would "bring the fighting to America." It then noted that bin Laden "prepares operations years in advance and is not deterred by setbacks." It warned that Al-Qaida members "— including some who are U.S. citizens — have resided in or traveled to the U.S. for years."

Scary stuff. And the briefing said there had been some intelligence which suggested that al-Qaida was making "preparations for hijackings or other types of attacks."

According to the liberals who hate President Bush he should have read that briefing and then gone into Harrison Ford mode (a la "Air Force One") and kicked some terrorist butt. Of course, there is no explanation of how he could have done so without arousing the wrath of the American Civil Liberties Union and other defenders of the jihadis. Remember, there was no Patriot Act then, and no real mechanism to pro-actively defend the country against a vague and fanciful conjecture that Mideastern mujahadeen could attack New York City and kill thousands of innocent civilians. The vanguard of laughing hyenas on late-night TV and in the cable jungle would have savaged the president viciously for his paranoid fantasies.

But not in hindsight.

In hindsight, the Democrats tell you, the president was wrong to be cautious. He should have canceled flights, put troops in airports, tapped phones, read e-mails. How dare he ignore the vague threat of the daily briefing? Instead he did nothing and led the country down the primrose path of over-confidence. He was a miserable fool who got us into trouble by underestimating al-Qaida, and then made matters worse by not going after al-Qaida harder in Afghanistan. In hindsight, the president led the country astray by getting us involved in a war in Iraq instead, and now he stubbornly refuses to admit his error and we have to depend on the wise heads of Congress to save us from the quagmire.

That's what hindsight would have you believe if you listen to Nancy Pelosi, John Murtha, Hillary Clinton, John Kerry, Bill Richardson, Joe Biden and all the other bright lights of the Democratic Party.

In hindsight, George Bush should have acted swiftly and decisively against the vague threat of al-Qaida in the United States. Probably nearly everyone really believes that, even most Democrats. But now that we have a real enemy, with not vague threats but definite ones, the Democratic leadership can think of no better solution than to pull head and feet into shell and go into Turtle Armor mode. Hindsight 20-20; foresight non-existent.

But you don't need foresight any longer; you just need to listen to the words of your sworn enemy — the words of Ayman al-Zawahiri, the architect of the Jihad against America — in his May 5 interview:

"The Jihad in Iraq today, by the Grace of Allah, is moving from the stage of defeat of the Crusader invaders and their traitorous underlings to the stage of consolidating a Mujahid Islamic Emirate which will liberate the homelands of Islam, protect the sacred things of the Muslims, implement the rules of the Shari'ah, give the weak and oppressed their rights back, and raise the banner of Jihad as it makes its way through a rugged path of sacrifice and giving towards the environs of Jerusalem, with Allah's permission."

Al-Qaida seems to think that the war in Iraq actually matters. They seem to think that if the U.S. pulls out of Iraq, then al-Qaida has won a major victory in its war to first conquer all the Muslim homelands and then to conquer Israel. And if you don't think an Islamic caliphate spanning three continents is a danger, you haven't been any more paying attention than Senate Majority Leader Harry Reid has. Indeed, after reading the interview with Zawahiri, it is obvious that he has a much better understanding of global geopolitics than Reid.

You remember Harry Reid, don't you? He was the first one to declare that the "war is lost," before Zawahiri took up the chant. This obvious parallel was left unspoken in most discussion of Zawahiri's proclamations, but if you see Harry

Reid and Ayman al-Zawahiri on the same side of an issue, what does that tell you? Anyone who cares about the continued existence of the United States cannot be happy to see our congressional leadership providing talking points for our sworn enemy. Which is why the momentous declaration of Zawahiri was barely reported by the left-wing media. It is dangerously inconvenient.

COME TO THE AID OF YOUR COUNTRY

May 20, 2007

I used to think we needed to leave the Constitution alone.

That was before the Senate decided to extend citizenship to as many as 20 million lawbreakers whose sole purpose in breaking the law was to gain U.S. citizenship. Talk about making the punishment fit the crime! This punishment fits the crime exactly — they are identical!

Forget about the billions of dollars it will cost the taxpayers of this country to give amnesty to illegal immigrants. Forget about the fact that it will forever change the nature of our country. Forget about the fact that if 9/11 terrorist Mohammed Atta had not blown himself up in the World Trade Center, he would have been eligible for a Z visa under the Senate's plan so that he could enjoy the fruits of American citizenship before he attacked us.

Forget about all that. Even forget the fact that this immigration bill was hammered out in the dark of night by senators who think they can make better law without interference from everyday Americans. Forget the fact that there is every indication that this bill is being bought and paid for by multinational corporations who want a source of cheap labor, and don't care about the future of the United States of America.

Just forget all that, and focus on the fact that for a few more short months, you still have a chance to make a difference.

Think about how unresponsive your government is, and how you have no confidence that your senators or even your congressman will do what is best for this country, and then ask yourself who is going to fix it if you don't.

Yeah you. Because I am pretty sure you scare the bejeezus out of Mr. Congressman and Mr. Senator.

If you are waiting for them to fix the problems in this country you will wait for a long time. The Senate and the House do not speak for you. They speak for the campaign contributors who financed them into office. It is time that the real rulers speak up, and that is "We the People."

It is time for "We the People" to run our own country for a change, and not assume that someone else is doing it for us. We can do that, if we do it quickly, by seizing control of the Constitution and stopping the Congress from giving away our country to the foreigners who have invaded it.

All it would take is a simple amendment to establish that citizenship shall not be granted to anyone who entered the country illegally. It should also establish that citizenship is not granted automatically to anyone born in the United States while their parents are here illegally. And finally such an amendment should spell out that it is the duty of the commander in chief to act to secure the borders of the country against foreign intrusions of any kind. The amendment could also establish the authority of the Congress to regulate legal immigration but rule out blanket amnesty of any kind for illegal residents of this country.

The problem, of course, is that such an amendment could never pass in Congress. Congress has no interest in securing our borders, and certainly the president has proven time and again that he has absolutely no desire to protect the rights of American citizens against the costly invasion from Mexico and elsewhere.

So that means we are doomed, right?

Not quite.

Listen to what the Constitution says about the amendment process:

"The Congress, whenever two thirds of both Houses shall deem it necessary, shall propose Amendments to this Constitution, or, on the Application of the Legislatures of two thirds of the several States, shall call a Convention for proposing Amendments, which, in either Case, shall be valid to all Intents and Purposes, as part of this Constitution, when ratified by the Legislatures of three fourths of the several States, or by Conventions in three fourths thereof, as the one or the other Mode of Ratification may be proposed by the Congress..."

As a matter of historical record, all of the 27 amendments ratified and joined to the Constitution thus far have originated with the Congress. But it may be time for the Legislatures of the several states to act, and act swiftly, to demand a constitutional convention to establish once and for all the will of "We the People." It would not by any means be easy to get 34 states to call such a convention, but this is do or die.

Every special interest group in the country would be terrified of what such a convention might do, but that is the point. It is time for the special interests to stop running this country, and for "We the People" to take it back. Thomas Jefferson would have thought we were long overdue. In a letter to James Madison in 1789, he said that "no society can make a perpetual constitution or even a perpetual law. The earth belongs always to the living generation." In the same letter he warned that the people's "power of repeal" was not of great value because it depended on representation in the legislature which was "unequal and vicious," and warned that the people's representatives were tainted by factionalism, corruption and personal interest. Today, we would call it party politics, campaign finance, and ambition, but the message is the same — don't trust the Congress to represent your interests. They have their own agenda.

Today, in this so-called immigration reform bill we have the best example we will ever need. This bill is not immigration reform; it is national reform — a fundamental change in the rules of citizenship — and it must not be allowed to stand.

WHY 'WE THE PEOPLE' MATTER ...

May 27, 2007

In the France of Louis XIV, the king could say without a shred of irony, "L'etat, c'est moi! The state, it is I."

In the years following the adoption of the U.S. Constitution, Americans could proudly say, "The state, it is we the people."

But in this day and age, who exactly is invested with sovereignty in the United States of America? Is it "we the people"? And if so, why do we feel so disenfranchised, so alienated, so used?

Or is it the president? Could it be? Then why does he look so drawn and haggard, so diminished and so beaten?

Or perhaps sovereignty today belongs to the Congress of the United States? Could our elected representatives have seized power from us, right under our noses, and left us none the wiser?

It sure feels that way to many of us who watched the Quentin Tarantino-choreographed pantomime in the Senate the past two weeks as all 326 pages of the "comprehensive immigration reform" bill were shoved down America's throat to the tune of "La Cucaracha."

The senators claim that America wants — no, demands — "comprehensive immigration reform," so the senators all have cleaned their hands just like jesting Pilate when he freed Barabbas and sent Jesus to his death. Only doing what America wants, they say. But America doesn't want reform that throws up its hands in surrender; it wants reform that enforces the law and enforces the border. It doesn't want immigration reform; it wants immigration control. It doesn't want a government that washes its hands; it wants a government that does its job.

Which is why last week I proposed that the people of the United States, through their state legislatures, ought to take back the reins of power and ask for — no, demand! — a convention to propose amendments to the U.S. Constitution — in particular, an amendment that requires border enforcement and denies citizenship to anyone in this country illegally, including those who were born here because their parents were here illegally.

If you think it is going to happen any other way, you are mistaken. And if you think the Constitution should not be handled by "we the people" because it is too fragile and too delicate, then you missed the point of having a Constitution. We are a self-governing people. It is not "we the dead people" who have the power in this country; it is "we the living."

But yet I have heard from many people who are afraid that a constitutional convention would give power to the wrong people — presumably the left wing of the Democratic Party or the right wing of the Republican Party — who would strip away all the liberties enshrined in the Constitution.

Such a fear is absurd for two reasons. First of all, it would never happen. The "convention to propose amendments" to the Constitution would do just that — propose. Any amendment proposed by the convention would still have to be ratified by three-quarters of the several states, which currently means 38 state legislatures would need to approve any changes. It is safe to assume that wholesale changes to our fundamental liberties would not survive such a process.

Second, it is absurd because such changes could only be accomplished if they represented the will of "we the people" — and to deny the will of "we the people" is to deny the whole principle, basis and intent of the Constitution in the first place.

God forbid that anyone tamper willy-nilly with that divinely inspired document, but also God forbid that anyone deny "we the people" the authority of self-government. Our forefathers did not write the Constitution to enslave us, but rather to empower us — and to protect us from either tyranny or mob rule.

In fact, you can think of the Constitution as the chariot which tamed the power of a pair of dangerous, belligerent snorting horses named Majority and Minority.

Those two stallions, not quite thoroughbreds, always want to go in opposite directions, and without the constitutional chariot of a republic to harness them, they would always be trying to overthrow each other. Majority is the bigger, meatier horse and has the natural advantage to dominate and destroy the much smaller Minority, but that does not mean the matter can be so simply decided. It turns out that even the tiny Minority can use terror and fear like a set of pincer teeth to keep Majority at bay, and in some ways that is an even more frightening picture.

So the strictures of the Constitution, which keep both the rough and tumble Majority and lean and hungry Minority in check, were clearly a brilliant feat of social engineering. You certainly would not want to tamper with it.

But on the other hand you probably would not want to leave it alone either, anymore than you would leave your 1967 Rolls Royce alone. You would not let just anyone mess with it, but you would surely expect a certified mechanic to do the necessary work to keep it running in smooth order.

That finally is what I realized about the Constitution, too. For a long time I mistakenly thought that if we had a constitutional convention, it would be like throwing dynamite into the chariot. But then I realized that a constitutional convention was not about tampering with the Constitution, but rather about bringing in an expert mechanic to look at it and figure out why it is chugging and clicking instead of whirring and purring.

Because the expert about the Constitution is not a blue-blood senator, and it is not the president, nor even the good men and women of the Supreme Court. The expert about the Constitution, and the one mechanic you would want to call in if things started to go wrong is "We the People."

Which is why a great many people who give lip service to the ideals of democracy quiver at the thought of actually trying it. Such people, and I'm not at all sure if they are mostly liberals or mostly conservatives, will tell you that the Constitution is too valuable and rarefied to be messed with by common folk.

But one thing our Founding Fathers were is ingenious. They seemed to anticipate many of the conflicts that would inevitably ensue in a constitutional republic, and provided safety valves in the somewhat ambiguously worded document so that if at all possible the Constitution would be self-correcting as the decades and then centuries passed.

Most obviously they provided for amendments to the Constitution to be made when experience and reason taught us that something was amiss. That amendment process has been used sparingly — just 27 times in the past 220 years — which is testament to the enduring quality of the workmanship in the original Constitutional Convention.

But we should not assume that a lack of change is automatically a good thing. It took, for instance, 78 years, from the ratification of the original Constitution to the admission in the 13th Amendment that slavery ought to be abolished. Other changes came more quickly, such as changing the way presidents and vice presidents were elected in 1804 or repealing the prohibition on liquor just 14 years after it was first passed in 1919.

Change is built into the Constitution, but for the most part the changes made have been relatively minor, relatively technical. Those which are most significant such as the addition of the income tax or giving women the right to vote show how powerful a document the Constitution is, and how much it shapes our society as a whole.

But up until now, all change to the Constitution has been in the hands of Congress. The amendments proposed have all originated there, and been approved by two-thirds of the members of the House and Senate, then ratified by three-quarters of the states. Considering that challenging process, it is surprising that any amendments have ever been approved, let alone the important ones.

That slow and deliberate quality has served us well, and protects us from mistakes which could harm or even imperil our great republic. But such mistakes, have, of course, been with us from the beginning, perhaps most recognizably in slavery and denial of full citizenship to women. Whether we act quickly or slow, we are subject to the same human foibles as all other people, and fool ourselves to think otherwise.

But we also possess the same human majesty which was celebrated and exemplified by our Founding Fathers, and by such token we should not be afraid to seize the power granted to us by our forbears and by God in order to revivify the words of Thomas Jefferson in the Declaration of Independence that "Governments are instituted among Men, deriving their just Powers from the consent of the governed" and "That whenever any Form of Government becomes destructive of these ends, it is the Right of the People to alter or to abolish it, and to institute new Government..."

It may be scary to think about changing the Constitution, but living in fear of consequences is a guarantee of paralysis, and paralysis is a guarantee of atrophy and ultimately dissolution. Jefferson was our foremost political philosopher at the start of our republic, and he argued forcefully for change in the Constitution that would keep it current and honest. Indeed, he promoted the idea of a constant freshening of government by the forced entry of We the People into the halls of power in every generation.

Thus, taking my cue from Jefferson, I am calling for a constitutional convention to quickly and once and for all establish the duty and necessity of the commander in chief acting to secure the borders of the country against foreign intrusions of any kind and establishing the authority of the Congress to regulate legal immigration but never to provide blanket amnesty of any kind for illegal residents of this country.

Such drastic action is necessary because it now becomes apparent that the people of the United States can no longer depend on the Congress of the United States to do our business. A constitutional convention may well be the only way to deprive the Senate of its plan to legitimize as many as 20 million illegal immigrants and change the face of America for all time.

The Senate's smug, secret plan was introduced two weeks ago with great fanfare, as if the people might not notice that our sovereignty was being sold for a mess of pottage. But even if that "comprehensive plan" goes away in defeat, the problem will remain. There is no enforcement of border security or of immigration control. We certainly cannot depend on the Senate to fix the problem.

Perhaps, the senators are so out of touch with reality that they are truly convinced that what they are doing is supported by the great mass of the American people. Or perhaps the Senate is convinced it can get away with anything it wants regardless of the people. I'm not sure which of those delusions is more accurate, but it leads me to decide that the time has come for Jefferson's ideal to be implemented.

Let's take back our Constitution, and take back our country.

SENATE PROVES IT'S NOT ON YOUR SIDE

June 10, 2007

If you ever had any doubt at all that the United States Senate does not represent you, you should have put that doubt aside forever on Wednesday.

That was when the Senate voted explicitly to extend blanket amnesty to convicted felons and criminals who have entered our country illegally.

This is not amnesty that clears the felony off their record; it is amnesty which says the United States of America does not care about your felony — we welcome you and your felony to our shores, no questions asked.

We don't just welcome your tired and your poor, your huddled masses — we welcome the thugs who stole their money, beat them up and treated them like animals in the first place.

If you ever made the mistake of thinking that there is no harm in leaving your front door open and then inviting whoever walked through the door to dinner, you will now have the chance to pay for that mistake — if the Senate gets its way.

Just incredible.

The Senate clearly does not represent the interests of the American people. Or if they do, how do they explain what good it will do for Americans to give a "path to citizenship" to gang members, drunk drivers, and fugitives from justice? Yes, the Senate ultimately passed an amendment that restricted some criminals from obtaining amnesty, but why is this even an issue? Why do the senators want any criminals to get legal status in our country?

As Sen. Jeff Sessions, R-Ala., astutely noted: "Nobody has a constitutional legal right to demand entry into the United States. It amazes me the lack of understanding and comprehension of what it's all about."

It would amaze me, too, except nothing does anymore. This is the logical outcome of a society based on trying to please everyone while doing no harm to anyone. (Hint: If you are saying, "What's wrong with that?" you are part of the problem.)

A small bit of good news for Montana, by the way. Our two senators broke from the lockstep to national suicide and voted for the amendment by Sen. John Cornyn, R-Texas, to bar criminals from gaining legal status. But the amendment lost 51 to 46. Baucus and Tester say they will oppose the immigration bill as long as it contains amnesty, so their votes should remain safe for a sane world.

Meanwhile, Sen. John McCain has taken leave of his senses as he dances once again with his new best friend in the Senate, Edward Kennedy of Massachussetts. McCain-Kennedy or Kennedy-McCain is rapidly becoming the new age mantra for politically correct bunk.

Cornyn did manage to get another amendment passed on a 57 to 39 vote. This one would change a provision in the original bill that barred law enforcement agencies from seeing applications for legalization from applicants who were rejected. Cornyn said authorities should know if applicants have criminal records that would warrant their deportation.

The weepy whiny pro-amnesty crowd said people might be afraid to file applications for legalization if they knew they night be deported when the truth about them was known. Imagine that. Afraid of the truth. Afraid they might have to leave our country because they were here illegally!

But don't worry. The truth will probably never see the light of day. The senior senator from Mexifornia, Dianne Feinstein, said that Cornyn's amendment was "not a deal killer" but that it would have to be changed in House-Senate negotiations to tidy things up.

As long as the illegal immigrants are taken care of, all is well in the world.

SILLY CONSPIRACY MAY JUST BE MOST DANGEROUS KIND

July 29, 2007

A successful conspiracy against power can only happen one of two ways:

Either the conspiracists are so closed-lipped that no one ever finds out about the conspiracy until it is too late, or else the conspiracy is so absurd and ill-considered that no one takes it seriously in the first place.

There appear to be relatively few successful conspiracies of the first sort, probably because it violates human nature too much. The larger the conspiracy, the more likely that someone will tell the wrong person too much and lead the authorities to the truth before the conspiracy can reach fruition.

It appears that the vows of the Islamist terrorists, being a sacred honor, make it possible for them to accomplish much more than other conspiracists through the weaponry of silence. Although the United States had enough intelligence about the 9/11 attacks to warn of an impending attack, there was very little certainty in that warning — not enough to make arrests and stop the attack in advance.

On the other hand, sometimes conspiracies are well understood in their intent and even practical application before they are accomplished, and yet the powers-that-be don't act in a manner fitting for self-preservation. These are the conspiracies that are most dangerous, the ones that are ignored or overlooked the way the brown recluse spider can hide in plain sight and be mistaken for a common house spider.

Such conspiracies are not always successful, of course, but they have a much better chance of success than those that are taken seriously by the authorities. A few simple examples are the rise to power of Adolf Hitler and the Bolshevik Revolution.

I'm not sure if we are in the midst of such a conspiracy today or not, but it seems that there are only two explanations for the Security and Prosperity Partnership of North America — one is stupidity and the other is conspiracy. That veil of stupidity, of course, is the perfect cover to make an actual conspiracy a success, so in a well-planned conspiracy it could actually be part of the plot.

If you don't know what the Security and Prosperity Partnership is, welcome to the crowd. Most people have never heard of it, even though it is clearly the framework by which three countries — the United States, Mexico and Canada — could give up their sovereignty in order to band together in some kind of new North American Union.

I was one of those people who used to laugh at the idea of a North American Union.

Longtime letter writer Linc France of Columbia Falls, who died a couple of years ago, used to send in a seemingly paranoid letter every month or two warning that the U.S. government was selling out the people, starting with a new international monetary unit called the Amero, which would replace the U.S. dollar. I laughed at Linc, along with I suppose many other readers, but if you do the research Linc was right. There is a movement underfoot to replace the dollar with the Amero, just as the start of the European Union was the creation of a new currency called the Euro.

And if you are foolish enough to talk about it in public, you are dismissed as a paranoid kook or a right-wing goon.

But despite the name-calling, sometimes you have to tell people what is happening and hope that it is not too late. Certainly, I have not met anyone who has any desire for a North American Union, where U.S. sovereignty would be subsumed into a greater collective with our neighbors to the north and south. I have met no one who wishes to replace the dollar with an Amero, and yet our government — our representative government — seems to be intent on accomplishing both those goals.

Did I mention our representatives? I shouldn't have. Congress has been silent on the Security and Prosperity Partnership, although it is an international treaty and should not exist without congressional approval.

But of course, the Security and Prosperity Partnership (spp.gov) insists that it is a harmless cooperative approach to terrorism, economic security, and cross-border convenience. The partnership has an entire Web page devoted to debunking so-called myths about its purpose. The goal of such a page, of course, is to reassure the masses that everything is under control until everything really is "under control."

Meanwhile, as long as we still are able to exercise our freedoms, I strongly encourage everyone to do your own research on the Security and Prosperity Partnership and the North American Union. President Bush is meeting with the presidents of Canada and Mexico in Montebello, Quebec, on Aug. 20-21.

Supposedly, opposition groups are being denied access to within 15 miles of the meeting, and though one of the purposes of the meeting is to reassure the public that nothing underhanded is under way, it is hard to fathom why President Bush continues to seek closer ties to Mexico when the public wants bigger fences.

There really is no way to know whether or not the Security and Prosperity Partnership is really just a harmless get-together, but there is no sense taking chances, so spread the word and — again — do your own research. Don't just play dead; Congress will do that.

It's time for the American public to take back the reins of government before it is too late.

BUSH GIVES AWAY THE FARM — AND THE HIGHWAY, TOO

September 9, 2007

You have to hand it to President Bush — he is persistent.

The Iraq war would be a good case of persistence, if not exactly a good war. But let's not get distracted by that war this week as there are many more examples of Bush's persistence which don't carry the emotional baggage of Iraq.

Without taking time to analyze each and every one of them, there were the nomination of Harriet Miers to the Supreme Court, the proposal to turn U.S. port security over to the Mideast city-state of Dubai, the dogged loyalty to Donald Rumsfeld and Alberto Gonzales, and the two failed efforts at "comprehensive immigration reform."

To those we may now add the president's continuing effort to break down the borders of the nation anyway he can.

I have already in this column written extensively on the foolishness of an open border with Mexico, the cupidity of the proposed North American Union, and the absurdity of putting Arabs in charge of shipping through U.S. ports.

But last week, with hardly anyone noticing, the president took another shot at chipping away at American sovereignty by opening our southern border to Mexican trucking firms in a pilot program that he clearly wants to expand quickly.

According to the Associated Press, "The U.S. plans to give as many as 25 Mexican firms permission [to haul their cargo anywhere in the United States] by the end of September and add another 25 companies each month until hitting 100 by the end of this year under the one-year program."

Let's be clear — this is one more rotten fruit of the NAFTA tree. It is that treaty, devised by Bush's father and shepherded by President Clinton, which said that roads in Canada, the United States and Mexico must be open to carriers from all three countries. Canada unfortunately already has full and total access to the U.S. trucking market, and now it looks like Mexico will follow.

171

So what's the problem?

Nothing, as long as you buy into the agenda of globalization. That's the template for all the changes being wrought in the name of multi-national corporations who want to take advantage of cheap labor. In the name of globalization, companies ship their manufacturing overseas to China or Thailand or Mexico where they don't have to worry about labor unions, or OSHA regulations or paying a decent wage. In the name of globalization, companies in the U.S. hire illegal Mexican workers to do "the jobs Americans won't do" (at slave wages). In the name of globalization, tariffs disappear, borders become meaningless, and sovereignty becomes a quaint 19th century whatnot.

This trucking invasion is just a variation on the riff that Bush and his corporate allies have been blowing for several years. Buy into the notion that we should not begrudge illegal immigrants their desire to work in America because, after all, we are all human and want the same things, then there is no reason to oppose giving American jobs to Mexicans who don't even live here at all.

Because make no mistake, American jobs are going to disappear. Once all those Mexican truckers can haul freight across the U.S. without restriction, there will be no need to pay Americans to do the same job any longer. Lots of manufacturing originates in Mexico, but even more importantly China will be able to ship its millions of cargo containers directly to Mexico for transport by Mexican drivers to Denver, to Kansas City, and to Bismarck. Why pay an American driver $17 an hour when you can pay a Mexican $7 or less? The Chinese are not stupid. Neither is corporate America.

There is also the disturbing question of the complete lack of controls on these drivers, who will be driving multi-ton vehicles that are potentially weapons of mass destruction. First of all, there is no requirement that they have to speak or read English. Yeah, English — the language which thank God we still use on street and highway signs in the United States, so when the message on the roadside says, "Prepare to stop ahead," there is no guarantee that our Mexican friend is not stepping on the gas instead.

In addition, there are virtually no controls in place to protect Americans from untrained or incompetent drivers. All that seems to matter to the president is creating a class of what can only be called "guest workers."

As Rep. Pete DeFazio, D-Calif., said, "This administration is hell-bent on opening our borders." DeFazio — who you may recall helped lead the fight to stop Dubai Ports World from running our major national port terminals — has been pursuing a legislative fix for months to protect us from the president's agenda.

With DeFazio's help, the House of Representatives passed the Safe American Roads Act of 2007 by an overwhelming and bipartisan vote of 411-3 way back in May. That would have mandated, at minimum, that Mexican drivers and carriers be required to meet the same standards of safety and excellence that we demand of our own drivers.

Unfortunately, for some reason known only to the power brokers in Washington, the Democratic-controlled Senate committee on commerce and transportation bowed to White House pressure not to hold hearings on the bill, thus effectively killing it. The provision is now part of the transportation appropriations bill for 2008, but there is no guarantee it will survive the legislative process.

Meanwhile, you have no assurance that the Mexican truck drivers are not convicted criminals or drug users. You have no way of knowing whether they have good driving records, and of course you have no way of knowing that they are not working for al-Qaida.

Considering the president's vaunted record in protecting us from terrorism, that is a particularly inexplicable blind spot. Of all presidents, you would think he would be worried about preventing explosives, nuclear material or chemical weapons from being shipped into our country, but that does not seem to be the case.

And thanks to the ever-troublesome Security and Prosperity Partnership of North America, there are 10 or so

FAST/express border crossing points where Mexican trucks will be able to enter the United States in as little as 15 seconds. No need to inspect those trucks for pesky drugs or weapons. The important thing is to keep the wheels of commerce rolling. American jobs, safety and security do not matter.

Maybe the president of Mexico knew what he was talking about last week when he said, "Mexico does not end at its borders," and planted a red, white and green flag in the heartland of the United States when he declared, "Where there is a Mexican, there is Mexico."

Kris Kristofferson wrote in "Me and Bobby McGee" that "Freedom's just another word for nothing left to lose." He was talking about the "freedom" you get when you opt to let your true love walk out the door, but he might as well be talking about sovereignty.

These days, we in America might want to start singing the new workingman's blues: Globalization's just another word for nothing left to lose." Kiss your wages good-bye. Kiss your jobs good-bye. "Nothin' ain't worth nothin' but it's free."

THIS **DREAM** COULD BE YOUR WORST NIGHTMARE

September 23, 2007

If you ever wondered what it would be like to live in an oligarchy, you can stop wondering.

We have met the oligarchy, and it is us.

Well, not exactly us, but the small part of "us" that we call Congress.

Oligarchy, in case you don't remember your high school history classes, is a fancy name for rule by the few — government by an elite segment of society which considers itself best qualified by education, experience, and family connections to make decisions for the rest of us.

You would not think that would apply to Congress, which is supposed to be a representative body answerable to "We the People." But if you really think that Congress — or your individual senator or congressperson — is answerable to "You the People," then you haven't been paying attention.

Consider this: According to a recent poll, Congress as an institution currently stands at 11 percent in popularity among the American people. That's right. Approximately one in 10 of us feel like we are being properly served by the people who are making all the laws that govern us.

Can you imagine a CEO who enjoyed one-tenth support from the board of directors of a major corporation? OK, it's a trick question. You can't imagine it because it is impossible — a CEO with 10 percent support would have been fired long ago!

But then there is Congress.

If we forget about the president for a minute (and I know some of you would like to), Congress in essence is the executive director of a corporation called "We the People," making decisions every day that affect our prosperity, our safety and our survival. And the board of "We the People" consists of the citizens of America. We are the ultimate boss; Congress works for us.

So, if only about one-tenth of the citizens of the United States think Congress is doing a good job as executive director, what happens?

If we were truly a "representative" democracy, or even a constitutional republic, that body known as Congress would have been reshaped long ago to more accurately "represent" us, just as an incompetent CEO is politely told to scram (often very politely, but that is another story!) The incompetent Congress doesn't go anywhere. The names change — slightly. The leadership changes — slightly. The party in charge changes — slightly. But nothing really changes. Bad government goes on year after year, and incumbents get re-elected over and over despite the fact that they don't really represent anyone except themselves and the special interests that support them.

Thus, my conclusion that we are ruled by an institutional oligarchy.

How this plays out in the legislative process is obviously complicated, but essentially Congress makes the rules not just for the country as a whole, but also for Congress. That means, over the years, multiple safeguards of congressional power and authority have been built into the system. That ensures a certain arrogance as well. Things get done when it benefits Congress; and things stand still when it suits Congress. The people be damned.

If you had reason to doubt the arrogance of Congress, you might ponder again the issue of illegal immigration. Here you have a case where the fundamental and paramount birthright of the American people — citizenship — is being auctioned off by Congress to the highest bidder. At least, it would be, if there hadn't been a peaceful uprising of voters this summer that got the attention of at least some senators.

But remember, those same voters were insulted and denigrated by the powers that be as racists, nativists, haters, fear-mongers, you name it. The proponents of "comprehensive immigration reform" used subterfuge and deceit to try to convince the American people that illegal immigration is such a mess that we ought to just pretend it doesn't exist. Or maybe they really believe that.

And so it is not surprising, in the wake of the defeat of the immigration bill in June, that some senators hope to slip through yet another amnesty program for illegal aliens before anyone notices what they are doing.

Sen. Dick Durbin has been trying to drum up support for getting the DREAM Act passed as an amendment to the pending defense authorization bill. That's DREAM as in "your worst nightmare." The ultraliberal senator from Illinois wants to make sure there are no sad little illegal immigrant children falling through the cracks of our mean-hearted society. That's why he wrote the bill, whose full title is the Development, Relief, and Education for Alien Minors Act of 2007.

At least, that's supposedly why he wrote it. But you don't even have to read the fine print to spot the flim-flam in this bit of legislative sleight-of-hand. Just start with the title. The bill is supposed to be about helping "Alien Minors," but that is a complete falsehood. George Orwell, meet Dick Durbin.

In fact, the bill actually benefits almost exclusively illegal immigrant ADULTS who first entered the United States before the age of 16, then lived in the United States for at least 5 years continuously, are under 30 years of age at the time of application, and most importantly, have been "admitted to an institution of higher education in the United States, ... earned a high school diploma, or obtained a general education development certificate in the United States."

That's right. The "Alien Minors" that Durbin is taking pity on are actually high school graduates or at the very least people who have a GED degree. Probably at least 95 percent of them will of necessity be adults at the time they apply. The only time they were a minor was when they snuck into this country illegally.

But even if the law did target those younger than 18 years of age, it still would be fundamentally flawed. Its purpose is to grant "conditional residency" (aka amnesty) to millions of illegal immigrants, each of whom would then be entitled to have the conditional status removed if they completed two years of college or two years of military service. Are we making U.S. citizenship contingent on college attendance? Or even on military service? Or is this just a convenient ploy to argue that these illegal immigrants are worthy of U.S. citizenship because they are such hard workers and so dedicated to improving themselves and helping the country they broke into.

Democrats object to having their Iraq policy called "cut and run," so I won't call their immigration policy "bow and grovel." Instead, we can call both policies by a plain-spoken word that is simple, direct and accurate — surrender. And, of course, there are plenty of Republicans who are happy to throw up the white flag, too. This is not a partisan issue; it is a survival issue.

Don't take my word for it — read the DREAM Act of 2007 for yourself at www.numbersusa.com/PDFs/DurbinSA2919.pdf and then call your senators to let them know you don't want them promoting a path to citizenship for lawbreakers. It's possible this could come up for a vote in the coming week, or it may go back under a rock until darkness falls.

My guess? Darkness is not far away.

A HEALTHY DEBATE ABOUT HEALTH CARE — OR: JUST SAY NO TO FREE STUFF YOU CAN'T AFFORD

October 28, 2007

The last time I looked, insurance was a business, not a social service.

But maybe I had better look more closely because after listening to Hillary Clinton, Arnold Schwarzenegger and numerous other politicians who are eager for votes, I am starting to think maybe health insurance is not a business at all, and not even just a social service, but actually an entitlement.

Here's how health insurance works, or at least how it had always worked until the government got involved:

It's really not that complicated. You pay money today as a gamble that you are going to get sick in the future. Insurance companies take your bet because they have statistics which show the likelihood you are going to get sick. The higher the likelihood, the higher your premiums (the money you put at risk).

If you don't get sick, then the insurance company has won the bet. You are out the cost of the premiums, and they don't have to pay you anything. Of course, you still have your good health and you didn't have to suffer any anxiety over how you would pay your medical bills if you did get sick.

If you actually got sick, on the other hand, then you would still be out the cost of the premiums, but the insurance company would have to pick up a large percentage of the cost of your actual medical care. In that case, the insurance company loses the bet.

That's good for you, but of course if the insurers lose too many bets they go out of business. That's why they base rates on actuarial tables to clearly delineate how much everyone should pay for their insurance to make it a profitable business. That's also why some people are uninsurable. If someone already has cancer, his or her premiums would basically have to equal or surpass the expected cost of the medical care or it would make no sense for the insurer to take the risk.

I don't know why I have to explain this. It should be pretty obvious to everyone. Insurance is not a new concept. But since Congress discovered they have way too much money on hand, politicians have been trying to think of new ways to spend all the extra dough. And because everyone gets sick some time, apparently some folks in government decided a good way to spend the billions of dollars of extra money would be to help the insurance companies pay for health care for people who don't have enough money to gamble on their own.

Notice: There are two fallacies in this proposal.

The first fallacy should be obvious to anyone. The government does not have any extra money! In fact, our government owes $9 trillion, give or take a few billion. That is what we call the national debt, but really, it is not owed by the government; it is owed by you and me. Every time some politician gets another bright idea to give away a million dollars here or $250,000 there, it comes out of your pocket. Don't just believe me; ask your pocket.

The second fallacy may be more subtle. What is being called "health insurance" by the politicians is nothing of the sort. As we have already established, insurance is a financial gamble where you put money at risk on the chance that you will reap a reward later. Notice the word "risk." But the only one assuming any risk in the "feel-good" version of insurance being proposed by Clinton, Obama, Edwards and the gang is the American taxpayer. What they are talking about is "free health care," not insurance. But it is only free for the sick person; instead of them paying for their own care, you and I pay for it.

That's a nice, pleasant sentiment, and I wholly support the government establishing an independent agency like the Postal

Service which can accept charitable contributions to be used to pay for health care. Everyone who thinks they have extra money that they don't need for their own families can send a check to the Charitable Health Service, and people who are sick can apply for money to be given out on the basis of need. A voluntary system of this sort, which clearly would have the backing of the entire Democratic Party, should be able to ensure that everyone can get health care, even illegal immigrants.

Which brings us to the unstated third fallacy of the health-care debate, the one which is pivotal and sadly which is accepted as truth by the vast majority of people. It is this: If there is something that is good for me, I am entitled to it, whether I can afford it or not.

Is there a medicine available that might extend my life by a month or two? I want it, even if it costs $200,000 per month. Is there a treatment which might, just possibly, give me a better chance to survive the lung cancer I got because I chose to smoke for 30 years? I want it, even if it costs $2 million. And I don't want to pay for it, so let's call it "health insurance." That way I can have it and not feel guilty for taking the free ride. Am I too sick to be insurable? Tough. I still want it. Am I not human?

But the fact of the matter is we cannot have everything we want just because it is good for us or just because we are human. Modern science has already doubled the average life expectancy in just over a century — without free health insurance! But if we expect every person to have the right to take advantage of every form of medical care ever invented, then we may as well just send ourselves to debtor's prison today, because we can't afford it. Or maybe we should just send ourselves to the asylum — because we are clearly insane. (At least there will be no cost for our care!)

Of course, pointing out that not everyone in the world can afford the same level of health care makes me a horrible person. I am well aware of that, so please let's get beyond the name-calling and into the facts of the argument. The fact is, there are many things in this world which would be good for us, but we accept that we cannot afford them, and move on with our lives.

For instance, it would have been good for me to be able to attend an Ivy League college, but my family couldn't pay the bill. It would be good for me (and my circulation) if I could afford to fly first-class, but I can't, so I ride in economy and stand up every half hour or so to stretch my legs. It would be good for me to eat steak every night (all right, maybe not good for me, but very tasty), yet I eat ramen about three nights a week and steak maybe once a month because it suits my budget better. I even think it would be good for me to be riding in a 2008 BMW instead of a 1996 Saturn, but my checkbook says otherwise.

This used to be called living within one's means. Today, it is called being a chump. I don't care what they call it. The fact of the matter is there ain't no such thing as a free lunch. All of that "free" health care is costing somebody plenty. If you want that somebody to be you, then call your senators and congressman and tell them to vote for national health insurance and send the bill to your house.

But opt me out. I can't afford it.

GIVING AWAY THE STORE, AND THE OCEAN, TOO

November 3, 2007

"Thar be dragons beyond here."

That's nautical lingo for slow down and pay attention before you fall off the edge of the world, and was featured on sea maps in the days before Columbus established the "globiness" of the globe.

You can't blame those old-time sailors for being terrified, because although there weren't dragons in the Atlantic or Pacific, there were real dangers if you sailed too far into the unknown. Dragons were just a symbol of peril, albeit a colorful one. It's just too bad that Congress doesn't have a "map-to-English" translator on the payroll. Otherwise, they might figure out that the Law of the Sea Treaty that is being fast-tracked through the Senate this month is the equivalent of one of those dragons that symbolizes the dangers of going too far without a map.

In fact, there are some things which are known about the Law of the Sea Treaty, which goes by the alarming acronym of LOST, and its proponents will tell you in a calm and soothing voice that you have nothing to worry about. Just trust the nations of the world to do the right thing.

Huh? When did that ever happen?

Fortunately, up till now, the United States has avoided the siren song that lures sailors to their deaths. Indeed, LOST has been floating around in one form or another ever since 1970, and was entered into force among the ratifying nations in 1994. The United Nations treaty created an international body which has regulatory power over the high seas and the seabeds. The convention established rules for settling disputes over navigation, fishing and economic development of the open seas and also established environmental standards to be maintained in the world's oceans. It further decreed that oceans are reserved for "peaceful purposes" (presumably in contradistinction to solid land, which as we all know is for military purposes).

What isn't known, and can't be fully known, is how various countries would use the treaty to control, blackmail and humiliate the United States if we were to join it, and how environmental groups would use it to shut down development of ocean resources or otherwise block activities which they find objectionable.

Sen. Dick Lugar, R-Ind., says the United States has no choice but to ratify the treaty because without it, "we are allowing decisions that will affect our Navy, our ship operators, our off-shore industries and other maritime interests to be made without U.S. representation."

The Bush administration agrees, and so does the Senate Foreign Relations Committee, which Lugar serves on. The panel voted 17-4 last week to approve the treaty.

Unfortunately, they are wrong. One hundred and eighty degrees wrong. In fact, if we JOIN the treaty convention, we will be "allowing decisions that will affect our Navy, our ship operators, our off-shore industries and other maritime interests" to be made with U.S. representation, but without U.S. consent. That is even worse, indeed much worse.

Face it, the United States would be just one of 156 nations participating in the treaty, and our one vote would have just as much weight as the vote of, let's say, land-bound Slovakia. That's promising, isn't it? We could practice the same politics of frustration that we are stuck with in the U.N. General Assembly, where repeatedly the democratic nations are out-voted by the Hugo Chavezes, Fidel Castros, Vladimir Putins and Saudi princes of the world. And, of course, if we are a signatory to the convention, we are stuck with it, and with any new interpretation of it that comes along in 10 or 20 years, just as we are stuck with the phony interpretation of the Geneva Convention that claims rogue bandit terrorists have the same rights as prisoners of war from a civilized nation that actually signed the convention.

Ultimately, if and when we ratify the Law of the Sea Treaty, what will be irretrievably lost will be any semblance of U.S. sovereignty. We may as well just go ahead and open the southern border, the northern border and our ports as well, because there won't be any real country left, just an empty semblance of a set of ideals and principals that had been fought for and died for starting in 1776 and then squandered, sold and destroyed one by one till there was nothing left except the now-meaningless piece of paper ironically called the Declaration of Independence.

In the wake of the immigration debate, it is already an open question whether sovereignty means anything to Americans anymore anyway. The amnesty fiasco was averted earlier this year, but the proponents of open borders have not given up the fight yet. Currently, the governor of New York is demanding to give drivers licenses to illegal immigrants. Tomorrow it will be a guest worker program. Then an earned right to vote. Then just a white flag of surrender. Bit by bit, the agenda of the United Nations will be imposed on our country until the world's last best hope of freedom and democracy will be just one more cog in the machinery of globalism.

Or... we could take a principled stand. We could continue to do what we have done in the past, protect the high seas for one and all, and at the same time protect our own national interests whenever we need to do so.

As I already noted, Sen. Lugar declared that, without the treaty, "we are allowing decisions that will affect our Navy, our ship operators, our off-shore industries and other maritime interests to be made without U.S. representation."

That is a confession of weakness and foolishness. The United States does not have to abide by treaties to which it is not a signatory. Indeed, if we allow decisions which affect our national security and interests to be made by other nations, then we are damned fools.

In the wake of the Cuban Missile Crisis, President Kennedy, a Navy man, declared on board the USS Kitty Hawk that, "Events of October 1962 indicated, as they had all through history, that control of the sea means security. Control of the seas can mean peace. Control of the seas can mean victory. The United States must control the seas if it is to protect your security..."

No one can say it any better today. And if we surrender that control to the United Nations, then we are truly lost.

TERMS OF SURRENDER:
AN EARLY ROUGH DRAFT

November 11, 2007

Last week, as the nation prepared to celebrate Veterans Day to honor our nation's war heroes, we learned that House Speaker Nancy Pelosi had scheduled another bill in the House to force the president to withdraw troops from Iraq. Although such a bill of surrender would be vetoed by President Bush, it is just a matter of time before he is no longer in office.

Therefore, in anticipation of a possible Democratic victory in November 2008, this column today provides a national service by offering up a draft of the terms of surrender which Congress can present to the new president for his or her signature before forwarding them to Osama bin Laden in his cave in Pakistan.

As much as possible, bin Laden's actual words were used in the surrender, so that people would know what they were surrendering to.

A Rough Draft
of Surrender

The United States of America does hereby concede that its military power and economic strength are no match for the tiny but indomitable foe known as al-Qaida.

We acknowledge and admit that the complaints made by the great warrior Osama bin Laden in his 1996 fatwa entitled "Declaration of War against the Americans Occupying the Land of the Two Holy Places" were entirely correct, that the United States was wrong to negotiate with the Saudi kingdom to place military bases there when we sought to free Kuwait from Iraqi domination, wrong to sell arms to Saudi Arabia and other Arab states, wrong to arrest the Muslim clerics and their followers who plotted our destruction, wrong to call members of al-Qaida "coward terrorists," and wrong to proclaim U.S. power when we could not even remain in Somalia after a few dozen soldiers were killed.

We acknowledge and admit also that the complaints made by the great warrior Osama bin Laden in his untitled 1998 fatwa declaring war against the West and Israel were just and justifiable and that the great warrior is beyond reproach and blameless. We admit that we occupied the holy land of Islam beginning in 1991 during the first Gulf War and stayed there like occupying Crusaders. We acknowledge that we tried to destroy Iraq in order "to serve the Jews' petty state and divert attention from its occupation of Jerusalem and murder of Muslims there." Moreover, we acknowledge and confirm that our many crimes and sins were "a clear declaration of war on God, his messenger and Muslims."

Therefore, the 1998 fatwa of Osama bin Laden calling on all Muslims "to kill the Americans and their allies — civilian and military" was entirely appropriate and the followers of the great warrior shall not be considered enemies but heroes for their part in making sure that "justice and faith in God" prevailed against the infidel foolishness of our previous U.S. leaders.

Moreover, we acknowledge that in the wake of the destruction of our centers of hatred and oppression known as the World Trade Center and the Pentagon, we falsely spread fear of Islam, which is a religion of peace. Let it be known that from this day forward, the people of the United States accept all religions equally and especially Islam, which is the greatest religion of all. Any insults against Islam or the Prophet Mohammed (peace be upon him) are the work of scurrilous dogs and will not be tolerated.

We acknowledge and accept the words of the great warrior Osama bin Laden from a speech posted on the Internet on April 27, 2006, regarding the Danish cartoons and other insults against the Prophet, when he said, "The freethinkers and heretics who defame Islam, and mock and scorn our noble Prophet — their case and the law concerning them have been clearly expounded by Imam Ibn Qayyim. He made it clear that the crime committed by a freethinker is the worst of crimes, that the damage caused by his staying alive among the Muslims is of the worst kind of damage, that he is to be killed, and that his repentance is not to be accepted."

We further acknowledge and confirm that we accept Osama bin Laden's wise words when he said, "Indeed, this is our Prophet's law regarding anyone who mocks him, and belittles Islam and scorns it... They should be killed... Take an example from Muhammad ibn Maslama and his companions [who assassinated the poet Ka'b ibn Al-Ashraf]. It is intolerable and outrageous that the heretics are among us, scorning our religion and our Prophet. Therefore, you must fear Allah and do His will. Do not consult anyone about the killing of these heretics.

Be secretive in carrying out that which is required of you. So much for the apostate heretics."

And finally, we do acknowledge that former President Bush is a liar and a master of deceit as the warrior bin Laden has declared, but also we admit that even before George W. Bush appeared on the scene, the American people had already "put themselves at the mercy of a disloyal government, and this is most evident in [Bill] Clinton's administration," as bin Laden told the world in an interview in May 1998. Bin Laden was correct when he declared then that the "[Clinton] administration represent[ed] Israel inside America. Take the sensitive ministries such as the Ministry of Exterior and the Ministry of Defense and the CIA, you will find that the Jews have the upper hand in them. They make use of America to further their plans for the world, especially the Islamic world. American presence in the Gulf provides support to the Jews and protects their rear. And while millions of Americans are homeless and destitute and live in abject poverty, their government is busy occupying [Arab] land and building new settlements and helping Israel build new settlements in the point of departure for [the] Prophet's midnight journey to the seven heavens. America throws her own sons in the land of the two Holy Mosques for the sake of protecting Jewish interests."

In conclusion, we acknowledge bin Laden's warning in 1998 that, "The American government is leading the country towards hell. ... We say to the Americans as people and to American mothers, if they cherish their lives and if they cherish their sons, they must elect an American patriotic government that caters to their interests not the interests of the Jews.... This is my message to the American people. I urge them to find a serious administration that acts in their interest and does not attack people and violate their honor and pilfer their wealth."

This administration confirms: Message received and heard. Our troops are coming home. Our tail is between our legs. Our future is in your hands.

•••

It should be noted that the preceding statement of surrender is a rough draft only. It is understood that the new

Democratic administration and Congress may have to insert additional groveling in order to fully satisfy the Islamic fundamentalists and to establish once and for all our national defeat and disgrace.

IT'S THE END OF THE WORLD AS WE KNOW IT, STUPID!

November 25, 2007

No one can forget the immortal words of James Carville when he was advising Bill Clinton how to get elected president in 1992: "It's the economy, stupid!" That certainly showed the power of brevity, didn't it?

So this week you get five shorter columns for the price of one longer one.

The common theme? It's the end of the world as we know it, stupid!

1) "It's the babies, stupid!"

Just when you were wondering what was causing global warming, the answer finally comes to us, via London's Daily Mail newspaper — It's the babies, stupid!

Toni Vernelli, who works for an "environmental charity," was the subject of a recent profile in the newspaper, and revealed that she had "terminated her pregnancy" 10 years ago in order to help "save the planet." She then valiantly had herself sterilized to make sure that she was not a vessel for the destruction of the planet.

For her it's a simple choice:

"Every person who is born uses more food, more water, more land, more fossil fuels, more trees and produces more rubbish, more pollution, more greenhouse gases, and adds to the problem of overpopulation."

I'm sure I speak for all right-thinking people when I echo the sentiments of her boyfriend after she was sterilized and say "Congratulations." We are sure you did the world a favor by not reproducing.

2 *"It's the Latin, stupid!"*

Pope Benedict XVI is considering restoring the Gregorian chant to a place of higher prominence in liturgical celebrations in the Catholic Church. This comes on the heels of a papal decision to allow churches to restore the Latin Mass if they wish to do so.

The director of the Pontifical Institute of Sacred Music, Monsignor Valentin Grau, applauded signs that the Gregorian chant had gained papal favor, and he said that the traditional church music of the sixth century "should become again the living soul of the assembly."

There's no denying the beauty and solemnity of Gregorian chants, but as far as becoming the "living soul" of the church, I think the pope might need to ask Monsignor Grau what part of "living" he doesn't understand.

Even 30 years ago when I was filling out my Gregorian chant collection, I was getting most of my records from what we called the "cut-out bin," the place where undesirable albums were sent for "deep discount."

The times they are a-changin' — and Gregorian chants will probably make a big comeback in the "living soul" of the church about the same time you and I start telling jokes in Latin.

3: *"It's the Middle Ages, stupid!"*

Speaking of the Middle Ages, we might want to move forward to the 7th century, so that we can consider the modern Islamic church, which has never budged one day past the death of Mohammed in 632 A.D.

As we have just seen in our discussion of the Catholic Church, this is not an uncommon tendency among religions in general. With a "received truth" in hand, there is really no impetus toward "progress" because what we call progress would necessarily also be a deviation from what is considered the law of God.

This is not a criticism per se, but rather a statement of fact.

In the case of Islam, the religion believes that the Prophet Muhammed is the last and most important messenger of God. Therefore, the faith adheres strictly to the teachings of Muhammed, and judges all actions and thoughts by how well they correspond to the Koran or other teachings associated with Muhammed.

To our tolerant Western society, it sounds harmless enough — until you realize that the Koran encourages, indeed demands, all kinds of medieval ideas which are anathema to free men and women.

Most recently, this was illustrated by the case of a 19-year-old Saudi woman who was sentenced to 200 lashes of the whip after being gang-raped by seven men.

What was the woman's crime? She was alone with a man to whom she was not related at the time the seven men attacked her and her companion. At first she only got 90 lashes, but then her lawyer complained about the sentence, so it was increased to six months in prison and 200 lashes, a potentially fatal assault. The lawyer's license to practice law was also suspended.

Saudi Arabia employs a strict reading of sharia law, or Islamic religious law, and so there is hardly any recourse available to the young woman. Only this: According to Saudi law, it is actually illegal for non-related men and women to meet in private, a concept known as "khalwa." Supposedly the man and woman actually met in public, until they were abducted and raped in private. If that is the case, the woman may win an appeal. If not, she has no hope at all because it is the law itself which has determined she has no rights.

The men who raped her, by the way, had originally received sentences between 10 months and five years. The appeals court did lengthen those sentences to between two and nine years, for what it's worth.

It should be considered a sign of the great difficulty the West faces in assimilating the world's 1.2 billion Muslims into the modern community that none of them could properly be offended by the young woman's sentence without renouncing the core of their religion.

Remember: The Middle Ages never ended; they just moved to the Middle East.

4: "It's a dictatorship, stupid!"

Hugo Chavez, the darling of the Hollywood elite, has grown more and more brazen in his disregard of fundamental human rights recently, and not a peep has been heard out of Sean Penn, Danny Glover or Cindy Sheehan.

Imagine that.

Chavez has already worked to shut down the free press, committed election fraud, and thrown out the concept of private property. Now, he is said to be confident of victory in a Dec. 2 referendum that will let him follow in Castro's benighted footsteps as "el presidente for life."

The Washington Post notes that under the so-called "constitutional reform," Chavez would have "broad powers to seize property, to dispose of Venezuela's foreign exchange reserves, to impose central government rule on local jurisdictions and to declare indefinite states of emergency under which due process and freedom of information would be suspended."

So how could the people of Venezuela possibly vote for this? Easy. Chavez has learned the lessons of socialism — promise people that they will get more for doing less. In this case, the referendum shortens the workday from eight to six hours. How do you say "Cool, dude!" in Spanish?

No need to rig elections when you can buy 'em.

5) "It's the end of everything, stupid!"

OK, this has to rank as one of my favorite stories of all time. Two professors of cosmology have recently reported in New Scientist magazine that the universe may be coming to a quicker conclusion than it would otherwise, thanks to the Nosy Parker instincts of none other than ... cosmologists!

You've got to put on your thinking cap to fully comprehend this one, but the good news is that you don't have to worry about 1 through 4 on your list any more, because No. 5 blows them all away.

As many students of basic physics already know, science has theorized for some time that we change things simply by looking at them. For those who want to try to comprehend the theory more fully, do a quick Google search for "Schrodinger's cat" and you will find out that the cat is both living and dead until someone looks at it, at which point the observer forces an outcome and the cat either drops dead or goes its merry way. (Well, sort of, but that will have to do for the short version.)

Now Professors Lawrence Krauss and James Dent have taken the theory of Schrodinger's cat and applied it to the big picture, the really big picture. In fact, they claim that because scientists have caught a glimpse of some "what-not" called "dark energy," they have speeded up our return to the formless void from which we came. If we had kept our peepers shut, we could have avoided the whole mess on the theory that a "watched pot never boils" (seriously!). But cosmologists are the Captain Kirks of science, going where no man has gone before and having fun doing it.

How do you say "trippy" in quantum physics? Or in Latin, for that matter?

WHAT WOULD TEDDY DO?

December 2, 2007

More and more these days, as the world turns topsy-turvy, I find myself asking, "WWTRD?" — What would Teddy Roosevelt do?

How would Teddy Roosevelt handle it if an American citizen were locked up in the Sudan for teaching a classroom of 7-year-olds who had named a stuffed bear Muhammad? Even forgetting about Roosevelt's interest in making sure that all such bears should be named Teddy, we can assume he would see the absurdity of the situation, which actually exists today for a British woman. Would TR let the woman suffer 40 lashes of the whip as originally intended by the "court"? Would he even allow her to remain in jail for the 15-day sentence while mobs roamed the streets outside with swords demanding her head?

And what would Roosevelt do about Osama bin Laden? How would he react to the death and destruction at the Twin Towers, just a few short miles from his birthplace in the Gramercy neighborhood of Manhattan? Would he be more concerned about offending Muslim sensibilities or more concerned about getting the killers no matter how hard it was or how long it took?

You don't even have to ask what TR would think about illegal immigration. He as much as told us in a letter to the American Defense Society in 1919:

"In the first place we should insist that the immigrant who comes here in good faith becomes an American and assimilates himself to us. He shall be treated on an exact equity with everyone else, for it is an outrage to discriminate against any such man because of creed, or birthplace or origin.

"But this is predicated upon the man's becoming an American and nothing but an American. There can be no divided allegiance here. Any man who says he is an American but something else also, isn't an American at all.

"We have room for but one flag, the American flag, and this excludes the red flag which symbolizes all wars against liberty and civilization, just as much as it excludes any flag of a nation to which we are hostile.

"We have room for but one language here, and that is the English language... and we have room for but one sole loyalty and that is a loyalty to the American people."

It is not too hard to imagine that Roosevelt would also expect immigrants to our country to follow the rules and regulations set up for them, thus not tolerate illegal immigration. Why exactly, after all, should we tolerate illegality in anything?

Of course, that is mere idle speculation, because Teddy Roosevelt could not exist today. His outspoken, some would say politically incorrect, manner; his racial Darwinism; his belief in the supremacy of civilization over barbarism; his willingness to use force to accomplish his goals — all of these would have disqualified him from a life of public service.

Even his time as a war hero would have worked against him. If it had occurred in this decade, the Spanish-American War would have been known as Bush's Blunder, and Roosevelt's participation would have been subject to endless congressional hearings to find out why he had not respected the enemy sufficiently. The Rough Riders unit he headed up would be considered roughly the equivalent of the so-called Blackwater mercenaries of the Iraq war, except they didn't get paid so well; they just liked to shoot and carry on.

But Roosevelt, nonetheless, remains an icon of the untamed American spirit — a man born of Eastern wealth, he had gone West after the tragedy of losing his mother and wife to disease on the same day in 1884. In a few short years in the Badlands of North Dakota, a stone's throw from Montana, young Roosevelt sponged up all the energy and excitement of the Wild West that he could. He was a rancher, a deputy sheriff, a raconteur and a big-game hunter.

Then he took that experience, went back east after a disastrous winter wiped out his herd of cattle, and wrote an influential four-volume history called "The Winning of the West." A few years later, he began his career of public service in earnest. He worked on the U.S. Civil Service Commission, was president of the board of the New York City Police Commissioners (where he played a key role as the reformer of a corrupt system) and then became assistant secretary of the Navy, where he prepared the Navy for the Spanish-American War. It was during this time that he made one of the many statements which would disqualify him for public office today: "I should welcome almost any war, for I think this country needs one." Under modern rules of etiquette, a country cannot need a war unless it is in the throes of a fascist dictatorship (also known as the Bush presidency in certain circles).

It was the Spanish-American War which cemented Roosevelt's reputation for being a man of action, as well as a man of ideas. It also catapulted him to a successful campaign for governor of New York in 1898 on the Republican ticket. His penchant for reform and rooting out corruption apparently made him unpopular with the Republican machine in New York and he was thus named as President McKinley's running mate in 1900. McKinley won in a landslide against William Jennings Bryan, but was assassinated late in 1901, elevating Roosevelt to the presidency.

It was there that he exercised his greatest influence on our nation and the world, accomplishing much through the sheer power of his will and according to the virtues of his own moral code. Indeed, it is impossible to imagine a modern president accomplishing anywhere near as much as Roosevelt did.

Quite soon, he developed a reputation as a "trust-buster," taking on corporate tycoons who had amassed wealth and power through the establishment of monopolies that prevented competition. He also pushed Congress to establish a system to regulate food and drugs which essentially is still in place today. It was, of course, also Roosevelt who promoted the establishment of the U.S. Forest Service and set aside 194 million acres for national parks and nature preserves. Such treasures as Glacier National Park owe their legacy of preservation to Roosevelt's foresight and love of nature.

It was perhaps in foreign affairs, however, that Roosevelt made his greatest impact of all. Certainly changing the world forever was the construction of the Panama Canal, a project made possible by willpower, money and a little bit of leverage to get Panama to declare its independence from Columbia. Of course, today we would be told that such a project is impossible, just as a border fence is impossible, but Roosevelt did not let impossibility stop him.

That stubbornness may also be how he won the Nobel Peace Prize, thanks to his bully negotiations to end the Russo-Japanese War in 1905. This conflict and a later conflict between France and Germany, which Roosevelt also helped to defuse, could easily have escalated into a world war.

It is well known that Roosevelt's motto was to "talk softly but carry a big stick." In such a manner, he was willing to use American force to project our power on the world without necessarily have to fight to do it. Most notably he greatly increased the size of the Navy and sent a fleet around the world to be gawked at by our friends and foes. He also established that the threat of force was sometimes enough, as in his standoff with the Moroccan renegade Ahmed ben Mohammed el Raisuli, which was popularized in the film "The Wind and the Lion."

Likewise Teddy declared that American power could be used to intervene in Latin American countries, but he was wise enough to not bite off more than he could chew. When elements in the Dominican Republic were seeking annexation in 1904, he said, in typically colorful fashion, "I have about the same desire to annex it as a gorged boa constrictor might have to swallow a porcupine."

The fact of the matter is that Teddy Roosevelt could not exist anymore, and neither could Teddy Roosevelt's America. We are neither smart enough, strong enough, or daring enough to do what is right no matter the cost. So although we may ponder, "What would Teddy Roosevelt do?" — we are stuck with the same old question as always, "What are we going to do?" and the same sad answer, "Vote for the lesser of two evils and hope for the best."

WHERE'S THE INTELLIGENCE? YOU DECIDE

December 9, 2007

You really have to wonder if the government of Iran could possibly be as stupid as the government of the United States.

But then you get a look at the declassified portion of the latest National Intelligence Estimate entitled "Iran: Nuclear Intentions and Capabilities," and you can stop wondering. There is no competition. Iran could not possibly match the stupidity of our own government.

Indeed, if global geopolitics were a television sitcom, then the government of the United States would be Boss Hogg, and Mahmoud and the gang in Tehran would be the Dukes of

Hazzard. We may have more money and power, but them Duke boys always seem to get the last laugh.

Last week, the laughter could be heard all the way 'round the world as the U.S. "intelligence community" let the Tehran regime off the hook for its nuclear ambitions, judging "with high confidence" that Iran halted its nuclear weapons program in 2003.

Sure 'nuff, and them Duke boys are just a couple of hayseeds who could never outsmart the big fat guy in the white hat (so said the big fat guy in the white hat anyway).

But before we get carried away, patting Iran's President Mahmoud Ahmadinejad on the back for being such a jolly good fellow, let's just look at the facts, as laid out in the National Intelligence Estimate, and see what they actually say.

The initial Associated Press story got it about right:

"Iran halted its nuclear weapons development program in the fall of 2003 under international pressure but is continuing to enrich uranium, which means it may still be able to develop a weapon between 2010 and 2015, according to a new U.S. intelligence assessment released Monday."

As soon as the announcement was made, of course, the mainstream media was doing a major blitz of the airwaves with the claim that Bush and Cheney had misled the American people and the world by saying that Iran was a nuclear threat.

My simple question to them is: "What part of 2010 don't you understand?"

Folks, that's two (make that TWO!) years away. Two years until Iran may develop a nuclear weapon! The only thing we could do to make Iran more of a threat would be literally to drive President Ahmadinejad to the Los Alamos nuclear laboratory, hand him the keys and a security pass, and tell him to enjoy himself.

It's true that the NIE concludes "with high confidence" that "in fall 2003, Tehran halted its nuclear weapons program." It's also true that the NIE concludes "with moderate-to-high confidence" that Tehran "at a minimum is keeping open its option to develop nuclear weapons."

We don't have any idea what kind of evidence the intelligence agencies are using to make these conclusions. It could be the same kind of bozos who said there were weapons of mass destruction in Iraq. It could be double agents who are working for the Iranian government in order to disseminate false information to over-eager American spies. It could be people who like getting paid for telling people what they want to hear. (If you think people who are tortured will say anything to stop the torture, just imagine what kind of lies people will confess to if you pay them generously enough.)

Be that as it may, even though we are not privy to the source of the information, let us assume it is all valid.

According to the NIE, Iran stopped its nuclear weapons program in 2003. But in the same report (on the same page, for goodness' sake) the National Intelligence Council tells us, "We assess [that] centrifuge enrichment is how Iran probably could first produce enough fissile material for a weapon, if it decides to do so." In the next sentence, the NIE tells us unblushingly, "Iran resumed its declared centrifuge enrichment activities in January 2006, despite the continued halt in its nuclear weapons program" (emphasis mine).

Does that mean what I think it means? That Iran has halted its nuclear weapons program... even though it is still doing exactly what it would be doing if it had a nuclear weapons program?

Is there some rule that intelligence estimates are supposed to be filled with gibberish and nonsense?

Here's another one:

"We judge with moderate confidence that the earliest possible date Iran would be technically capable of producing enough HEU [highly enriched uranium] for a weapon is late 2009..."

The report concludes that this is not likely to occur, but that's irrelevant. We are not talking about whether or not Iran WILL create a nuclear bomb; we are talking about their capacity to do so. And once they have the capacity, we may well have crossed beyond the point where nuclear war could be prevented. Besides, if they have the capability to produce a bomb, then they already have a nuclear weapons program, whatever you call it.

That's why President Bush and our European allies have been working so diligently to convince their counterparts in Tehran to abandon their nuclear ambitions now. Later is by definition too late.

Of course, what has raised the hackles of the left wing in this country is that this NIE report seems to raise the specter that President Bush has been misleading the public and the world about Iran's real threat level. Certainly, you have to concede that the National Intelligence Council seems to be writing propaganda for Iran rather than the United States in the way it framed the report. There it is in black and white that "in fall 2003, Tehran halted its nuclear weapons program."

So it is not surprising that the report has fed the left's fears about the president by suggesting that Iran really has no such weapons program, and that therefore President Bush has just been trying to justify another war because he is insane or an idiot (I don't think I am exaggerating the rhetoric of his opponents).

But let's carefully compare the "key differences" between the "key judgments" of the 2007 NIE and the previous NIE issued in 2005, and see why it is this report itself which is the propaganda blunder. It is the intelligence community which should be tarred and feathered, not the president.

The new report says that, "We judge with moderate confidence that the earliest possible date Iran would be technically capable of producing enough highly enriched uranium (HEU) for a weapon is late 2009, but that this is very unlikely."

Now listen to the 2005 report: "Iran could produce enough fissile material for a weapon by the end of this decade if it were to make more rapid and successful progress than we have seen to date" (emphasis mine).

So the difference between the two reports on this point is... absolutely nothing! The conclusions are identical! Iran could produce uranium for a bomb by the end of this decade (also known as "late 2009"), but it is not likely to do so! BOTH REPORTS SAY THE SAME THING!

So why can't the endless liberal commentators who have lined up to bash Bush for the past week read the report for themselves? Why can't they understand plain English? And why would the intelligence community frame the report in such a way that it makes the president (the U.S. president, that is) look bad? Could it be incompetence? Or must every Boss Hogg have a Sheriff Rosco on the payroll to make himself look smart? (Sorry, that's my last "Dukes of Hazzard" analogy.)

If you think I am over-estimating the foolishness of this probably multimillion-dollar intelligence report, take a look at the final "key judgment" of the 2005 and 2007 NIE reports, and see how the evil King George has misled us.

In 2005, the National Intelligence Estimate concluded that the intelligence community had "moderate confidence" in projecting that Iran is unlikely to make a nuclear weapon "before early-to-mid next decade."

Then in the new report issued last week, dated November 2007, the NIE concluded "with moderate confidence" that "Iran probably would be technically capable of producing enough HEU [highly enriched uranium] for a weapon sometime during the 2010-2015 time frame."

So the dramatic new evidence that has Washington all a-twitter is that it turns out Iran is probably capable of producing a nuclear weapon sometime between 2010 and 2015 instead of "early-to-mid next decade."

Far be it from me to point out the obvious, but "IT'S THE SAME THING!" Early-to-mid next decade IS EXACTLY THE SAME as 2010 to 2015, no more and no less.

If this is the best we can get out of the National Clandestine Service, the National Security Agency, the National Geo-Spatial Intelligence Agency, the Defense Intelligence Agency, the Bureau of Intelligence and Research, and the director of national intelligence, then we would be better off kicking the whole lot of them out the door and start over again with some recent college graduates who at least know how to read a calendar.

CONFESSIONS OF A SERIAL KILLER

December 16, 2007

America has been waiting and waiting for a confession from a suspected killer.

Did he or didn't he do it? It appears that he is guilty beyond a shadow of a doubt, but a few people just don't believe it. They want more evidence, better evidence, a full confession.

No, I am not talking about Drew Peterson, the now-retired Chicago cop who is a suspect in the death of his third wife and the disappearance of his fourth.

Drew Peterson may or may not be a serial killer, but there is one man alive who is a far more successful killer than Peterson, O.J. Simpson or any other suspected or convicted murderer in the world.

Of course, I am talking about Osama bin Laden. Like another charismatic leader, Charles Manson, Osama prefers to get others to do his dirty work, but responsibility for murder can't be avoided by having someone else pull the trigger.

Still, by staying holed up in Afghanistan, Pakistan and other Third World countries for many years, bin Laden could make a case that he has "plausible deniability" when bombs explode in Baghdad or planes hit buildings in New York. It also certainly has helped his "mystique" that he got support from the United States many years ago when he was fighting the Soviet Union, leading some people to conclude that he was either a patsy or a stooge of the U.S. government on Sept. 11, 2001, when his soldiers killed nearly 3,000 people.

Thus, we have the so-called "9/11 Truth Movement," which automatically denies the truth of any theory that doesn't blame the U.S. government (or forces therein) for masterminding and executing the whole tragic scenario of 9/11. The near-endless variety of theories that have been proposed, and the casual acceptance of many patently absurd scenarios by the movement, raises the specter of a Rube Goldberg style conspiracy which is held in place by bubble gum and started into motion by burnt bread bouncing out of a defective toaster.

It doesn't matter to these people that bin Laden had pledged to go to war against the United States years before 9/11. It doesn't matter that study after study has looked into the claims of the "9/11 Truthers" and demonstrated that most of them are based on misunderstandings, coincidence, error, or lies. You can blame space aliens for 9/11 but that doesn't make it so — despite the entertaining conspiracy theories of David Icke, who supposes that the "Global Elite" rulers of earth are actually reptilians from the constellation Draco.

Truth of the matter is, nothing will satisfy the 9/11 Truthers. Probably even a full confession by George W. Bush that he ordered the attack on the World Trade Center would be met with skepticism. After all, Bush is a known liar, right?

But it may satisfy some of the mainstream Americans who have been persuaded by the 9/11 Truth Movement to know that there has been a full confession of responsibility for the terror attacks. On Nov. 29 of this year, Osama bin Laden issued an audiotape in which he took full responsibility for the attacks. The purpose of the tape was to convince America's European allies to abandon their efforts to assist the U.S. military in Afghanistan. His point was that the former Taliban government of Afghanistan did not attack anyone, so other governments should not have invaded Afghanistan. He said, in part:

"[Afghanistan was] invaded without right by your unjust governments, without stopping to think about or reflect on Bush's claim that this invasion was a response to the events of the 11th, although — as I mentioned previously — the events of Manhattan were a response to the American-Israeli coalition's murder of our people in Palestine and Lebanon.

"And it was I who was responsible for 9/11, and I stress that all Afghans — both government and people — had no knowledge of those events and America knows that, because some of the Taliban's ministers fell into its hands as captives, and they were interrogated and that became known."

He then concludes his statement by proclaiming that "the American tide is ebbing, by the grace of Allah, and ... they shall soon depart for their homeland beyond the Atlantic and leave the neighbors to settle their accounts with each other."

Could it be any plainer that Osama bin Laden is an enemy of the United States? That he planned and plotted the Sept. 11 attacks? That as long as we support Israel's right to defend itself and to exist, he will think it appropriate to kill our civilians? That if we depart Afghanistan (or Iraq) there will be a bloodbath of monumental proportions?

But yet we dither and doubt. We worry about George Bush and let bin Laden off the hook. We plan for imminent withdrawal from Iraq and forget about the immediate past in Manhattan. We imagine there's "nothing to kill or die for, and no religion too" and walk like sheep among people who think there is something to kill and die for, and are willing to do it, too.

WHY NOT ASK CANDIDATES WHAT THEY BELIEVE?

December 23, 2007

As we prepare to celebrate the birth of Christ, it is worth looking around and considering what Christ would think of the mess we have made.

First of all, because of his insight into the nature of man, we have to assume he would not be surprised. There is no indication anywhere in the New Testament that Jesus was naive. On the other hand, there is also no suggestion that he would just shrug the mess off and tell us to do better next time. Instead, he would expect us to do better this time.

Jesus had fairly high standards, for himself and for his followers. He told us to pick up our own cross and follow him — and that meant being willing to suffer for our beliefs, being willing to die for them if necessary, and always remembering to put our own will in second position to the will of God, just as Jesus had to do.

Jesus was no chicken. He didn't join any armies, and he didn't lead the expected war against the Roman Empire that some of his followers wanted, but he took a stand. He didn't just go along to get along. He said what he believed, and believed what he said.

Perhaps, most importantly, he had a moral code that gave him strength, substance and certainty. Indeed, the moral code he lived and died by was so powerful that it ultimately changed the world, shaped Western civilization and helped our founders create the nation we live in today.

Unfortunately, that moral code — like the cross itself — is now foolishness to the Hollywood elite and a stumbling block to our politically correct leaders. More and more we see Christians mocked for their beliefs, or pressured to keep quiet. Former Gov. Mike Huckabee, for instance, had to explain repeatedly to the mainstream media last week why his Christmas greeting advertisement in Iowa had "hidden" Christian symbolism.

Not the "hidden" Christmas tree plainly visible at his side. Not the "hidden" words coming straight out of his mouth which explained that "what really matters [about Christmas] is the celebration of the birth of Christ." No, it was the bookshelf in the background that looked like a cross to some viewers that made media pundits see deviltry in Huckabee's Christmas ad.

Turns out these folks were convinced the "floating cross" was an attack on former Gov. Mitt Romney, who is a Mormon. Oddly enough, no one has explained how the cross symbolism hurts Romney, whose church is officially known as the Church of Jesus Christ of Latter-day Saints and who has publicly professed that Jesus is his personal savior.

Probably, the people making such allegations are actually trying to kill two candidates with one well-aimed stone. It is unlikely they are trying to protect Romney from Huckabee, but rather trying to protect the nation from what they perceive to be two kookie religious zealots who will use their "moral code" to govern with principle rather than simply by doing what is convenient or popular.

Indeed, it has become something of a truism of late that we should not select our political leaders because of their religious beliefs. Even Romney gave a speech this month in which he said, "A person should not be elected because of his faith nor should he be rejected because of his faith."

Certainly, it is plain in the Constitution of the United States that "no religious test shall ever be required as a qualification to any office or public trust under the United States." That is a wise and useful prohibition. We the people should be able to elect whoever we want, and should not see our favored candidates excluded because of their faith or lack of it.

But there is a difference between a requirement for office and a requirement for what each individual voter expects of the candidates they will support. There, it seems vital that the electorate should consider the moral qualifications of the candidates, and specifically the moral code or world view that each candidate subscribes to. After all, it is the beliefs which a candidate has before being elected which will inform his or her choices after taking office. If you want abortion to be legal, for instance, you should not vote for someone who believes abortion is murder. If you want to improve border security, you should not vote for someone who believes that all people have a God-given right to migrate wherever they choose.

Some people will say that a person's religion is a private matter, and of course it is. But when you run for public office you shed a certain amount of privacy, and what matters to the public is not what a candidate will do in church, but what they will do in public as a result of their belief system. If our democracy is going to have any meaning, then voters must consider what moral creed a candidate follows.

Toward the end of that same Sermon on the Mount where Jesus advised us to "judge not lest ye be judged," he also had this to say of false prophets: "You will know them by their fruits. Grapes are not gathered from thorn bushes nor figs from thistles, are they?" In other words, he taught us that in place of haughty judgment we could substitute wise discernment, and recognize that not all those who come to lead us are suitable for the job. Even those in "sheep's clothing" may inwardly be "ravenous wolves."

It is foolish to think that when choosing our public leaders we should not consider their moral character. Who would want to elect immoral leaders, after all? Yet in large part, moral character is shaped by one's religion or one's decision not to follow a religion at all. This doesn't give a free pass to those who profess to be religious. As Jesus implied, it is often those who pretend to be religious who are the most dangerous among us. But likewise it does not mean we should select our leaders based on some kind of religion-free criteria.

Don't forget, our national leaders are moral leaders as well as political leaders. And it is easy to see that moral character does matter to the American people by looking at the presidencies of Richard Nixon and Bill Clinton, among others. Nixon and Clinton were perhaps the most skilled politicians of the last half-century. Nixon was one of the most successful presidents in our history when it came to pushing an agenda through Congress, yet he was ultimately forced to resign in disgrace because of a moral failing. President Clinton did not accomplish as much as Nixon, but he governed over a period of prosperity and optimism and had great personal popularity, yet he too was disgraced by a moral lapse and was only the second president in our history to undergo the ordeal of impeachment.

As we select our new president, in this coming year, in seems we should first think about our own moral values, then ask which candidate will promote those values in his character and his policies. This does not mean voting only for candidates who are of the same religion as us, or who have the same world view, but it does mean realizing that we can't just pretend our values don't matter. If we don't publicly vote for our values and embrace them, they are not values at all. They are window dressing.

FENCE FIASCO: OR FELIZ AÑO NUEVO

December 30, 2007

The decline of American sovereignty would typically be a big story in any year, but with all the news coming out of Hollywood this year, maybe it was a bit overshadowed by more significant events.

I mean, how can the virtual surrender of a 231-year-old nation to the Pollyanna-ish forces of political correctness possibly compete with the dramatic real-life struggles of Brittany Spears, Angelina Jolie, Tom Cruise, and the nation's hot new nymphet, Brittany's baby sister, Jamie Lynn Spears?

But every once in a while, when Fox News could get their cameras to focus a little higher than their blonde news anchors' ankles and thighs, a significant story would slip through by accident.

Most recently, we learned that Congress — that hallmark of American integrity — had pulled a fast one on the voting public by undermining the border fence which it had so ostentatiously supported before the 2006 midterm elections.

Back then, Congress voted to approve two layers of reinforced fencing, as well as additional physical barriers, roads, lighting and electronic surveillance" across portions of the border totaling 700 miles.

The president signed the bill, too, even though he has generally been an obstructionist on any issue that involves the United States standing up to its neighbor to the south.

That's because the voting public was getting restless, wondering how the government could justify allowing 20 million illegal aliens to take up residence in our country, utilize public services, and demand their "right" to U.S. citizenship!

Back in October of 2006, I wrote a column subtitled "Lies about the fence," in which I warned that the bill authorizing the border fence did not provide any funding for it, and was just one more political shell game.

I was partly wrong. Despite my warnings, apparently FIVE MILES of the purported 700-MILE fence has actually been built in the last year, for which, I suppose, we should be grateful. At this "frenetic" pace, we can get the entire 700 miles built by the year 2147. Perhaps the descendants of Vicente Fox and George Bush can hold a picnic as the last fence post is put into place in the 22nd century while they toast the 100th anniversary of the founding of the United States of North America.

There has never been any doubt that President Bush was against the fence, and Mexico's former president Fox said at the time the bill was passed in 2006 that the fence was an "embarrassment."

Heck no, the embarrassment is that this country CAN'T build a fence.

Just as predicted by advocates of border security last year, the project has been met with one bureaucratic or congressional stalling tactic after another. The latest sleight-of-hand was seen in the $555 billion spending bill signed by President Bush last week.

Remarkably, the Republican senator from Texas, Kay Bailey Hutchinson, added language on a voice vote that essentially strips the 2006 Secure Border Fence of any teeth it had. Here's what she added about funding for the fence:

"Nothing in this paragraph shall require the Secretary of Homeland Security to install fencing, physical barriers, roads, lighting, cameras, and sensors in a particular location along an international border of the United States, if the Secretary determines that the use or placement of such resources is not the most appropriate means to achieve and maintain operational control over the international border at such location."

In other words, it leaves total discretion for whether to build the fence or not to the administration that opposed the fence in the first place. Way to go, Congress, and feliz año nuevo.

MCCAIN TO ILLEGALS: MAKE US CRY, AND YOU CAN STAY (FOR A FEE, OF COURSE) ...

January 13, 2008

John McCain, one of the leading Republican candidates for president, is thought to be tough as nails because he survived 5 1/2 years of abuse at the hands of the North Vietnamese when he was a prisoner of war.

Everyone pays appropriate homage to him for his service to his country, but since he is running for president he also deserves a serious look at his record and his proposals.

And on the subject of enforcing immigration law, McCain is not as tough as nails; he is squishy as a jelly doughnut.

Accused of supporting amnesty in the McCain-Kennedy bill and in subsequent immigration "reform" bills, McCain typically denies it was amnesty because the illegal immigrants had to pay a $5,000 fine, but then he says that under his plan no one would be able to avoid following the law. "There is no special right associated with my plan," he says.

Except... he always adds a squishy exception.

In one debate, he said he wouldn't deport the grandmother of a soldier fighting in Iraq because she was illegal. In another, he said he wouldn't deport the wife of a soldier fighting in Iraq because he was possibly missing in action.

Apparently, McCain believes in "rule of law" unless you have a really compelling story. Then you get a free pass. Call it the Oprah factor. If you can make us cry on a talk show, we like you too much to send you home.

But maybe someone should tell McCain that every one of us has a compelling story, every one of us has a grandmother who loves us, and every one of us believes in true love. That doesn't mean we can avoid our legal responsibilities; it doesn't mean we can cross borders with impunity; and it doesn't mean you can come to America if you are willing to pay $5,000.

Nor do you get to stay in America just because you have a compelling story; you get to stay here if you followed all the rules and you have a green card.

Heck, if we are going to sell legal residency in the United States to the highest bidder, we should be able to do much better than $5,000. Why don't we hold an annual auction where we sell a limited number of green cards to the highest bidder? I think we might be able to get as much as $50,000 for each card. McCain is clearly not seeing the big picture! We could probably solve the deficit with this plan.

And why stop with green cards? We could even sell citizenship. No need for people with a big fat wallet to pass those silly tests about American history and culture, is there? After all, once they get here, they don't even have to speak English, so why bother pretending they care about fitting in?

Most of the other Republican candidates are firmly against amnesty, but they are afraid to challenge McCain too loudly on this issue because they think he might win the nomination and pick them for his running mate.

But at least illegal immigration is an issue in the Republican primary; for the Democrats it doesn't even exist.

Literally.

When Hillary Clinton was in Las Vegas last week prior to the Nevada caucuses, she was told by a man that his immigrant wife was "illegal."

"No woman is illegal," replied Clinton to cheers in the Mexican restaurant where she was campaigning.

Wow! That is some blanket statement. But what exactly does it mean? Of course, the man did not mean that his wife was "against the law." He meant that she was in this country illegally. He, at least, understands the law, but we may have to ask whether Hillary Clinton does.

But it is no surprise that Clinton, Barack Obama and John Edwards all support amnesty for illegal immigrants. It's too hard for them to say "no" to 12 million potential voters, and mean it. Maybe Democrats are just not tough enough to be president.

But then again, apparently neither is John McCain._

PRESIDENTIAL PERSPECTIVES; OR, OOPS, I WAS WRONG

January 20, 2008

For me, this year's presidential election is quite a bit different than the one in 2004. That time I had a clear candidate — someone who I thought offered hope for the future, would be tough on terrorism, and put principles ahead of politics.

In 2008, of course, George Bush is not running for president, but it may come as a surprise to some of you that the candidate I supported in 2004 wasn't George Bush at all — and it wasn't even a Republican.

What a difference four years makes.

Today, I am known as a knuckle-dragging conservative, someone with the audacity to hope for secure borders, jobs for Americans, protection against mass-murdering hooligans, less money wasted on government handouts, more common sense in the media, a return to civility in our common discourse, and a return to morality in our common understanding.

But four years ago, I was looking for a candidate who could replace George Bush. I had learned to like the president well enough after Sept. 11, 2001, when he seemed to be able to bring the nation together in a moment of crisis. But that was three long years before the 2004 election. In the meantime, we had not just invaded Afghanistan to look for bin Laden, but had invaded Iraq to look for democracy. And as everyone knows, we had seen slight sign of either. As a result, our own nation was clearly fracturing into "red" and "blue," and it appeared that President Bush did not have the political skills to put Humpty-Dumpty together again.

Don't get me wrong. I supported President Bush in principle, but found him to be a terribly flawed leader who had mishandled NOT the war in Iraq or the war against al-Qaida, but the war against lethargy.

Lethargy is the tendency toward apathy, or toward laziness if you will, that can silence passions and cause a person or a nation to "lose the name of action." I was worried by the forgetfulness which I had seen follow quickly on the heels of the righteous outrage after 9/11 and did not think that President Bush, despite his good ideas, had the stamina or the intestinal fortitude to take the fight to the American public. He seemed to be content to remain in the White House and was not willing to take his agenda to the public, to sell his ideas and use the "bully pulpit" to bring the nation together in common purpose.

What every good leader knows is that a good idea is worth about as much as the winning entry in the "Tell us how you would improve the world in 25 words or less" contest. Without the ability and will to put even the simplest plan into action, it remains forever a good idea, and never becomes a good thing. President Bush has had many good ideas, but he has accomplished very few good things.

So in 2003, I started following the career of a still little-known senator from North Carolina, and decided he might have the charisma and sincerity to sway the American people to do what we needed to do to conquer challenges both home and abroad. John Edwards seemed to have a sincere appreciation of the importance of the war on terror, yet promised to wage it more effectively than President Bush. He also had an apparent concern for the plight of the working man and woman, although he himself was a millionaire. Although it would be easy to see Edwards as an ambitious potential demagogue, I instead took him at face value and envisioned him as someone who just might inspire a better society while at the same time protecting us from our enemies.

As I have said before — that was then, this is now. The current version of John Edwards is a disaster waiting to happen, but fortunately the early voters have decided he will have a long time to wait.

Of course, it didn't take me until this 2008 campaign to realize that Edwards was weak on defense and strong on spending other people's money. In fact, it all became quite clear as soon as he was selected as John Kerry's running mate in the 2004 election. Edwards quickly changed all of his spots for political convenience, thus unintentionally revealing his true nature as a political opportunist.

Oh well, you can rank that as my second greatest election-year mistake. The first? Voting for the worst candidate in the 2000 presidential election — but not my good buddy George Bush. I refer, of course, to Mr. Doom and Gloom himself, Al Gore.

And now you know the rest of the story.

FLIP-FLOPPERS, CONSISTENCY AND THE AMERICAN WAY

January 27, 2008

Last week, I made the shocking revelation that once upon a time I had — eek! — changed my mind.

It was done partly in fun, because I thought it was about time that people who try to pigeon-hole me as a Bush lackey found out that four years ago, I had been hoping Democrat John Edwards would unseat the uninspiring chief exec who still haunts the Oval Office like a pale ghost of former presidents.

But it was also done partly as a cautionary tale — to make the case that — most importantly — we don't know what is in each other's souls, and secondarily that we can't really anticipate how changed circumstances will affect our own deeply held views.

So yes, although I have supported President Bush in the war on terror more or less faithfully since 2001, I voted for Al Gore not Bush in 2000. And when I thought Bush was losing the war for the hearts and minds of the American people, I saw Edwards as a charismatic leader who might be better able to sell the need for continued action against Islamic terrorists. Predictably enough, these revelations pleased neither Republicans nor Democrats, as they now know that I cannot be

213

trusted to follow a party line. And because Edwards eventually proved himself to be a pandering politician who would say whatever he thought was necessary to feed his ambition, I also had to publicly acknowledge my own bad judgment and return back to President Bush as the only, if not the best, hope for victory in the war on terror.

Of course, if I were running for public office, such a confession would earn me the dread title of "flip-flopper." Poor me. Flip-floppers are considered dangerous folk. Mitt Romney, for instance, changed his mind about abortion after becoming governor of Massachusetts and has never lived it down since. Mike Huckabee tried to give a tuition break to a couple dozen illegal immigrants when he was governor of Arkansas, so according to his opponents, he can't possibly be honest when he says he's for strong border security and no amnesty today.

The examples are endless. From what I can tell, being a flip-flopper largely means you had the audacity to hope you could use your own mind to reach a conclusion based on current data, instead of regurgitating what you said yesterday under different circumstances. Considering the flak they get for sticking their head out of the trenches, maybe the politicians are right to just do what is politically expedient and not follow their own conscience. After all, getting elected is easy; being faithful to yourself is hard.

If we were being honest, we would have to ask what kind of a president we want, and not just which candidate we think will win. If we were being honest, we would have to ask ourselves if we want Rush Limbaugh or Tim Russert picking our presidents for us, or whether we should squeeze into the election booths beside them, so that we may have a small say in our own future. If we were being honest, we would have to admit that "truth squads" are just "spin doctors" without the medical degree.

The truth, it turns out, is more complicated than a 30-second sound bite. You might even say that the truth has as many sides as a politician who hasn't seen the morning polls yet. As Ralph Waldo Emerson said of people who try to conform themselves to the general opinion: "This conformity makes them not false in a few particulars, authors of a few lies, but false in all particulars. Their every truth is not quite true. Their two is not the real two, their four not the real four; so that every word they say chagrins us, and we know not where to begin to set them right."

Goodness, that reminds me of a politician or two, but why bother to name them when their own words condemn them much more convincingly than anything I could say. It also is worth remembering when we judge politicians that being consistent is not the greatest virtue, or as Emerson more famously said, "A foolish consistency is the hobgoblin of little minds."

Emerson died 125 years ago, but we can be glad he lived at all. If you want some clarity about the American character, not to mention the human condition, you could do worse than to open a book of his essays and take a deep breath of inspiration. Imagine how the mass-media pundit poobahs would holler if word got out that we do not have to get all of our information about the meaning of life from cable television!

And, of course, if we did not read Emerson's essay "Self-Reliance" from which that famous quote comes, we would not know that the full saying is: "A foolish consistency is the hobgoblin of little minds, adored by little statesmen and philosophers and divines."

Yes, it is the politicians and the pundits who insist on making consistency a big thing, but there is one thing politicians and pundits cannot do, and that is to make the world around us unchanging. So if the world changes, so too will I change, and I will not worry too much about what anyone else thinks about it. The same cannot be said of most politicians, so if you find one who seems to be really alive, who is not afraid to speak his mind, or even to admit that he has one, you might consider yourself lucky.

"Why drag about this corpse of your memory, lest you contradict somewhat you have stated in this or that public place? Suppose you should contradict yourself; what then? ... Speak what you think now in hard words, and to-morrow speak what to-morrow thinks in hard words again, though it contradict every thing you said to-day. — 'Ah, so you shall be sure to be misunderstood.' — Is it so bad, then, to be misunderstood? Pythagoras was misunderstood, and Socrates, and Jesus, and Luther, and Copernicus, and Galileo, and Newton, and every pure and wise spirit that ever took flesh. To be great is to be misunderstood."

I think what we are all looking for as we scan the horizon for a true leader is someone who will risk being misunderstood, someone who will say what he or she thinks without consulting a poll, someone who is spontaneous and original and not just a suit of clothes filled up by hot air, someone who (as Emerson said) will "affront and reprimand the smooth mediocrity and squalid contentment of the times."

I've followed politics closely since at least 1968, and I can assure you there are such worthies, though they are few and far between, and none quite as perfect as our hopes for them. You can start the list with Gene McCarthy and Bobby Kennedy from that tumultuous year, then move ahead from one lost cause to another to see what happens to those who follow the beat of a different drummer.

My own conscience led me almost invariably to support candidates who were either outside the mainstream or promised to shake it up. George McGovern, Morris Udall, Jerry "Gov. Moonbeam" Brown, John B. Anderson, Pete DuPont, Gary Hart, Joe Biden, Jack Kemp, Bruce Babbitt, Pat Buchanan, Ross Perot, Steve "Flat Tax" Forbes, John McCain circa 2000, even Jesse Jackson somewhere along the way — my chosen standard-bearers were all doomed to failure, partly because they were rebels, but also partly because to a greater or lesser extent they never quite got the knack of consistency.

With a track record like that, I suppose it's kind of surprising that I am not supporting Ron Paul this year. If he weren't such an isolationist, I might be tempted, because many of Paul's "kooky" ideas are just what the doctor ordered, but I am wise enough now to know that no candidate of Paul's persuasion will ever win the White House (and if he did, certainly not live to talk about it).

Which brings us to this year's election — certainly one of the most interesting and competitive races in many years, full of sound and fury and possibly signifying quite a lot.

But one of the most important lessons I have learned in politics is to doubt everything, even my own judgment. There was no way I could have figured out in 1980 that Ronald Reagan would not just be a good president, but a great one. So how can I possibly know whether Barack Obama would inspire a generation like John Kennedy did? Or whether Mike Huckabee would be able to deliver on his promise to demolish the IRS?

For many of us, the current field of candidates remains a jumble, and things could shake out in a number of different ways — some encouraging, some frightful. Which for me, at least, makes it worth pondering.

But as I watch the turns and tides of the next few weeks or months, I'll pay heed to one last piece of advice from Emerson, who encouraged us all to be our own masters and slaves to no one:

"A political victory, ... or some other favorable event, raises your spirits, and you think good days are preparing for you. Do not believe it. Nothing can bring you peace but yourself. Nothing can bring you peace but the triumph of principles."

POLITICS AS USUAL? UGH

March 30, 2008

Last week, I raised questions about whether Barack Obama had the judgment to be president after seeing that he had been duped by his pastor for 20 years.

But the truth is that Obama is not the only top candidate for president who we should be worried about. The last 10 days should have been an eye-opener for anyone out there who has been laboring under the misapprehension that our top candidates are actually the best-qualified people to run this country.

Obama's total befuddlement over the fact that his pastor and friend, Jeremiah Wright, is a racist and anti-Semite was the most prominent political story of the last two weeks, but it was by no means the only one that should scare you.

Obama's Democratic opponent Hillary Clinton was also skewered publicly by her own overactive imagination. You all know the story by now. Sen. Clinton has been regaling audiences with the tale of her dangerous arrival in Bosnia under sniper fire in 1996 as part of her sales package for her foreign policy "experience" as first lady.

"I remember landing under sniper fire," she told a political gathering recently. "There was supposed to be some kind of a greeting ceremony at the airport, but instead we just ran with our heads down to get into the vehicles to get to our base."

In fact, as we all know now thanks to the archival footage, she arrived at Tuzla military air base with a smile and her 15-year-old daughter Chelsea and no one was running for cover. Instead she was greeted by children and other well-wishers. In fact, it was so evident that Clinton had misspoken, she did what no politician ever does — she admitted she was wrong!

But the questions raised about her character and fitness to be president are just as serious as those raised about Obama. She claims she is prepared to make serious, world-changing decisions when the phone rings at three in the morning, but then she claimed she was just "sleep-deprived" when she made the misstatements about Bosnia.

But hold on! This wasn't an isolated case. She had made similar claims before the Iowa caucus and on other occasions. But comedian Sinbad, who was with Clinton on that trip along with musician Sheryl Crow, blew her cover earlier this month when he joked about Clinton's statement that, "We used to say in the White House that if a place is too dangerous, too small or too poor, send the First Lady."

In any other political year, being proven to have completely fabricated a life-threatening experience would be disqualifying for a presidential candidate. This year, it's just one more lah-dee-dah moment, as the electorate sleepwalks toward judgment day on Nov. 4.

I'm not a psychiatrist, but telling lies when you don't need to is one of the defining characteristics of a sociopath, isn't it? Or maybe I'm wrong. Maybe it's just a defining characteristic of being a Clinton. In either case, does anyone really want to vote for this woman?

But if you can't vote for either Obama or Clinton, you are just left with John McCain, right?

Not so fast.

McCain had his own foreign policy blunder last week, and it was a doozy, all caught on videotape. While in Jordan, he made a statement on the Iraq war's insurgency that was flat-out wrong and should raise serious questions about his "attention to detail."

McCain told reporters that al-Qaida operatives were receiving training in Iran and then being sent back into Iraq to do battle against U.S. led forces. Now this is certainly possible (in the same sense that an asteroid hitting the Earth while you are reading this column is possible) but it is highly unlikely considering that al-Qaida is a Sunni Muslim operation and Iran has a Shiite Muslim regime, and Sunnis and Shiites hate each other slightly more than Boston Red Sox fans hate the Yankees.

Yet there was the man who would be president saying it just as if it was true. And then came the truly embarrassing moment — the TV hook — when a gaffe went from dopey to dangerous.

Sen. Joe Lieberman, playing the role of Nancy Reagan to McCain's "Ronnie," leaned over and whispered into McCain's ear what sounds like: "You said the Iranians are training al-Qaida; they are training extremists"

That prompted McCain to correct himself: "I'm sorry. The Iranians are training extremists. Not al-Qaida."

I suppose if we were sure that Joe Lieberman was going to be appointed as McCain's secretary of state, this episode might have some positive value to show that McCain's handlers could keep him out of trouble, but the fact is we just have plain old McCain on the ballot, and what we seem to have is a senator who is plainly confused about the facts.

Nor can the matter be glossed over as simply a momentary gaffe such as any of us can make. The fact is that the day before,

McCain had made the same assertion on the "Hugh Hewitt Show," saying: "As you know, there are al-Qaida operatives that are taken back into Iran, given training as leaders, and they're moving back into Iraq. I think Americans should be very angry when we know that Iran is exporting weapons into Iraq that kill Americans."

As for me, I think Americans should be angry that we are now stuck with three candidates for president who have all proven themselves to be less than ideal candidates. Is this really the best we can do?

SEN. MCCAIN TURNS HIS BACK ON GOP; WILL THEY RETURN THE FAVOR?

May 11, 2008

Some diehard Republicans like Sean Hannity (who admittedly doesn't realize he is one) are puffed up with excitement over the long, drawn-out knockdown battle between Hillary Clinton and Barack Obama.

They figure that whatever is bad for the Democrats is good for Republicans.

And it certainly looks like the rancorous race for the nomination on the Democratic side is a slow trainwreck in progress. Most polls show that about one-fourth of Obama's supporters won't support Hillary Clinton if she gets the nomination. An even higher number of Clinton's supporters, usually about one-third, say they wouldn't vote for Obama in the general election.

Taking it for granted that those numbers will decline after the nomination is settled, there is still considerable reason to think that Democrats are much weaker today than anyone expected five months ago when the primaries started.

Which is why the one-track mind of Mr. Hannity, radio talk show host and Fox News personality, envisions a glorious victory for Republicans in the fall.

The problem is that, even if the Republicans win, they have already ensured it won't be a glorious victory. Instead it will be a victory bought with abandoned principles, lost causes, and (almost certainly) personal attacks.

John McCain, the luckiest man on the planet, only stumbled into the GOP nomination because Rudy Giuliani imploded, Fred Thompson forgot the magic words ("We have ignition!), Mike Huckabee decided to "play nice," and Ron Paul pulled away conservative votes from other, more viable, alternatives to McCain. Indeed, it seems like most Republicans had coalesced around the slogan "Anybody But McCain," but forgot to find a "body" they could all agree on.

So the guy who engineered the national re-emergence of the Democratic Party with campaign finance "reform," who stalled conservative nominees from being appointed to court seats as one of the founders of the "Gang of 14," and who tried to give amnesty to 20 million illegal aliens against the wishes of the American people — this guy turned out to be the nominee of the once-proud Republican Party.

The pundits, of course, said that conservative Republicans would have to come home and vote for McCain because — after all — where else could they go? Hillary Clinton does appeal to working-class swing voters because, after all, she is pugnacious and mostly sincere in her beliefs, but she is also Hillary Clinton, and that's hard for most Republican voters to swallow. As for Obama, and his much-vaunted non-partisan "politics for a change," most people now give that about the same credence that Nixon's "secret plan" to get us out of Vietnam deserved.

The secret plan to get us out of Vietnam turned out to be to bomb the heck out of the Cambodians, the Vietnamese and anybody else who got in the way of our negotiated surrender. Obama's "change you can believe in" is apparently the change from corrupt, partisan Republican leadership to corrupt, partisan Democratic leadership. If you believe in more "change" than that — if you believe that Obama can really somehow stop conservatives from caring enough about their principles to fight for them, or can stop Democrats from trying to benefit from their positions of power — then you probably also need a change... in your medication.

But this column is not about the problem with Obama, but rather the problem with McCain, who seems to be constitutionally incapable of being on the right side of any issue that is important to his own party.

Of course, throughout the contentious early primaries, McCain kept his mouth shut so that he would not aggravate the Republican "base" — because the fact is, every time McCain speaks his own mind he sounds like he is doing the bidding of the Democratic Party. But for the past month, McCain HAS BEEN speaking his own mind, and Republicans — or at least the conservatives who usually vote Republican — have been cringing as a result.

Last month, McCain accused the North Carolina Republican Party of being "out of touch with reality and the Republican Party" for running an advertisement that used comments by the Rev. Jeremiah Wright, Obama's former pastor, to raise questions about Obama's judgment, and thus the judgment of those who endorse Obama. The ad actually was intended to blast two N.C. Democratic gubernatorial candidates who had endorsed Obama, and suggested that Obama was "too extreme" for America."

McCain told the North Carolina GOP chairwoman, "we need not engage in political tactics that only seek to divide the American people." Apparently McCain prefers to engage in political tactics that divide his own party.

McCain's "holier than thou" moment was not his first, and won't be his last. He seems to be confirmed in his belief that Republicans are nasty, small-minded people who are the human equivalent of pit bulls — they should either be caged or put down. As to why he bothers to remain in a party that he seems to detest, that is an interesting question, but perhaps the fact that he was able to win the party's nomination for president is answer enough.

On the other hand, if he is going to win the general election, he almost certainly has to resort to ads very similar to the one that aired in North Carolina. We have not heard the last of Rev.

Wright, and when the GOP and its allies start airing those ads in September, Sen. McCain is going to have to add hypocrisy to his list of character flaws.

But for many Americans, there is no need to wait for September to disown McCain.

Last week, the senator finally went too far for many Republicans (Sean Hannity not necessarily included) when he announced he would be attending the national conference of La Raza, a Hispanic lobbying group that doesn't just support amnesty for illegal immigrants, but also is the leading force behind the reconquista idea, which encourages Mexicans to settle in the Western United States in order to establish a majority presence and, in effect, reconquer these areas for Mexico. The name La Raza literally means "The Race," and even if it means "The People" (as its defenders claim) it is still a name which promotes separatism rather than assimilation for Mexican-Americans.

But maybe John McCain knows all this. He told the American people he "gets it" now when it comes to their anger about illegal immigration and non-assimilation, so this could be his chance to prove it.

On July 14, when he addresses the National Council of La Raza, McCain could surprise everyone and use some of his famous "straight talk" to tell all those assembled why a border fence is not just necessary but a good idea, why English should be our national language and why illegal immigrants are not welcome here. He could do that, but he won't, which is why Republicans don't have to worry about who the Democrat nominee will be; they have to worry about who the Republican nominee is, and just how they can possibly vote for him.

One amusing solution came from Gene Holt on the Internet:

"Now that John McCain is embracing La Raza, conservatives will not only need to hold their noses if they vote for John McCain; they will now need to walk into the polling place backwards with a bag over their head."

And even that may not work.

PRESIDENTIAL PUZZLE — WHO CAN RUN?

July 13, 2008

Every presidential campaign generates its share of unique stories that are fodder for trivia contests, if nothing else.

As an example, consider the following: Which presidential campaign featured two major-party candidates who both faced allegations that they were ineligible for the office?

Answer? You guessed it — our very own John McCain and Barack Obama.

Or maybe you didn't guess it, because the story has largely flown under the radar. Is it possible that only constitutional law wonks care about whether a candidate is eligible for the highest office in the country?

Maybe so, but it can be an amusing puzzle for the rest of us as well. Here's why. The Constitution provides only three qualifications for those who can serve as president. One of those qualifications is straightforward; you have to be 35 years old. The other two are a bit more vague, leaving them up to the interpretation of courts.

Here's the entire relevant verbiage from Article II of the Constitution"

"No person except a natural born citizen, or a citizen of the United States, at the time of the adoption of this Constitution, shall be eligible to the office of President; neither shall any person be eligible to that office who shall not have attained to the age of thirty five years, and been fourteen Years a resident within the United States."

The last part of that has never been relevant to my knowledge, but I think it could someday be up to a court to decide if those 14 years of residency were meant to be consecutive and immediately prior to running for the office, or cumulative and in any order.

But the sticking point this year is the "natural born citizen" part of the equation.

John McCain, it turns out, was born in the Panama Canal Zone in 1936, when his father was stationed on a U.S. military base there. You would think that would not make him ineligible to be president, because after all both of his parents were U.S. citizens.

Ultimately, the language of the Constitution also seems to be a bit ambiguous in another regard as well — namely the commas that set off the phrase "or a citizen of the United States" in the paragraph about qualifications.

Grammatically speaking, the sentence's meaning is that, "No person except a natural born citizen ... at the time of the adoption of this Constitution, or a citizen of the United States, shall be eligible to the office of President."

In other words, by the logic of grammar, the phrase "or a citizen of the United States" stands alone and should mean that any citizen of the United States whether natural-born or not should be eligible to serve.

Of course, this has never been the interpretation of the clause, and would result in the possibility of immigrant presidents, but don't rule that out from happening based on some future court's decision about the meaning of the comma between "a citizen of the United States" and "at the time of the adoption of this Constitution."

Chances are McCain would be found to be eligible in any case, but a law professor from the University of Arizona says he isn't so sure. Gabriel J. Chin discovered a 1937 law which conferred citizenship on children of American parents who were born in the Canal Zone after 1904. He claims this meant that McCain was not a citizen at the time of his birth in 1936.

Of course, everyone knows that Congress passes many unnecessary laws, and this may just have been one more in a long line of them. Just because Congress "granted" citizenship to McCain and others in 1937 doesn't mean they didn't already have it by some other means previously.

As for Barack Obama, his case is in some ways even more interesting, but only if you believe in skulduggery and deception in high places.

Unfortunately for Obama, some people have questioned whether he was actually born in Hawaii. If he had been born in Kenya, where his father lived, he would actually not be eligible to be president under the common interpretation of "natural-born" citizen.

And oddly enough, Obama would not even be a U.S. citizen at all if he had been born in Kenya to an American mother because the relevant law that grants citizenship to foreign-born children with one non-American parent is pretty clear that the American parent at that time needed to have spent at least five years in the United States past the age of 14, although some sources say 16. Since Obama's mother was just 18 when he was born, she could not have fulfilled this rule in either case.

Because of the importance of the issue, Obama's campaign posted what is supposed to be his birth certificate at barackobama.com (do an Internet search for "Barack Obama birth certificate" to find it for yourself). But the posting has done nothing but inflame the controversy.

For one thing, the birth certificate is of recent vintage, not an original one, or even a copy of an original. In addition, the certificate number has been blacked out so that it cannot be validated against any original. Moreover, there is no embossed seal or signature vouching for the authenticity of the birth certificate by any official of the state of Hawaii.

You would think it would be relatively easy for a man who wants to run the free world to obtain a certified birth certificate, but that does not seem to be the case.

Is this irrelevant or immaterial?

Gee, I hope not. Let's get this straight again. There are three requirements to be president of the United States. All elected presidents have to meet all THREE requirements. If Obama were 33 years old, could we just say it's not a big deal and pretend he is 35? Fat chance.

So let's all be serious about both of these candidates and make sure we know what we are getting.

At a minimum it would be nice to know who in the government verifies eligibility to run for the highest office in the country. Or are we supposed to just hold the election first, and then sort it out later? Gee, that would be nice — another election decided by the Supreme Court! Nothing like a good stiff constitutional crisis to wake you up in the morning.

Nonetheless, it is fairly apparent that most people aren't serious about this issue, and don't really care whether the candidates are in fact eligible to be president. All they really want is to see their candidate elected, and the devil take the hindmost.

Of course, you could make the case that another qualification for president is willingness to swear the oath of office, as dictated here in Article II:

"Before he enter on the execution of his office, he shall take the following oath or affirmation: "I do solemnly swear (or affirm) that I will faithfully execute the office of President of the United States, and will to the best of my ability, preserve, protect and defend the Constitution of the United States."

Hopefully, all of our candidates can meet that qualification at least. If not, we are doomed beyond my ability to describe.

ONE MAN, ONE VOTE, ONE MESS: SENATOR PUTS A 'HOLD' ON LOGIC

August 17, 2008

It was Ronald Reagan who famously said, "Trust but verify."

Those words could very easily be used to describe a Homeland Security program which allows employers to check new hires for their eligibility to work in the United States.

It's important to note that the E-Verify system isn't used to screen applicants, but used to verify the legal status of people after they are hired. Applicants get the benefit of an employer's "trust" that they are telling the truth during the application process, but employers get the comfort of knowing they can "verify" that they are indeed hiring legal workers.

And everyone should be comforted to know the program cannot be used to discriminate against anyone. Once signed up for the program, employers must check all new hires, not use it on a few applicants based on outward appearances such as race or language.

The program began in 1996 and has proven to be an effective tool for employers to make sure they are not running afoul of immigration and employment laws. There are more than 75,000 employers signed up, with as many as 1,000 new employers signing up each week, according to Department of Homeland Security administrator Michael Chertoff.

So what's the big deal?

The clock is ticking on E-Verify, and the program will expire in November unless it is reauthorized by Congress. The House of Representatives actually voted on July 31 to extend the program for five years by a vote of 407-2.

Unfortunately, one lone senator, Robert Menendez of New Jersey, using the arcane rules of the Senate, is holding the bill hostage. Menendez has put a "hold" on the bill because he wants the bill tied to an effort by him and his Democratic colleague, Rep. Zoe Lofgren, to create 550,000 new legal immigrants. Forget the fact that the economy is in a downturn, and those 550,000 new residents will be competing against Americans for jobs. Let's just keep it simple. Vote on separate proposals based on their merits, not on politics.

It's up to everyone to put pressure on Menendez to let this program come to a vote. His mail address is Sen. Robert Menendez, 317 Hart Senate Office Building, Washington, D.C. 20510. His phone number is 202-224-4744. He can also be reached by webmail at http://menendez.senate.gov/contact/contact.cfm

But don't stop there. Let Sens. Max Baucus and Jon Tester of Montana know what you think as well. Our two Democratic senators have both seemed to recognize the need for sanity in immigration laws, and have often voted against amnesty and other programs that make it easier for those who have broken the law. They should be called upon now to persuade their Democratic colleague from New Jersey that he should put the interests of the country ahead of the interests of foreign workers.

You can contact Baucus's office from Montana using a toll-free line at 1-800-332-6106. Or by sending webmail through http://baucus.senate.gov/contact/emailForm.cfm?subj=issue To contact Tester, call toll-free from Montana at 1-866-554-4403 or use webmail at http://tester.senate.gov/Contact

Time is of the essence since senators are in recess until after Labor Day, and will return for only about 15 days of legislative work before they recess again for electioneering.

There is no need to turn this into a partisan battle. Those who promote the rights of illegal immigrants often blame employers for hiring undocumented workers, and say they should be punished rather than the workers. Here's a chance to make sure that employers are doing the right thing. That's why I say it is a no-brainer to make this program mandatory in the future.

If the illegal hiring stops, the illegal aliens will eventually go home. That's as easy to understand as supply and demand. Let's do the right thing for our country, not for our party.

BUSH, BARACK, BIG MAC: ### RECIPE FOR DISASTER ... ?

August 31, 2008

Who knows how much more damage George W. Bush can do to the country before he leaves office in January. Take your pick: A war with Iran. A war with Russia. Surrender to Mexico. Close Gitmo. Pardon Osama bin Laden's chauffeur.

Anything is possible.

I always get a kick out of those polls that ask, "Is the country going in the wrong direction?" Democrats point at the large numbers of people who respond affirmatively as evidence that the country wants liberal change, but in fact millions of people are sick of George Bush exactly because they think he governs too much like a liberal.

Want more spending on government programs? George Bush is your man. Want more open borders? George Bush is your guy. Want to improve the lives of people overseas whether they like it or not? George Bush is with you on that one. Want to spend billions of dollars to force schools in Montana and other states to indoctrinate children? George Bush agrees, and hopes there is No Child Left Behind. Want to increase the role of the federal government in every other sector of modern life, too? So does George Bush.

Call him Barack Obama Lite.

It's no wonder there were leftist activists at the Democratic convention protesting the coronation of Obama at Invesco Field. They are afraid that, despite his "change" rhetoric, Obama will just be George Bush Lite. Certainly, Obama's choice of career politician Joe Biden as his vice-presidential running mate did not help to dissuade the skeptics, who think the two-party system is really just a charade to keep the masses otherwise occupied while they are being robbed blind.

As for the other Republican in the race (Obama IS running against Bush, isn't he?), John McCain certainly doesn't instill any confidence that he will change the system. Remember, he is part of the national crisis also known as Congress. Despite his rhetoric against earmarks and his reputation as a maverick, McCain is an establishment politician who is just as goofy as Bush. He has bought into the liberal rhetoric about global warming, for instance, and he is one of the prime movers for the program of amnesty for illegal aliens. Lord knows, any conservative who plans to vote for McCain has to be both wearing blinders and holding his nose at the same time and is almost certainly motivated simply by dread terror of Barack Obama.

But that is in the future. For now, we just have to worry about Bush, and the do-nothing (except cause trouble) Congress. The two things I am most worried about are an attack on Iran's nuclear facilities and some puling act of surrender to Mexico.

Hitler disregarded the sage advice of his generals in 1941 and attacked Russia before he had concluded his takeover of

Western Europe. The rest, as they say, is history. Britain, under Churchill, withstood Germany's aerial onslaught until the United States entered the war after Pearl Harbor, and Russia sacrificed tens of millions of its citizens to defend the motherland from the butcher of Berlin. Eventually Hitler was crushed and the United States got to foot the bill for healing Europe's wounds from World War II in the form of the Marshall Plan.

To complete the analogy, Bush is already fighting his war on the western front in Iraq and is fighting a limited war on the eastern front in Afghanistan. The difference with World War II is that both wars are against the same enemy, the Sunni Muslim leadership represented by al-Qaida and the Taliban. If Bush, however, authorized an attack on Iran, or sanctioned one by Israel, he would be opening a true second front — a war against the other major branch of Islam, the Shiite sect. This could easily spread into a conflagration that would stretch from Lebanon to Indonesia and beyond, and President Bush would be safely retired to Crawford, Texas.

Not likely to happen? Maybe not, but if we are going to fight a new world war, I would rather not see George Bush at the helm. Despite his occasional good intentions, he has proven himself to be a dismal failure at what his father called "the vision thing." He may not want to destroy his country, but you don't have to want a car crash in order to have one. Cowboy-style provocations without the capacity to follow through with measured and unified pressure on the enemy could easily result in a domino effect that would end with a flattened world (and not in the comfortable sense intended by author Tom Friedman).

As for Mexico, who knows what to expect? Anything is possible from the Bush administration, up to and including ceding the Gadsden Strip back to our southern neighbor (adios, Tucson!) as a sign of our enduring regret over America's heavy-handed 19th century applications of Manifest Destiny. It's also entirely realistic that the president would use his constitutional power of amnesty to give a blanket pardon to any and all illegal aliens within our borders.

But what I am most afraid of is that he will do something quiet and simple like send Congress the 2004 agreement he negotiated with Mexico to give Mexican citizens the right to receive Social Security Benefits for work done in the United States. This so-called Social Security "totalization" agreement allows workers from both countries to use work done in either country to amass credits toward Social Security retirement payouts, and there is no explicit ban on illegal work being used in the calculation. Like most Bush-designed programs, the devil is in the details. But one estimate puts the cost of the program the first year at $100 million. Considering how close our Social Security system is to bankrupt, that's $100 million too much.

Thanks to Congress giving up its constitutional authority to ratify treaties, Bush doesn't even need to get congressional approval on this baby. He just has to get it before the do-nothing Congress for 60 days and hope the citizens of the country don't notice. After the two months pass, if Congress doesn't say otherwise, the treaty is a done deal. Kind of reminds me of the way Congress votes itself pay raises without actually voting.

Sadly, even if President Bush forgets to send his "King George" treaty to Congress before he goes home, the next president still could. President Obama certainly would, and President McCain might just ask George to do it on his last day, as a personal favor.

Like I said, the country is going in the wrong direction, but not because we need to get more liberal.

MRS. PALIN GOES TO TOWN

September 7, 2008

Don't count out small-town America.

That was the message of Sarah Palin as she addressed the nation for the first time Wednesday night at the Republican convention in preparation for accepting the party's nomination as vice president.

She quoted an unnamed writer as saying, "We grow good people in our small towns, with honesty, sincerity and dignity." She might have gone on to add energy, strength and pugnaciousness to the list, because she showed herself to be a fighter and a formidable opponent.

It was a message addressed partly to Democratic presidential candidate Barack Obama, whose campaign had been somewhat condescending to Palin before her speech, but probably won't be again.

Obama once infamously quipped that people from small towns "cling to guns or religion or antipathy to people who aren't like them or anti-immigrant sentiment or anti-trade sentiment as a way to explain their frustrations" when politicians make promises they can't keep. Well, there is no doubt that politicians often mislead voters, but that doesn't mean you should dismiss the values of the voters. Instead, you should discount the promises of the politicians.

Maybe that's why Gov. Palin didn't spend a lot of time making promises in her speech; she instead talked about who she is. And it was clear when Gov. Palin spoke of her values, she did not do so out of frustration, but out of love — love of her country. If she believes in policies that are not the same as those espoused by Barack Obama, it is not because she is afraid or frustrated, but because her beliefs are based on her own values, small-town values, frontier values, the values that made America the great nation it is.

The same talking heads who dismissed suggestions that Obama is not qualified to be president after one term as U.S. senator wasted no time laughing at the "inexperience" of a woman who has held elective office almost continuously since 1992, winning two terms as city councilor, two terms as mayor and a term as governor. When not in elective office, Palin chaired the Alaska Oil and Gas Conservation Commission, and in the meantime, she has also raised a family of five children and enjoyed a successful 20-year marriage to her high school sweetheart, Todd.

Not too shabby for a woman with "no" experience. And everyone knows that what the media is really saying is that she is a Republican "woman" with no experience. If Montana's Democratic governor, Brian Schweitzer, had been tapped by Barack Obama to be vice president, would the Washington establishment be talking about his inexperience as a first-term governor? Or would they be celebrating his maverick credentials and his bolo tie?

The fact of the matter is Barack Obama SHOULD have picked Brian Schweitzer to run for vice president instead of Joe Biden. Biden is a career politician; Schweitzer is a breath of fresh mountain air. If Obama is the "change" candidate, he should have put some thought into what kind of change the American people want to see.

It is apparent that John McCain did just that. Despite the pundits telling him that he ought to pick someone safe like Tim Pawlenty, the milquetoast governor of Minnesota, McCain went for "Fire and Nice," a sometime nickname for Gov. Palin.

Is she ready to be vice president? You bet. She has all the qualifications. She is more than 35 years old, a natural born citizen and has lived in the United States for more than 14 years. That's what the Constitution asks for, plus one more thing... She needs to win a majority of the electoral votes cast for the office. To do that, she needs to be vetted — not by John McCain, not by the media, not by Barack Obama, but by the people of the United States of America. If we think she is ready to be vice president, then by God she is. And all the whining about it from the Daily Kos, MoveOn.org, MSNBC and the Democratic National Committee won't make a bit of difference.

That remains to be seen, but as Palin said in her acceptance speech Wednesday, "Here's a news flash for all those reporters and commentators: I'm not going to Washington to seek their good opinion — I'm going to Washington to serve the people of this country. Americans expect us to go to Washington for the right reasons, and not just to mingle with the right people."

It reminds me heartily of the story of Longfellow Deeds, the folk hero of American cinema who was turned by Gary Cooper into a plainspoken voice of the common man in the movie "Mr.

Deeds Goes to Town." As you probably remember, Deeds was a small-town Vermonter during the Great Depression whose worldly experience consisted mainly of writing greeting-card doggerel and playing the tuba. Like Palin, Deeds was thrust upon the world stage, in his case by inheriting $20 million, and like Palin, Deeds was mocked by the big-city journalists who found him too simple by half, and too decent by far.

But Deeds was an all-American who stood on the shoulders of small-town country folk like Lincoln and Thoreau. One famous scene takes place at Grant's Tomb, the burial place of Ulysses S. Grant, which his girlfriend tells him is "an awful letdown" to most people.

Deeds tells her, "that depends on what they see" and then tells her what he sees:

"Oh, I see a small Ohio farm boy becoming a great soldier. I see thousands of marching men. I see General Lee with a broken heart, surrendering, and I can see the beginning of a new nation, like Abraham Lincoln said. And I can see that Ohio boy being inaugurated as President — Things like that can only happen in a country like America."

The pundits in the media don't understand it, but that's what ordinary folks see when they watch Sarah Palin, too — a woman who raised herself up from a simple Idaho and Alaska upbringing to become governor of a great state and to inspire the nation with her example. Or maybe (and this is scary) the folks in the media do get it, and they just say the hurtful things about people like Sarah Palin because they don't care about anything except ratings.

Longfellow Deeds was hurt by the newspapers, too, but realized there was no point in worrying about them or what they would say because "they'll go on writing [those hurtful articles] until they get tired." But he didn't just stop there. In the script by Frank Capra, Deeds asks a question that is still resonant 75 years later:

"What puzzles me is why people seem to get so much pleasure out of hurting each other. Why don't they try liking each other once in a while?"

The same puzzlement probably intruded on the sincere joy and excitement of Sarah Palin last week as she thought about how she lives in an America where "every woman can walk through every door of opportunity." But I suspect her consternation didn't last long, even when the media attacked her family; she is, after all, a woman of character, and like most Americans a born optimist.

"Politics isn't just a game of clashing parties and competing interests," she said. "The right reason" to serve in public office "is to challenge the status quo, to serve the common good, and to leave this nation better than we found it."

Sarah Palin, as a national figure, is only a week old, but it's clear already she wasn't born yesterday. For an "average hockey mom," she makes a pretty darn good vice-presidential candidate.

McCAIN'S IGNOBLE FAILURE TO IGNITE

October 12, 2008

What is wrong with John McCain?

No, I don't mean his physical ailments, partly brought on by age and partly by the vicissitudes of torture at the hands of his captors in Hanoi 40 years ago. And I don't mean his policies, although God knows he has some explaining to do there as well.

I am talking about his inability to carry the battle to his enemies — to look a man square in the eye and tell him, "You are wrong." He hasn't yet determined how to run a campaign aimed against Barack Obama's many flaws, and time is running out. Heck, even Joe Biden understands that McCain looks weak and ineffective on this score.

Biden, the Democratic vice presidential candidate, pointed to "all of the things they said about Barack Obama... on the TV, at their rallies, and now on YouTube, and everything else they're doing before the debate, all the things they're saying after the debate" and noted that "John McCain could not bring himself to look Barack Obama in the eye and say the same things to him."

But most pointedly of all, a McCain supporter at a rally in Waukesha, Wisconsin, on Thursday stood up and told McCain to his face what almost all of his supporters are feeling — take off your gloves and fight!

"I'm mad! I'm really mad!" said the unidentified man. "When you have Obama, [House speaker Nancy] Pelosi and the rest of the hooligans up there going to run the country, we have to have our head examined. It's time that you two represent the rest of us," he told McCain and his running mate, Sarah Palin, "So go get 'em!"

Huh? A plan that you and Obama have? Say what?

Sen. McCain, here's the problem. The people who support you for president don't trust Barack Obama, and if you DO trust him, then they don't trust you either. The last thing Republicans want is a plan endorsed by Sen. Obama. So how do you win an election that way?

Probably you don't.

Barring some unforeseen testosterone transfusion, McCain is destined to keep thinking his enemies are his "friends" and that his self-appointed role as the oxymoronic "maverick moderate" will somehow pay off in votes instead of snickers.

It had looked for a while like Pitbull Palin would pull McCain across the finish line, but now it seems safe to assume that McCain will put a muzzle on her and turn the final three weeks of the campaign into a race for last place.

Face it, the McCain campaign is not going to have any help from the national media. With probably a hundred stories or more circulating on the Internet and talk radio about Barack Obama's past associations and mistaken judgments, the only thing the celebrity reporters can focus on is "McCain's negative campaign."

Huh? Say what?

McCain has missed opportunity after opportunity to go after Barack Obama's tax policy, his education policy, his foreign policy and his fiscal policy, let alone his association with ACORN and its fraudulent voter registration campaigns, his 20 years of friendship with the radical Rev. Jeremiah Wright and his ties to the domestic terrorist and lifelong communist William Ayers.

The national media has already painted McCain as a negative campaigner, but the funny thing is, they do it without ever investigating whether the allegations against Obama are true. Doesn't the truth play some small role in whether a campaign is negative or not? I mean, if someone in Russia had called Josef Stalin a mass murderer, would that be considered negative campaigning? Yes, it's a negative statement, but in deciding your future, isn't the truth relevant?

Ugh. It's becoming almost ridiculously silly out there.

This time, I am afraid, America will get the government it deserves, and that — my friends — is a scary thought.

WHERE DO WE GO FROM HERE?

October 26, 2008

As we head into the final 10 days of the election, it might be healthy to remember the words of Bob Dylan — "You're right from your side — I'm right from mine."

Too often in this current political climate, people forget that. They figure to some extent the best way to win an argument is to tell the other guy to shut up. Even when they do engage in a discussion, it seems most people don't bother to do an analysis of issues, but rather just take sides.

It makes decision-making rather easy if you feel free to voice opinions without needing to substantiate them. If you like Obama, you can just support him no matter what the facts reveal. If you like McCain, you can vote for him without worrying about his policies.

It also means that no matter how much evidence opponents amass and put in front of your face, you can blithely — perhaps willfully — ignore it and just label it as a partisan hatchet job. No need to bother studying the information presented then. No need to refute it with your own arguments and your own evidence. Just call it stupid. Or worse yet, call it Republican. Name-calling is much more effective at winning arguments than analysis is.

I wish I had some solution to offer to this intellectual impasse, but I don't. The fact of the matter is there are serious, significant differences between Barack Obama and John McCain. They can't both be "right" about outcomes. If McCain is right, Obama would lead us to socialism. But Obama obviously disagrees with that conclusion. If Obama is right, McCain would lead us to class warfare. But McCain obviously finds that possibility absurd.

Nonetheless, they can both be right about their own beliefs — they can be right that they intend to do good for the country, and that they think they will do a better job than their opponent.

If we can remember this distinction between outcomes and intentions, we will all be much happier on the day after Election Day. If Barack Obama is elected, he will have accomplished much, but only a fraction of what he will have to accomplish in the days ahead. If John McCain is elected, he will have overcome much, but only a fraction of what he will have to overcome when he takes office.

And for the rest of us? If we survive this election, we will have seen the best and worst of American democracy, but we are likely to have both better and worse times ahead. The challenges are obvious; the solutions are difficult. Whether Obama or McCain is elected shouldn't matter as much as having a successful president, one who will leave the country stronger than he found it.

In that spirit, may the best man win.

Epilogue

BUSHWHACKED: MY YEARS WITH W

July 9, 2009

What is it about George W. Bush that drives people crazy?

The number of times I defended Bush the Younger in this column could probably be counted on one hand, maybe one finger, but in the minds of many of my liberal readers, I am a slack-jawed, mind-numbed rabid Bush enthusiast.

That's because I supported the War on Terror, and continue to support it under President Obama.

But, hey, let's be honest. There's a difference between supporting a war cause and calling George Bush a successful president. I was consistently complaining about the Bush presidency for at least the final three years of his presidency, so I find it rather amusing when readers now say I never blame George Bush for anything.

Um, yes, that's true as far as it goes, but let's keep in mind that George Bush isn't president any longer, so I usually don't have anything to say about him. Nonetheless, in the interest of keeping my liberal readers at bay for one more week, I throw them this red meat: A collection of the greatest "hits" taken by President Bush in this column over the past four years.

Remember the 2006 boondoggle when Bush wanted to turn U.S. port security over to an Arab-owned company based in Dubai? I wrote of Bush, "...the idea of putting our ports of entry into the hands of a foreign government, any foreign government, is absurd. And when that foreign government has ties to al-Qaida and the Taliban, the terrorists who we are at war with, then it is beyond absurd. It is downright criminal."

Indeed, much of my disdain for President Bush centered on his policies for border security and illegal immigration, and my criticism of him was as vehement as anything I have said about President Obama in the last few months.

Don't believe me?

"Everyone who is concerned about the future of the United States of America already knows what needs to be done, and everyone who likes the idea of amnesty for illegal aliens [such as President Bush] has already sold out the country anyway."

I even went so far as to say that President Bush's homeland was in doubt. In a column about the Security and Prosperity Partnership of North America, I wrote: "President Bush's recent trip to Mexico was something of a homecoming for him. After visiting Brazil, Colombia and other countries in Latin America, Bush made a stop in Mexico, and it must have seemed to him like he had returned to the motherland. After all, Mexico and Canada are part of the Security and Prosperity Partnership of North America, which the president is promoting as the first step in a virtual merger of our three nations."

That 2007 column also mocked President Bush's fumbling performance abroad as he met with Mexican President Calderon:

"...[Bush] had the audacity to publicly assure the Mexicans that he was working for them in the immigration battle: 'Mr. President, my pledge to you and your government — but, more importantly, the people of Mexico — is I will work as hard as I possibly can to pass comprehensive immigration reform.' Say what? Isn't it a might unseemly for the president of the United States to be making pledges to push the agenda of a foreign government?"

And even though I had supported President Bush in his fight against terrorism, I did not think he was an effective leader in that war, as I expressed just after Barack Obama was elected in 2008:

"...it can be stated somewhat authoritatively that after 9/11 President Bush gained a certain stature as commander-in-chief which he squandered in a series of feckless, if not reckless, decisions about how to wage the war on terror."

Even before that, I had publicly admitted that I supported a Democrat in the 2004 primaries to unseat President Bush: "Don't get me wrong. I supported President Bush in principle, but found him to be a terribly flawed leader who had mishandled NOT the war in Iraq or the war against al-Qaida, but the war against lethargy... I was worried by the forgetfulness which I had seen follow quickly on the heels of the righteous outrage after 9/11 and did not think that President Bush, despite his good ideas, had the stamina or the intestinal fortitude to take the fight to the American public."

For the record, I also criticized the Republican-controlled Congress such as in this quote from a column after the mid-term elections of 2006:

"...while I personally would have preferred a Republican victory in the recent congressional elections, I am entirely ready to be proven wrong by the Democrats taking action to save our country from the train wreck that is in progress. Let's face it, the Republican Congress had a dismal record of inaction, corruption, and overspending. It's hard to see how the Democrats could do much worse."

In that same column, I offered up this summation of my non-affiliation with either party:

"...Our leadership is the only thing between us and total chaos, and if I have to root for the Democrats to come to their senses and save our country, then I will do so, just as I have rooted for President Bush, even though he has proven himself to be a flawed president."

Whether you agree with me or not about the problems we face, I clearly established my own belief that our national crisis is not partisan when I wrote:

"...in a way, I suspect we are better off to have a Democratic Congress in place for a few years, so that the Democratic Party can take part of the blame for the problems the country faces. There's no reason why anyone should think these are Republican problems. Instead, they are problems that have occurred over the past 50 years, as presidents both Republican and Democrat, have dithered."

I predicted that the United States was on the verge of a collapse into a second-rate power, and then asked: "Am I too pessimistic? I hope the Democrats prove me wrong. Maybe they can stave off the coming collapse with a well-placed tax-raise here or another government program there."

Now the Democrats have their chance. With a Democratic president, a Democratic House and a filibuster-proof Democratic Senate, there is nothing standing between us and that collapse except, well, Democrats.

I wish them success in their efforts to save the nation, but please don't expect me to agree with them even when I think they are wrong. If it was fair to call President Bush a criminal and a sellout, then it should be OK to call President Obama the "nanny in chief" of the welfare state. But that is for another column...

FOR MY EXTENDED ASSESSMENT OF
PRESIDENT BARACK OBAMA,
PLEASE READ THE NEXT VOLUME OF THE HEARTLAND DIARIES:
"WHY WE NEEDED TRUMP, PART 2:
OBAMA'S FUNDAMENTAL TRANSFORMATION: FAR LEFT."

About the Author

Frank Miele is a conservative columnist at RealClearPolitics.com. He is also the moderator of www.HeartlandDiaryUSA.com. He worked as an award-winning community journalist for most of four decades, including 34 years at the Daily Inter Lake in Kalispell, Montana, where he was managing editor from 2000 to 2018. Miele's "Editor's 2 Cents" column was a regular feature in the newspaper from 2004 to 2018 and won him a broad following among conservatives across the nation. He lives with his wife and children in Kalispell.

Made in the USA
Coppell, TX
07 November 2019

11069821R10143